COMRADES

INSIDE THE WAR OF INDEPENDENCE

ANNIE RYAN

LIB
ERT
IES

In memory of all those who lived through the War of Independence
with a story to tell

First published in 2007 by
Liberties Press
Guinness Enterprise Centre | Taylor's Lane | Dublin 8
www.LibertiesPress.com | info@libertiespress.com
Editorial: +353 (1) 402 0805 | sean@libertiespress.com
Sales and marketing: +353 (1) 415 1224 | peter@libertiespress.com
Liberties Press is a member of Clé, the Irish Book Publishers' Association

Trade enquiries to CMD Distribution
55A Spruce Avenue | Stillorgan Industrial Park | Blackrock | County Dublin
Tel: +353 (1) 294 2560
Fax: +353 (1) 294 2564

ISBN for PB: 978–1–905483–14–3
ISBN for HB: 978–1–905483–22–8

2 4 6 8 10 9 7 5 3 1

A CIP record for this title is available from the British Library

Cover design by Liam Furlong at space.ie
Set in Garamond

Printed in Ireland by
Colour Books | Baldoyle Industrial Estate | Dublin 13

Contents

	Acknowledgements	7
	Note on Military and Police Forces	8
	Foreword by Diarmaid Ferriter	9
	Introduction	11
1	Executions and Deportations	13
2	The Prisoners' Return	19
3	Lining Up	27
4	Political Action: The By-elections	32
5	Loyalties Transformed, Identities Confirmed	37
6	Michael Collins, the Castle and the Spies	50
7	Sections, Companies, Battalions and Brigades	59
8	Active Service	66
9	The Rebel County	79
10	Kerry	89
11	The RIC, Ned Broy and Others	100
12	The War in the West	115
13	Establishing the Threads of Government	126
14	Legal Adjustments	136
15	At the Interface	142
16	The Ulster Context	151
17	The Truce in the Northern Context	165
18	Conflicting Loyalties	176
19	Meath and North Dublin	183
20	Westmeath, Longford, Roscommon and the Offaly Area	191

21	KILDARE AND LAOIS	200
22	CARLOW AND KILKENNY	207
23	WEXFORD AND WICKLOW	214
24	WATERFORD	221
25	THE TESTIMONY OF THE WOMEN	227
26	THE CAPITAL CITY	244
27	IN RETROSPECT	258
	APPENDIX: THE WITNESSES	269
	SUGGESTED FURTHER READING	279

ACKNOWLEDGEMENTS

My gratitude to all those who were so kind as to encourage me to undertake *Comrades: Inside the War of Independence,* almost before my publishers had time to get my first book, *Witnesses: Inside the Easter Rising,* on to the shelves of Irish bookshops. Again, people like Dr Margaret Mac Curtain and Professor Donal McCartney were very kind. Colette O'Daly of the National Library, who was such a help when I was putting *Witnesses* together, could see no reason why I should not proceed at once to renew my acquaintance with the interesting people whose stories were to be found in the archives. The generous validation provided by Martin Mansergh and Diarmaid Ferriter further impelled me towards a task which, I must say, was a thoroughly enjoyable one.

The National Archives in Bishop Street is a remarkably congenial place, warm and comfortable – a perfect place to spend time with these engaging people who were generous enough to leave us their stories. I am deeply grateful to the staff at the National Archives.

I am conscious of the great debt we owe the Bureau of Military History, firstly for putting together the Military Archives and then for taking such good care of them.

I would like to take this opportunity of thanking old friends and relatives of my own generation for their memories. Most of my generation are fortunate enough to have known many of the people who feature in *Comrades.* It was heartening to find that, for example, an extraordinary man like Tomas Malone was remembered by my old friend Julie O'Halloran of Nenagh, County Tipperary. If *Comrades* succeeds in stirring old memories, it will have achieved its purpose.

My thanks also go to my husband for his listening gifts and to my brothers and sisters for their unfailing interest in the progress of *Comrades.*

PUBLISHERS' NOTE

All quotations from the Bureau of Military History 1913–21 witness statements are reproduced courtesy of Military Archives, Cathal Brugha Barracks, Rathmines, Dublin 6. Thanks to Commandant Victor Laing and the staff of the Military Archives for their generous assistance with images, and to Orlaith Delaney and Sam Egan for editorial support.

NOTE ON MILITARY AND POLICE FORCES

Volunteers Members of armed units of the unilaterally declared Irish Republic, the Irish State proclaimed in the Easter Rising in 1916 and re-affirmed by the Dáil in January 1919. These units came to be known collectively as the IRA.

RIC The Royal Irish Constabulary was one of Ireland's two police forces in the early twentieth century, alongside the Dublin Metropolitan Police. The RIC was disbanded in 1922 and replaced by two new police forces: the Garda Síochána in the Irish Free State and the Royal Ulster Constabulary in Northern Ireland.

B Specials Initiated in 1920 as a vigilante force locally recruited from ex-members of the Protestant Ulster Volunteer Force, later funded by the Northern government. A Specials and C Specials completed the Ulster Special Constabulary.

DMP The Dublin Metropolitan Police was the police force of Dublin from 1836 to 1925, when it became part of the new Garda Síochána.

Black and Tans Because of the enormous strain of guerrilla warfare on the RIC in 1920, the government found it necessary to obtain reinforcements in England. The new recruits were mostly unemployed ex-servicemen. They came to be known as the Black and Tans because of their uniforms, which were a combination of police and army uniforms. A more elite force was later recruited. These were ex-officers and became the Auxiliary Division of the RIC.

Cumann na mBan Cumann na mBan, a women's league associated with the Irish Volunteers, was founded by Countess Markieviez in association with Agnes O'Farrelly, Jennie Wyse-Power and Louise Gavan Duffy. It had the same aims as the Irish Volunteers but was a separate organisation. As well as learning first aid, the members drilled and learned how to load, unload and clean guns.

FOREWORD

In March 1959, eighty-three steel boxes were locked into the strongroom in Government Buildings in Dublin. They contained the 1,770 statements of the Bureau of Military History, which, with the backing of successive governments, had organised the collection of the statements from those who took part in the Irish revolution from 1913 to 1921. There was only one problem. No agreement had been reached about when the statements should be released. It was a problem that remained for nearly half a century.

In 1967, the historian F. X. Martin bemoaned 'the official iron curtain . . . cutting off the findings of the Bureau from all outsiders. The papers of the Bureau have now become a miser's hoard'. But he also maintained that the material would prove to be 'a gilt-edged investment, increasing in value with the passage of the years'. The statements were finally released in 2003, and, as Annie Ryan has demonstrated in this absorbing, original and engaging book, F. X. Martin's prediction was accurate.

Here, we see the Irish War of Independence laid bare: the triumphs, the sorrows, the idealism and the brutality, the bravery and the pain. What makes this book important is that the stories are told through the voices of those who participated directly. It is a period of Irish history still much disputed, but a lot of the research to date has excluded the voices of those who were fuelling the Irish republican engine.

The value of this book lies not only in the determination to allow the voices of the participants to emerge, but also the acknowledgement that there were many layers to this revolution. It was, like all wars, complicated and difficult, and the certainty expressed by so many in its aftermath was rarely evident at the time. There is much defiance, resoluteness and bravery on display in this book, but also uncertainty and vulnerability. It is to Annie Ryan's credit that she has not sought to simplify or romanticise what was such a painful period for many, marked by pride, but also by suffering and conflicting allegiances.

This was overwhelmingly a revolution of the young and the inexperienced. As the author acknowledges, many of them took huge risks for little or no reward, but the bonds of friendship and common purpose that they shared helped them in their quest. It was a war fought on different levels. There were the activities of the IRA Flying Columns, or, in the words of Seamus Robinson, one of those who gave a statement to the Bureau, 'the ghostly army of sharpshooters', but also 'the occasional chivalrous enemy'. There was often a pitiful shortage of weapons, and communications problems between IRA GHQ and the regional Brigades. There was also an intelligence war fought, and a crusade to undermine the Royal Irish Constabulary, many of whom were rightly regarded, as pointed out by Ned Broy, as 'personally honest and decent men with discipline and self-respect'. There was also the attempt to supplant the British administration in Ireland in the areas of local government and the administration of justice, with Sinn Féin courts in Leitrim, for example, 'held in a local disused granary on the mountainside'.

The author has done justice to the many regions and counties involved, by examining events north, south, east and west, but also individuals who were away from Ireland, serving in the British army, such as the mutineers in the Connaught Rangers in India. Many had joined for reasons that had little to do with politics or imperialism; in the words of Maurice Meade, who joined the British army in 1911, 'any private thoughts I had were given up to the hope of gaining my own independence'.

There were chilling executions also, such as that of RIC Sergeant King in south Roscommon, shot dead when cycling to his barracks on the morning of the Truce in July 1921, and the publican in Borris, County Carlow, shot dead because he would not support the IRA. There was anger about alleged spies and informers, and sometimes a resistance to the IRA when it was deemed not to be acting in the interests of the communities it claimed to represent. There were many resourceful women in Cumman na mBan whose structures proved efficient and reliable, and whose role in transporting despatches was indispensable. As Leslie Price discovered, the safest way for these messages to get to Cork was through Celbridge, and 'to test its efficiency she cycled every yard of it herself as far as Cork'.

Annie Ryan's commitment to making these Bureau statements accessible and putting them in context has resulted in an honest and illuminating book that, by focusing on the ordinary Volunteers, will greatly enhance our understanding of the various dimensions of the Irish War of Independence.

Diarmaid Ferriter, IRCHSS Fellow, April 2007

10

INTRODUCTION

Comrades: Inside the War of Independence is the second book to be based almost exclusively on statements submitted to the Bureau of Military History by men and women who had been involved in the movement for independence in the early years of the last century. The statements, which had been locked away for so many years, are now accessible at the Military Archives in Cathal Brugha Barracks in Rathmines, Dublin, and at the National Archives on Bishop Street, also in Dublin. The material assembled from these statements by the Bureau of Military History in the years between 1947 and 1957 was far from exhausted by *Witnesses: Inside the Easter Rising*, the companion volume to this book. I found it impossible to walk away from the rest of the story, as told by a new group of men and women, dealing with new events and offering new perspectives on the period, in which men and women from all over the island were involved in one way or another.

Apart from the carefully organised infiltration of the postal services, and the cooperation of some members of the RIC, unexpected help for the nationalist cause came from unsuspected quarters: from secret sympathisers who held funds for the Volunteers and took huge risks for little or no reward. Information was imparted from unlikely quarters, as is described in Seamus Robinson's witness statement, for example.

What emerges above all from the testimonies of the men and women is the wide circle of friends and colleagues which grew out of their activities. A labyrinthine grid of mutual assistance developed over the whole island, supported by a remarkable consensus of outlook. The unity of purpose which emerged was never so marked as at the time of the threat of conscription in 1918, but the deep foundations of trust amongst these men and women essentially lay in their long connection with the Gaelic League, the Volunteer movement and Sinn Féin. One of the most important organisers of the embryo State, Seamus Ua Caomhanaigh, remarks that, through his long-standing connections, 'There was hardly a parish in the country in which I did not know someone who would act as a cover.'

11

The bonds forged by the shared experiences of time spent in prisons and internment camps proved invaluable – and were carefully fostered by nationalist leaders like Michael Collins, who appeared to find the re-organisation of the IRB at Frongoch useful for his purposes. Moreover, the Cumann na mBan of the time were able to forge country-wide connections without the aid of secret societies. This network enabled them to provide the long-term recuperative nursing care, in safe surroundings, which many of the men who had been on active service required.

It is true that the differences which arose in the national movement at the time of the Treaty sundered the bonds which had been built up since before 1916 – a fact of which the men and women who submitted their testimonies to the Bureau of Military History in the 1940s and 1950s were well conscious. An air of ineffable sadness hangs over many of the statements. Most of them stop short of the Treaty negotiations, choosing to conclude on the date of the Truce. One or two make painful references, such as Michael Hynes from Borrisoleigh, County Tipperary, who remarks: 'No one ever thought that civil war would develop and that things would become so bitter.'

The rifts left by the Civil War began to close during the Second World War. These witness statements, together with contemporary documents, press cuttings, photographs and a few rare voice recordings from people who had been active in the national movement between 1913 and 1921, are a gift which the army has collected and kept safe for us. There is much in these archives to unite us, and much for us to admire.

Annie Ryan, April 2007

1

EXECUTIONS AND DEPORTATIONS

On 3 May 1916, almost as soon as the Easter Rising was over and while Dublin lay in smoking ruins, the first of the executions of the rebel leaders took place. Spread out over two weeks, they had a profound effect not only on the participants and would-be participants in the Rising but on public opinion as well. The initial reaction to the Rising had been one of shock. It was different in Britain: there the reaction was one of fury – hardly surprising in the year of the Somme and in the middle of the Great War. As a result, martial law was introduced throughout Ireland. The principal Irish newspapers demanded retribution.

The last of the executions took place on 12 May 1916. The country was quiet. As Elizabeth Bloxham, a young Protestant nationalist from the west of Ireland, put it: 'There was great agony of spirit in Ireland at that time.' As a student in Dublin, Bloxham had known many of the leading figures involved in the Rising.

On 8 May, Ignatius Callender, who had been a dispatch carrier for the rebels during Easter Week, was

> so horrified by the announcement of the execution of my Company captain and intimate friend Sean Heuston, that I decided it was time something should be done. . . . I called on a priest friend and discussed the situation with him; we decided on certain action.

In 1954, when Callender gave his testimony to the Bureau of Military History, he

> was happy to say that as a result of the priest's action and the speech made by John Dillon in the English House of Commons, on 11 May, that Asquith promised that, with the exception of the two men already sentenced, no other executions would take place.

Whether the priest was as influential as Callender believed or not, the executions came to an end on 12 May, when Sean McDermott and James Connolly went before the firing squad.

Before the Rising, Callender's mother ran a restaurant that was heavily patronised by the British military. Callender recollected that:

> On the third of May, 1916, when the Stop Press *Evening Mail* appeared, announcing the execution of P. H. Pearse, T. MacDonagh and T. J. Clarke, my mother on hearing the news exclaimed 'May the Lord have mercy on their souls'. One of the British HQ Command chauffeurs, who was having lunch in my mother's restaurant, said 'What is that you said?' My mother repeated the prayer for him. He immediately left, without finishing his meal, remarking as he left, 'that is more than you said for our poor fellows who were killed'.

Soon after this incident, the Lucan Restaurant, as it was known, was 'put out of military bounds by order of the British authority'. It closed at the end of June.

Muriel McSwiney, widow of Terence McSwiney, who made her statement in Paris in 1951, remembered the feeling of revulsion that was generated in Cork and elsewhere by the executions: 'The news was posted up on the pavement in front of the *Cork Examiner* office, day and night, and the crowd gathered to hear it.' People all over Ireland were hungry for news of the rising and its aftermath. Miss Dulcibella Barton, who was a sister of Robert Barton (later to be a noted political activist) and a cousin of Erskine Childers, had a very clear recollection of events:

> I was very interested in the fact that there was a rebellion in progress. I spent about a week in the city. I think it must have been at the end of the week that I met Father Sherwin of University Church and he asked me where I was going. I said I was going into town to buy an *Irish Times*. He asked me to get one for him. When I got to the *Times* office there was a great crowd and as I hate standing in a queue I got a little boy to get the papers for me. He did and I gave him something for himself. The paper was a single sheet and I brought one back to Father Sherwin.

Dulcibella Barton left for home, in Annamoe, Glendalough, County Wicklow, the next day. A policeman stopped her at Roundwood and asked her for news from Dublin. She refused to give him any. After all, Barton was a great friend of 'Con Markievicz, and whenever I wanted a bed in

Dublin I had one in her house in Leinster Road'. Barton also took care of her dog, a brown spaniel, whenever the Countess was in jail.

Elizabeth Bloxham was working as a teacher in Newtownards, County Down, in 1916. When she read news of the Rising in the *Evening Telegraph*, she was shocked 'into a state of unreality by the bald report in the paper'. There was no one to whom she could talk:

> Then came the time when each day's paper brought news of the execu-tions. I made what I thought was a successful effort to hide my feelings from people who I knew were unsympathetic. But later on the woman of the house told me that whenever she entered my room at that time she felt I was as one watching by the dead. I said I thought my manner to her was the same as usual. 'It was,' she said, 'but I knew that the moment I closed the door you were again watching by the dead.'

Marie Perolz (née Flanagan), who had missed the Rising in Dublin because she had been sent to Cork on courier business, was arrested on the day Tom Clarke was executed. She was sent to Kilmainham before being moved to Mountjoy, and eventually on to Lewes Prisons in Sussex in the south of England. Perolz remembered:

> At Kilmainham I was very depressed when I knew the men were being executed. I could neither eat nor sleep. Only for Brighid Foley I would have died. She kept up my courage and tried to force me to eat.

Ignatius Callender escaped arrest despite his activities during Easter Week. Not so lucky were many others throughout the country who had not taken part in the Rising but were sympathetic to its aims. All over Ireland, after the rebellion had collapsed, there was a round-up of sus-pects by the RIC and the British army.

In many places, these suspects had tried hard to get to Dublin, with every intention of taking part in the rebellion. For example, Edward Moane describes how in Westport 'the Rebellion came upon us and still found us without any proper armaments and, worse still, without any orders'. By Wednesday of Easter Week, Moane's IRB Circle knew that fighting was taking place in Dublin. They held a meeting to discuss what they could do but concluded that it would be hopeless to attempt any-thing. In the subsequent round-up, Joe McBride, a brother of Major John

McBride, who was executed for his part in the Rising in Dublin, was arrested, whereas Moane was not. Moane did not escape completely, however. Early in the spring of 1917, when all the other prisoners had been released, Moane was imprisoned for three months for singing a seditious song at a concert.

According to Robert Holland, the nineteen-year-old who had fought so valiantly at the Marrowbone Lane Distillery:

> everyone and anyone who had anything to do with any organisation participating in the Insurrection were liable to arrest . . . the prisons in Ireland and England were packed . . . in Dublin men and women suspected of sympathising with the Insurrection were dismissed from their employment.

Many of the prisoners' relatives were finding it very hard to get the necessities of life. Holland was beginning to think that 'we, in prison, were better off than some of them'.

It is little wonder then that people like Kathleen Clarke, Tom Clarke's widow, had begun to organise aid committees for the relatives even before the executions had ceased. Those members of Cumann na mBan who were not imprisoned got down to work immediately. Aine Heron, who was a Captain in Cumann na mBan, was involved in the founding of the Volunteer Dependants Fund. This fund, together with the National Aid Committee, was invaluable in restoring some kind of morale for the stricken families and friends of the prisoners. Heron found it difficult at first to establish contact with the relatives of the Volunteers:

> When we called at the houses sometimes the inhabitants denied all knowledge of the Volunteers in question, as they did not know us and they thought we might be setting traps for them. Gradually it became easier as the sympathy of the public had veered round to the victims of the rebellion. Especially, the Masses for the men of Easter Week did a great deal to give courage to all these people. They gave them the only opportunity they had of coming together and exchanging news from the various prisons.

Eilis Bean Ui Connaill, vice-commandant and member of the Executive of Cumann na mBan, had a very similar story to tell in her witness statement:

news of men killed in action, of soldiers shooting our innocent people in their homes as occurred in our area in North King Street, execution of our leaders, deportations, raids, arrests and all the mock trials etc. We seemed helpless at this stage.

The National Aid Fund was established to relieve distress among 'the dependants of persons killed in action, executed, sentenced or deported', as Ui Connaill notes. Voluntary helpers assembled in Exchequer Street and issued an appeal to the whole country – to which there was a huge response. Ui Connaill continues: 'Many of our members helped on that committee. Each went around in her own area, investigating the cases of distress. We met with great difficulties.' Many of the relatives were terrified of being identified with those who took part in the Rising 'as the military and police were still very busy making raids and arrests'.

Ui Connaill first noticed a change in attitudes towards the prisoners through the size of the Cumann na mBan church-door collections for the National Aid Fund:

> People who had refused to subscribe before now gave generously and sympathetically. This gave us great courage and resulted in [us] filling several boxes on Sundays instead of merely one.

Prisoners such as Robert Holland were deeply grateful for the existence of the National Aid Fund. While he was in prison, he worried for his mother, who was an invalid, and his twelve-year old sister. Others too began to be aware of the hard times their families were going through. Holland's testimony informs us:

> We heard at this time that the National Fund had been started, that a kind of means test was in operation with the object of relieving the most necessitous cases first. As time went on and money came in, every deserving case was relieved to some extent; we in prison thanked God and said many a Rosary for those who gave their time and money to help our destitute people.

No one was more appreciative of the help and support received from the Fund on their release than Seamus Ua Caomhanaigh, Secretary 'Defence of Ireland Fund'; Accountant to the Sinn Féin Executive; Secretary, Local Government Department, Dáil Éireann. The support began for him on the boat home from Britain. The night before

17

Christmas Eve, Ua Caomhanaigh and his comrades were paraded from Frongoch Jail to catch the train to Holyhead. It was a terrible night, and the ex-prisoners stood for two hours at the station in a blizzard of sleet and snow until their train arrived at eight o'clock. By the time they embarked on the mailboat, the comrades were saturated. The boat was packed with people going home to Ireland for Christmas and, to the former prisoners' surprise, their fellow passengers were very nice to them. Ua Caomhanaigh had no difficulty in remembering the details:

> We were not long on board when a man came up to me and asked me would I like a cup of tea. I said I would. He went away and brought it back to me in no time. Then a lady gave me an enormous hunk of rich Christmas cake. Another gave me a large piece of cheese. I was literally starving, as we had [had] no refreshment of any kind since leaving Frongoch. . . . I drank the tea and with the cheese in one hand and the cake in the other I would take an alternative bite out of each and by the time I had got it all down I was feeling fine.

It was even more pleasant for the former prisoners to meet old friends. Ua Caomhanaigh goes on:

> Some of the girls who had been released were going home on the same boat. I remember talking to Miss Helena Moloney and I think also Miss Kearney. It was a very rough passage. The night was wild. There were no lights showing anywhere on board as this was in the middle of the first Great War

They arrived in Dublin on Christmas Eve.

2

The Prisoners' Return

It was hard for Seamus Ua Caomhanaigh to put his memories on record for the Bureau of Military History. He found it extremely painful to recall the experiences of the War of Independence, especially the lead-up to the truce and the Treaty. A fit of terrible depression would descend on him whenever he heard or read anything relating to the happenings of those years: 'I could not read a book nor look at a movie without experiencing it.' He told the Bureau to feel free to scrap his statement if they thought it was no good. Luckily, the Bureau accepted his contribution. Ua Caomhanaigh's account of his time in Frongoch and his return to Ireland on the mailboat is only part of his enthralling story. His full statement covers his life from his birth on 21 April 1888 in St Michael's Lane, not far from St Stephen's Green, up to the formation of the Department of Local Government under the first Dáil, and the Truce in 1921.

When his mailboat reached Dublin's North Wall on Christmas Eve, 1916, Ua Caomhanaigh was met by Paddy McGuirk, who had been his next-door neighbour in Stafford Jail, and had been released earlier: '[McGuirk] had an outside car waiting to bring me home, where I arrived in a short time.' Ua Caomhanaigh did not return alone. He brought Joe Duffy, another prisoner friend, home with him:

> When we reached Dublin Joe had no place to go. He was a stranger to Dublin, never having lived there except for the short time he had been in Larkfield, Kimmage.

It was at Larkfield, on the Plunkett estate, that the men who had returned to Ireland for the Rising set up camp.

Ua Caomhanaigh was in prison when he learned of the birth of his son. He had not known that his wife was pregnant at the time of his deportation; by the time he returned, the child had been christened and named Seamus Diarmuid, after Sean McDermott. On the day Ua Caomhanaigh arrived home, a Christmas hamper was delivered to the house. It was provided not by the National Aid Fund 'but by one of the societies of women who were working so hard at the time in the national cause'. The National Aid Committee, however, sent him an 'order for a complete new outfit'.

Within a few days, Ua Caomhanaigh was appointed secretary to the ex-prisoners' committee. He was given the task of examining the cases of all the former prisoners and their dependants 'and seeing that nobody was left destitute'. Ua Caomhanaigh had found his niche. He was kept happily occupied during the spring and summer 'having things done properly and quickly'. It was at this time that Michael Collins had been appointed secretary of the National Aid Fund; Ua Caomhanaigh heartily approved of Collins's selection for this post, as it made his own job much easier. Amongst his many other talents, Michael Collins was an extremely efficient administrator.

People like Ua Caomhanaigh were already beginning to look to the future rather than the past. Before they could do this, however, it was necessary for some to analyse the events, unhappy as they were, of Easter Week. Robert Holland had gone into the question in some depth whilst still in Knutsford Jail. Indeed, even before the surrender, towards the end of Easter Week, as the fight was beginning to wind down, Holland and Con Colbert (who was later executed) drew up lists of their men who had and had not turned out for the Rising. In Knutsford, Holland had learned:

> all that had happened in the two sections of the South Dublin Garrison, also all about the battle at Ashbourne and in fact, before the middle of May, we knew all that had taken place in the country during and after the insurrection – of the fate of the men they termed our leaders – of prison sentences of the group of less important [rebels]. We got this through small groups who were being picked up in Ireland and were still being transferred to Knutsford Prison.

When Peadar McMahon, who had fought in the Rising under Commandant Michael Mallin, was released from Frongoch in the autumn of 1916, he found himself out of a job. The shipping firm that had employed him before the Rising refused to re-hire him due to his involvement in the Rising. Whilst visiting the widow of Tom Clarke, one of the leaders of the Rising who had been executed, McMahon met Miss Madge Daly, who was desperately looking for help with running the bakery business:

> She said that her brother was executed; her uncle, John Daly, had died and some assistance was required to run the business. I decided to go to Limerick. . . . While in Limerick I assisted in the formation of a second Battalion in the city and a number of Battalions in the adjoining country.

Ernest Blythe, who had been imprisoned in Reading Jail for his pre-1916 activities, expected to be released with the other leading figures who were held there. But the governor of the jail informed Blythe that, because the order under which he had been deported a fortnight before Easter 1916 had not been lifted, he could not return to Ireland. He was, however, free to go where he liked in England. But Blythe decided to take a chance and went to Dublin with the rest. On Blythe's arrival there, Sean T. O'Kelly invited him to his home for breakfast; Blythe later went out to Bray to see his old friends, the FitzGeralds. From there, he went 'up North' and spent a week at his father's house in County Antrim, 'the police having lost sight of him'. The police caught Blythe when he went to Belfast 'to see if I could find Sean Lestor' (an old friend from pre-1916 days who was afterwards Secretary General of the League of Nations, and the father-in-law of Douglas Gageby, who was editor of the *Irish Times* and also wrote Lestor's biography). Blythe was then picked up, taken to the police station and put aboard a train for Dublin and conveyed to Arbour Hill. At length, after many negotiations and undertakings, and withdrawing of undertakings, the British Commander sent a 'DMP man . . . who told [me] that the order to leave Ireland had been suspended'. Blythe could now go where he liked. He decided to go to Limerick:

> The Dalys of Limerick had written asking me to spend a while with them. I accepted the invitation and arrived in Limerick just after the end of the Clare election.

In the first few weeks after his return to Ireland, Blythe knew little of how matters stood with the Volunteer organisation. His visit to the Dalys afforded him the opportunity of observing activities at close quarters. Blythe found:

There was a great deal of strained feeling between the officers of the Volunteers, as there was prior to the Rising, and a great many people who found fault with their attitude and action at that time. I thought there was no use in discussing the past, but I agreed that the complete inactivity of the existing body of Volunteer officers was wrong.

In his testimony, Joe Barrett from Clare, who had, like so many others in 1916, mobilised for a Rising on Easter Sunday, only to wait in vain for further orders, gives us a fairly clear indication of what might have been the bone of contention in Limerick:

> When we learned that the Limerick Volunteers had surrendered their arms to the British authorities, the Volunteers in my area entirely disagreed with this action.

Edward Moane of Westport, County Mayo, delicately suggests that something of the same kind happened only ten miles from him in Castlebar:

> We knew there was about thirty rifles in the Castlebar area, but [as to] where they were located or what ammunition was available we had no information. Some of these rifles were surrendered to the British authorities after the Rebellion.

The surrender of arms was a severe embarrassment to the Volunteers, none more so than to those in Cork. Muriel McSwiney, the widow of Terence McSwiney, who died on hunger strike in 1920, remembered that:

> It was towards the end of Easter Week that the Volunteers surrendered their arms. Some of them gave up wooden instruments wrapped in stuff and kept their rifles.

The Catholic bishop of Cork, Thomas O'Callaghan, in some way became implicated in a deal with the British military whereby it was promised that, if the arms were ceded, there would be no arrests of Volunteers. This involvement soured relations between the leaders of the Volunteers in Cork and the bishop for many years afterwards.

Henry O'Brien from Athlone had been active in the Volunteer movement since 1913. About a week or so before the Rising, a priest called Father O'Reilly managed to procure arms for the Volunteers in Athlone.

On Easter Sunday morning, they 'mobilised about thirty strong. . . . Our first task was to cut the railway and telegraph and telephone wires outside Athlone.' The rifles and shotguns had been sent on to Shannon Bridge, where the Volunteers were to meet Liam Mellows after cutting the wires. But at 2.30 PM, 'we received a message that the whole affair was off'.

O'Brien was arrested immediately after the Rising but was released, and returned home in time to witness the surrendering of arms:

> Mr Chapman, who owned the printing works in Athlone, and one of the friars from the Abbey, acted as liaison officers between the RIC and British authorities, and the Volunteers, and through them the rifles and ammunition were surrendered to the British authorities.

Timothy Houlihan from Ballybunion, County Kerry, was careful to record that, even if the town was not particularly active up to 1916, its honour was saved by a Volunteer leader from Listowel:

> After the Easter Week Rebellion, when the order came to surrender all arms in the country, a man named Paddy Landers, who was in charge of a Company in Listowel before Easter Week, sent out to Ballybunion two BSA rifles and five hundred rounds and a lot of cartridge and wads by a man named Joe Mahoney, a native of Ballybunion. The stuff was dumped at Eddie Horagan's, a farmer who lived near the town. Horagan looked after the stuff. He was never under suspicion as he was regarded as pro-British.

The opinion held by Patrick McElligot (a member of the IRB from 1911 and of the Volunteers from 1914, and OC of the Listowel Battalion) of Paddy Landers is unambiguous, however. According to McElligot, Landers made no attempt to save the arms but was in fact determined to surrender all the guns to the RIC:

> Landers sent for the RIC and handed over the stack of broken guns, at the same time informing the RIC of the missing nine rifles . . . . The Volunteers were more afraid of Landers than the RIC as he was constantly in touch with them.

Another Kerry man, Matthew Finucane, was careful to record that in Duagh, where the Volunteer Company had been reorganised by Ernest Blythe in the early months of 1916:

the order to surrender all arms in the Company was never carried out, as the RIC were not aware that there were any arms in the possession of the Volunteers here in Duagh.

Almost immediately after the release of the prisoners, the work of reorganisation began; indeed, some would say that it began before the general release, which took place at Christmas 1916. Certainly the Committees that were set up to assist families that had been left without means of financial support after the Rising helped to draw the remnants of the revolution together.

The significance of imprisonment on the development of the Volunteers cannot be overlooked. William Mullins, quartermaster of Duagh Company of the Irish Volunteers in County Kerry and OC of Kerry No. 1 Brigade, from Moyderwell, Tralee, was emphatic about the role of the prisons and detention camps, particularly Frongoch. He states:

> I am fully convinced that Frongoch made our whole organisation into what it eventually reached. The comradeship that developed in Frongoch and the knowledge we got of each other from different parts of the country, the military aspect of things and being brought into close contact with men whom we used only hear about previous to that, was a binding force for the future.

Many of the Volunteer leaders, when they made their way home after their time in jail, found everything in order. In Duagh, the Volunteers were reorganised for a second time, Mullins remembers:

> The Company strength was about forty men. Up to the end of 1917 and all through 1918 we held meetings, received drill instruction and paraded from time to time.

Matthew Finucane was appointed quartermasterof Duagh Company in 1919 and made responsible for the collection of all shotguns and arms in the area. As Henry O'Brien found in Athlone, in almost every area where the Volunteers had been active before the Rising:

> nearly all our members became active again . . . . We held regular parades for drill, in secret of course. We had no arms and each member paid a small subscription towards a fund for the purchase of arms. Concerts, dances and so forth were run with the assistance of the Cumann na mBan.

Patrick Egan, who had hid out in the hills above Ticknock after the Rising, was able to attend a meeting in early 1917 in Cathal Brugha's house in Dublin when things became more normal. At that meeting, the reorganisation of the Battalion began and 'the election of officers for C Company took place'.

Oscar Traynor, who was later to become commandant of the Dublin Brigade and a member of the Army Council, was released on Christmas Eve, like the great majority of the internees. He remembers:

> Shortly after my arrival in Dublin I made contact with the Volunteer organisation again. My old Company, while meeting from time to time, was very much below strength.

The renewed activity of the Volunteers did not escape the notice of the authorities. In early January 1917, the Volunteers – or, as they were beginning to be known, the Irish Republican Army – started a reorganising campaign in Tralee and the surrounding country districts. Joseph Melinn, vice-commandant of Kerry No. 1 Brigade, recalls that he:

> was actively engaged in this when I was again taken prisoner, and deported with twenty-seven others from other counties, to different parts of England, on February 22nd, 1917. By arrangement, the Irish Republican Brotherhood got us in touch with friends in London and Manchester who offered assistance to enable us to escape back to Ireland.

Joseph Melinn, with fourteen others, escaped on that occasion and 'reported back to headquarters on the morning of May 5th, 1917'.

A pattern was beginning to emerge: arrest, imprisonment, escape. This pattern did not, however, impede the growth of the IRA. By December 1917, the Battalion in the Westport area alone numbered

> three hundred and fifty strong and [was] organised in nine Companies. . . . I (with two others) organised these Companies, travelling here and there, sometimes on cycles but more often across country on foot

according to Edward Moane, Vice Commandant of the West Mayo Brigade of the IRA.

25

In Limerick, Peadar McMahon and Ernest Blythe, after a good deal of discussion with the other senior Volunteers, decided that the only way to get over the inactivity of the existing Volunteer body in Limerick was to organise a second Battalion from amongst 'young men who were not Volunteers and who were not being encouraged to join', as Blythe notes. Eventually, they were able to establish 'a number of Battalions in the adjoining country'.

Later, Blythe expresses some uncharacteristic doubts about his actions in Limerick. He felt that he could have handled the situation better:

> Perhaps if we had continued to urge the existing officers to undertake some activity, our appeals, plus the changing temperature, would have sufficed to induce them to make the moves [begin a new campaign with new officers].

3

LINING UP

Dan Breen, best known later for his book, *My Fight for Irish Freedom*, describes in his statement to the Bureau of Military History an important element in the drive for action that seized several of his comrades. All over Ireland, people like Sean Treacy (one of the leaders of the South Tipperary Brigade during the War of Independence) felt impelled to carry on from where the men and women of 1916 had left off. Treacy was later shot dead in Talbot Street, at the height of the war which he so ardently desired. Dan Breen recalls in his statement:

> At this time, following 1916, I was Treacy's chief, if not his only confidant, and he discussed everything freely with me. I remember him talking about the Rising of 1916 and calling it 'another '98', meaning that this was another failure, as 1798 had been, and yet he was insistent that everything was not yet lost and that we might still do something to retrieve [the failure of the 1916 Rising].

Seamus Robinson puts it in another way:

> I would say that it was the leaders of the 1916 Rising by their heroic deaths after an historic fight that left us survivors. . . . [and with] no honourable alternative but the slogan 'They shall not have fought and died in vain'.

In his testimony, Robinson attempts to answer how, when and on whose authority the hostilities began after 1916. During his imprisonment in Reading Jail, Robinson was in a good position to assess the thinking of his fellow prisoners. These included Arthur Griffith, Sean T. O'Kelly, Ernest Blythe, Herbert More-Pim, Darrell Figgis, George Nicholls, Sean Milroy and others – all of them leaders in Sinn Féin. These men – Sean T. O'Kelly excepted – were, in Robinson's opinion, convinced that a 'united passive resistance policy was all-sufficient to win our independence'. Robinson was at pains to make his own position, and that of younger men, clear. He and his young comrades had a tremendous regard for the intelligence, clear-sightedness, integrity and zeal of these eminent older men. In his opinion, it was only common sense that the Volunteer army needed a vigorous political party in order to withstand the 'pro-British partisan propaganda of press and pulpit'. They could see the importance of the 'moral-legal support of an elected government. . . . "the Constituent Assembly" of Arthur Griffith's talks to us'. They could also see the necessity of having 'the will of the people behind the coming struggle'. This was of equal importance with the existence of a well-organised and well-equipped army, if the revolution was to succeed. Robinson lists the officers in Reading at the time who were in favour of the political movement 'as the nation's second arm'. He lists them:

> Terence McSweeney, Tomas MacCurtain, J. J. O'Connell, Eamon O'Duibhir, Joe Robinson, Seamus Pender, Mick Brennan, Padraig O'Maille.

According to Robinson, when the prisoners came home to Ireland after their release, the Volunteers quickly became aware of the immense support that the people as a whole gave to Sinn Féin: 'It soon was unnecessary for the Volunteers to waste their time on it'. So they concentrated on building up their own forces instead.

In October 1917, Sinn Féin's annual convention, or Ard Fheis, was held in Dublin – the tenth such convention that had been held by the party. Under cover of the Ard Fheis, the Volunteers also held a convention. In fact, many of the delegates held dual membership of the two organisations. The attendance at the Ard Fheis included several people who were also members of the Irish Republican Brotherhood; many were members of all three organisations.

Monsignor Patrick Browne, president of University College Galway, who used to meet Arthur Griffith fairly frequently after 1916, 'generally in the Bailey smoke-room', was certain that Griffith was out of sympathy with 'the Resolution to proclaim the country independent and follow a Republican policy'. Griffith expressed his considerable distaste with the idea of declaring Ireland a republic then, as he also did in 1919, just before the Dáil proclaimed the Republic. He professed his disbelief that

the Irish people wanted such an arrangement. It was on Griffith's proposal that de Valera was made President. Browne added that, 'as time went
on, Griffith fell in with the policy and, when de Valera was in America,
[Griffith] was Acting President'.

Seamus Dobbyn's testimony regarding the IRB makes interesting
reading. Dobbyn's membership of the IRB stretched back to the
Dungannon Club, where, in 1907, he met men like Sean McDermott,
Denis McCullough and Bulmer Hobson. Dobbyn had done his best to
join the Rising but had been frustrated in his attempts in this area. He had
been one of the first to be imprisoned after the Rising but was released
in the autumn of 1916. In May 1917, Dobbyn was sent to Dublin to meet
three members of the Supreme Council of the IRB: Diarmuid Lynch,
Mick Collins and Sean McGarry.

Dobbyn recalls that 'I was asked by them to go on a six-month tour
of inspection of the nine Ulster counties'. Dobbyn made his report on
this tour a few months later. Things were not good with the IRB in Ulster.
The main trouble was that, although they were doing nothing of any significance for the national movement, 'a number of them thought themselves superior to the IRA and were not even supporting the IRA'. Soon
after this tour, Dobbyn was co-opted as a member of the Supreme
Council of the IRB.

Seamus Robinson was even more critical of the IRB organisation as
a whole. According to Robinson:

> The IRB had lost prestige after Easter Week 1916, their authority mori-
> bund where not already dead. Many had apparently shirked the Rising.
> There had been some movement started in Frongoch which aimed at
> reviving and getting a change in control of the IRB. Shortly after the
> release from internment, young chaps mixed among us broadcasting the
> news that every member of the 'Organisation' was requested to attend
> a meeting in Parnell Square – No. 44 I think. At that meeting I saw
> young fellows with notebooks rushing round and about the ground
> floor (there were about 150 present) buttonholing individuals with anx-
> ious whispers – 'We must make sure that no one will be elected an offi-
> cer of the Volunteers who is not a member of the "Organisation".' As
> if that were something new or something that we would be allowed to
> forget.

Robinson was not impressed. He did not wait for the meeting to
begin and walked out in disgust. He never again 'bothered about the IRB'.

When the Volunteer Executive was elected at the Ard Fheis in October 1917, Robinson considered the authority of the IRB redundant and illegal for the Volunteers. Stronger still, he stated: 'After the Oath of Allegiance to the Dáil, the IRB became a sinister cabal.'

Whatever Robinson might have thought about the IRB, the organisation continued. Dobbyn was given the job of reorganising the IRB in Ulster. He was then asked to add the inspection of the IRA to his IRB duties. 'This I believe was given as a cover for my activities with the IRB,' he says.

As for the Sinn Féin Ard Fheis in October 1917, Dobbyn is certain that

> IRB men were instructed to have themselves elected delegates to that Convention, if possible, and to vote for the election of de Valera as President. I was ordered by the Supreme Council, and carried out the order, to give instructions to suitable IRB men to join the local Sinn Féin Club and, if possible, to have themselves elected to that Convention

Whatever certain members of the Volunteers (or the IRA, as it was beginning to be called) thought of the IRB, on occasion almost everyone was glad of its help, particularly in organising prison escapes outside Ireland. Liam McMahon, Centre (head) of the Manchester Circle of the IRB, was born in 1878 in Kildimo, County Limerick. He emigrated to Liverpool, where he worked for the butter merchants Dowdall Brothers as a clerk. He became a member of the Gaelic League in Bootle, Lancashire, and later joined the GAA. He was picked to play for Lancashire against Kilkenny in the All-Ireland Hurling Championship in Croke Park in 1905. It was while crossing back to Liverpool after this match that McMahon was inducted into the IRB by a man called Paddy Lively. As McMahon says:

> After a short conversation, during which he explained the aims and objects of the IRB, he asked me if I had any religious scruples about becoming a member. I said I had not. There and then, he administered the oath, as we stood by the rails looking out to sea.

Later on, McMahon's firm appointed him to their Manchester office and the IRB transferred him from the Liverpool Circle to the Manchester Circle. Sean McDermott visited Manchester some five years before 1916, and 'from time to time, we purchased war material – mostly revolvers and ammunition – and sent it across to Dublin'.

Unlike the men at the Kimmage camp and, indeed, Michael Collins and other members of the IRB, McMahon was 'not summoned to take part in the Rising'. He met Collins through the National Aid Society:

> I was made Honorary Secretary to that Society for England and Wales, and through that I met Michael Collins. Our association afterwards, up to the signing of the Treaty, was most intimate.

Michael Collins was not the only republican leader who was in touch with McMahon. McMahon describes how Éamon de Valera involved himself in the development of the movement:

> Some time after Mr de Valera's release from jail in June 1917, I got a letter from him, through Harry Boland, saying that he thought Sinn Féin in England was rather dangerous. It was proclaimed and all that. He suggested we should form the Irish Self-Determination League. He asked me, as Honorary Secretary of Sinn Féin, to call the officers of the different Irish Societies there and to start a provisional executive, which I did.

The first meeting of this executive, which was held in Manchester, was a huge success. Two halls, the Free Trade Hall and the Albert Hall opposite, were packed out. Arthur Griffith, Laurence Ginnell MP and Harry Boland came over from Dublin to speak to this large gathering. The League spread rapidly: 'At one time we had over four hundred branches in England and Wales.' McMahon describes his modus operandi:

> We decided that the best plan was to use the League, not openly but surreptitiously, for IRB purposes. All our organisers were IRB men. They were to report likely persons to start a Company of Volunteers. If we got a good man, whom we thought was reliable, we would initiate him into the Volunteers.

In the capable hands of McMahon, the Irish independence movement in Britain flourished. The contacts made, and the networks established, were invaluable later on, not least to Michael Collins when he and his comrades managed to 'spring' de Valera from Lincoln Jail.

4

Political Action: The By-elections

There is nothing like a contest against a common enemy for welding different elements of a movement into a united front. The first three by-elections after the Rising were ideal for this purpose. By the time that some extremely sensitive issues came to be discussed at the Volunteer Convention, the delegates were able to deal with them comparatively easily. Major Patrick Colgan, a veteran of 1916, attended that meeting and in his statement reports:

> Éamon de Valera presided at the meeting. A long discussion took place on a proposal that Eoin McNeill should be tried by a Volunteer Court for his action in countermanding the Manoeuvres which were to be held on Easter Sunday, 1916.

But the time for that kind of discussion was past.

Seamus Ua Caomhanaigh, who by this time must have been settling in nicely at home after his prison experiences, not to mention into his new job at the centre of events, considered that:

> The first of the more important things that happened was Count Plunkett's name appeared in the papers as a candidate, a man named Gallagher, a draper with a place of business in George's Street, called to see me. He told me he was a native of Roscommon and that he continued to take an active interest in the affairs of the county. He asked me was Count Plunkett all right from the Sinn Féin point of view, 'for', said he, 'if he is, he's already elected. I know all about his sons Joe, George and Jack. But you know many a son reared a bad father, and I want to make sure he won't sit in the British Parliament if elected.' He said his word went far in the county and if he put in a favourable word for the Count his election was assured.

Ua Caomhanaigh was able to get him an assurance from Headquarters that Count Plunkett was indeed sound. He won the election with 3,000 votes against 1,700.

Miss Brighid O'Mullane, who had lived in Leinster Road in Rathmines, Dublin, at the time she gave her account of her work in Cumann na mBan, remembers that she:

> had just left school in Sligo, after my mother's death, when the Roscommon election was held. I was asked to assist on the organising committee of a banquet that was to be given to Count Plunkett and his wife some weeks after his victory. The Corporation had decided to confer the freedom of the city on him.

The second by-election in 1917 was in South Longford. The candidate, Joseph McGuinness, was a prisoner in Lewes, England, and his election campaign used the slogan: 'Put him in to get him out'.

Eilis Bean Ui Chonaill was a personal friend of Joseph McGuinness, and this was her home constituency. She took a week's leave, and set off for the country without delay:

> I made a personal canvas of my native parish and the surroundings, and the fact that I knew the candidate was almost sufficient to convince the people to go to the polls.

No one gives a clearer account of this by-election than Judge Charles Wyse Power, who, as he describes, was given a watching brief:

> My role was generally to watch the legal position of the candidate as he was still serving his sentence of penal servitude in lieu of the death sentence which had been passed on him in 1916, and it was feared that there was a possibility that the Redmondites might raise the point that he was a felon and therefore incapable of being a candidate.

Nobody in fact raised the point, but the count after the election proved to be one of the most exciting in the history of County Longford. Wyse Power was there:

> The first declared result announced that the Redmondite had been elected by a majority of thirteen. The votes had been counted in bundles of fifty placed on each side of the table. When this was announced, the Redmondites, inside and outside the courthouse, physically danced for joy. Looking out of the window I saw Arthur Griffith and our supporters looking very glum on the other side of the street.

But Griffith and his friends had no need to be downcast. Joe McGrath, who later ran the Irish Sweepstakes, had calculated that there must be fifty missing votes:

> The fifty votes were found immediately and they were McGuinness's, thus altering a minority of thirteen against McGuinness to a majority of thirty-seven for him.

Leo Baxter, who lived in Longford when he testified in 1950, was one of those men who joined the Volunteers after 1916. He joined a small Company in Ardagh, consisting of about thirty men that had no arms of any kind. This did not prevent them from engaging in military exercises, however. Baxter states: 'Our instructors were a couple of British army men who were also members.'

The membership of this Company overlapped completely with the Sinn Féin Club in Ardagh. According to Baxter: 'The Volunteers took a big part in the McGuinness election in South Longford and were active in canvassing and other duties on his behalf.'

The people, including the clergy, took their elections seriously in County Longford. Bean Ui Connaill recounts the story of one priest, Father Terry Meehan, who paid for the transport of sympathetic voters out of his own pocket:

> On the Saturday previous to the election, in his enthusiasm, he overlooked the time for Confessions in his parish and he was, as a result, shortly transferred to a parish in the back of beyond.

The next by-election, the one in East Clare, was to demonstrate a shift in public opinion which was to become altogether more apparent in the general election in 1918. The Irish Parliamentary Party (or the Redmondites, as the supporters of Sinn Féin still called them in 1950) were never to recover electorally from this shift.

The East Clare election took place on 11 July 1917. Wyse Power remembered: 'The announcement of the result of the poll . . . went through Ireland like wildfire, for Mr De Valera had polled three to one.'

Joseph Barrett of Kilrush, County Clare, in his testimony explains:

> The prisoners who were sentenced after the Rising were released and numbers of these, as well as the men who had been released from internment earlier, came to Clare to assist in the election. The presence

of all these around the county, as well as the meetings held in connection with the election, gave a great fillip to the morale of the volunteers in the county. Thousands of new recruits joined the ranks that time.

The volunteers in County Clare got such a head start at the time of the by-election that there was little to do in the line of recruiting in 1918: 'all the available young men had already joined up', says Barrett.

The first incidents of any consequence in the bitter fight which was soon to take place in Ireland were connected with the celebrations that followed the election victories. One such incident took place in Ballybunion, County Kerry, when people from the town and the surrounding country gathered for a victory parade. As the parade passed the RIC barracks, some RIC men there became so annoyed that they opened fire on the people and shot one man, a certain Scanlon, dead. The story of the inquiry and the court case which followed is told by Judge Wyse Power in his witness statement.

It was in 1917 too that Thomas Ashe died on hunger strike. Ashe was born and reared on the Dingle Peninsula. In 1916, he led the Volunteers in battle in Ashbourne, on the outskirts of Dublin. He was subsequently condemned to death, but the sentence was commuted to life imprisonment. He was released from Lewes in June 1917 and, like the other Volunteers, helped in the by-elections. His sister, Nora Aghas, describes how he made a political speech in Ballinalee 'for which the police were after him'. He was picked up in Dublin and sentenced to two years' hard labour in Mountjoy. Almost immediately, he and the other prisoners went on hunger strike. He died before his sister could get to see him.

Patrick Walsh from Annascaul describes the funeral:

We had the Volunteers reorganised, our ranks began to swell, and then came the death of Thomas Ashe. He was one of our own, and on the day of his funeral we sent representatives to Dublin but we also organised a procession to the Ashe family burial ground at Kinnard. We had a great muster of Volunteers. They came from Dingle, Ballyferriter, Lispole, and some came by boat from Cahirciveen. An oration was delivered at the graveyard.

Years later, Nora Aghas remembered her brother as he had been when he was at home in Kerry:

He always went home for holidays. He always had nice setters and a good gun and he used to range the mountains – himself and Padraig

35

Aghas, a second cousin who lived next door – after game of all kinds, woodcock, snipe etc. He also had a set of bagpipes and used to go up on Kinnard hill, which belonged to our farm, and walk along it playing the pipes. The neighbours all over the parish used to listen to the music and missed it greatly when he was dead.

In Dublin, the public funeral took up most of the day. The members of Cumann na mBan were much in evidence. Eilis Bean Ui Chonaiil remembered:

We met on the Sunday morning – I think it was at 12 o'clock – in Exchequer Street. And we were there a considerable time before we moved off to join the Procession. . . . We were dismissed at 6 PM

It was the first death of a republican on hunger strike.

5

Loyalties Transformed, Identities Confirmed

At the beginning of 1918, the First World War was continuing on its seemingly unstoppable course. The nature of the war demanded more and more servicemen, and recruiting continued unabated. The war had only an indirect impact on the majority of the people who gave witness statements to the Bureau, however. Robert and Dulcibella Barton, who were brother and sister, were an exception in this respect. The war, still raging, affected their lives almost as much as the conflict in Ireland, which was just getting under way. Erskine Childers, whose son was later to become President of Ireland, was their double first cousin. His parents had died 'when he was only twelve or thirteen'. Dulcibella Barton describes her family:

> Erskine, his brother Henry and his three sisters came to live with us, as my father was their guardian. In that way they were brought up as members of our family. . . . A governess took care of the girls' education and none of us went to school. One of my sisters went to college in Oxford. The boys went to school.

Dulcibella had been in France when the First World War began. She remembered the 'tocsin ringing out. That was a sign that war was declared'. When she made her witness statement, she was seventy-four years old:

> one year and three months older than my brother Bob. Two of my brothers, Erskine and Thomas Barton, younger than Bob and I, are buried in France, having been in the British army. . . . Neither of them had anything to do with the Irish War of Independence. . . . How we got to know about Sinn Féin was that we took in the Sinn Féin paper in the early days.

Like his two brothers, Robert Barton also served in the British army. His friend, Colonel Larry Esmond, appointed him 'OC Prisoners' Effects' in Dublin immediately after the Rising. Barton became more and more involved with Sinn Féin, and in 1918 stood for election in Wicklow and won the seat for Sinn Féin. His cousin Erskine Childers had joined the Volunteers before the split in 1914. Dulcibella relates: 'When the war broke out Erskine went back to England and was in the air arm of the navy or something like that.' Shortly before the outbreak of war in 1914, he had run in the guns at Howth in his yacht, the *Asgard*.

Conscription marked the final parting of the ways for Childers and the British authorities. William Mullins from Kerry records:

> At this time – the beginning of 1918 – the British government is hav-ing recruiting meetings, and around the County Kerry these recruiting meetings are being broken in disorder

The recruiting attempts were unpopular, but it was the issue of con-scription which infuriated so many. Politically, the attempt to introduce conscription in Ireland completely undermined the Irish Parliamentary Party's position. Combined with what had happened since 1916, its main impact seems to have been to swell the ranks of the Volunteers, not to mention Sinn Féin.

Volunteers like Eamon Morken, who had fought in the 1916 Rising and had been detained in Frongoch, were not slow to take advantage of the situation. He was appointed by his employers, the National Bank, to their branch in Birr. Having contacted Michael Collins and other leaders in Dublin, he started to organise a unit of Volunteers there. At the same time, his wife started a branch of Cumann na mBan. When the British government was thinking of putting the Conscription Act into operation, Morken and the Volunteers arranged to

> have a recruiting meeting in the town of Birr, at which Madam Markievicz and Joe McDonough spoke. The meeting was a great suc-cess as far as numbers were concerned: over 1,200 men paraded in mil-itary formation, and a number of these became members of the Volunteer organisation.

On the following Monday, Morken was suspended from his duties at the bank. The suspension lasted for only a week. Morken continued his

Sinn Féin activities, until eventually he was arrested and detained. A Court of Inquiry was held, and Morken was duly deported to Durham Jail, where he met a number of old friends who had been there since May. These had been arrested in connection with what was known as the 'German Plot', which the Volunteers believed had been concocted by the British authorities to facilitate the detention of their leaders.

The First World War came to an end whilst Morken was still in Durham. He remembered:

> the governor of the jail, very excited, came in to announce the news that an armistice had been signed. I think he was quite surprised to find that this news did not appear to be so important to me as it was to him, and he expressed disappointment at our detachment.

In May of 1918, there was no thought of an end to the war, and it was in that month that the Conscription Bill was passed at Westminster. With this Bill came a decided shift in opinion amongst the clergy of the Catholic Church. Although there had always been some support for Sinn Féin amongst the younger priests, the higher clergy and the bishops had been somewhat hostile to national developments up to this point. By coincidence, the by-election in East Cavan fell due in May. Sinn Féin put Arthur Griffith forward for election. Monsignor Patrick Browne describes the impact of the Bill:

> It [the election] was on at the same time as the meeting of the bishops in Maynooth. The bishops held a special meeting in May 1918 to consider the question of what attitude they would take with regard to the conscription of Ireland becoming law. To that meeting came the members of the Mansion House Conference on Conscription. One of the results of that meeting was that the bishops broke up Maynooth and gave holidays to the students. It looked as if there would be a fight. It was partly to give the students a chance to help.

Browne himself decided to help out in the East Cavan election, as there was a great shortage of election workers. Most of the usual helpers were jailed as suspects in the 'German Plot'.

To Browne's delight, Griffith won the election. Browne was even more delighted to report:

The general feeling of the bishops was to rejoice that Griffith, the Sinn Féin candidate, had been elected, on account of the conscription crisis, instead of the Party candidate. The bishops behaved wonderfully at that time. Stephen McKenna said they behaved 'like Irish gentlemen'. The form of the Resolution was very strong.

The anti-conscription meetings continued throughout the year. In Kerry, according to William Mullins, these meetings were very large:

> the biggest of them being held in Tralee, at which one of the local priests was in the habit of speaking and warning the youths to prepare to resist to the last.

Mullins also records:

> During this time too, we collected a number of firearms, principally shot-guns, and some very costly ones too. These were taken from private owners and from gunsmiths. . . . We always gave receipts.

Almost simultaneously with the Armistice, signed on 11 November 1918, the Great Flu struck. At this time, Ernest Blythe was once more in jail. The epidemic greatly interfered with his plans for escape, as it caused the breakdown of all regulations within the prison. He recalls:

> Very few escaped the flu. Up to a certain point we had full parades every day. Then there came a morning when half a dozen were sick. By the time the evening parade was reached, the half-dozen had grown to twenty. At last, out of the two hundred in the prison, barely thirty were on their feet. [Austin] Stack fell ill early. I visited every cell each day but fortunately did not fall ill. A lot of the prisoners were very bad, with a great deal of bleeding from the nose. Two men went off their heads and had to be removed to a mental institution. We had, however, no deaths.

Blythe felt that brandy, which the prison authorities supplied 'with the greatest liberality', contributed to the survival of the sick prisoners.

Dr Kathleen Lynn, who had fought as a member of James Connolly's Citizen Army in 1916, was 'on the run' when the flu epidemic broke out 'at the end of October 1918':

> At the flu epidemic, as doctors were so badly needed, I just decided that I would go home, and I did. I was arrested immediately and brought to Oriel House. I was told I would be deported.

As Dr Lynn put it, everybody 'kicked up an awful shine' and Dr Lynn was allowed to remain in practice in Dublin.

The epidemic was so devastating in Dublin and throughout the country that Cumann na mBan, whose members had Red Cross training, offered their services. Mrs Sean Beaumont – or Maureen McGavock, as she was at the time of the epidemic – was a member of the Cumann na mBan Executive:

> We established a Bureau in 6 Harcourt Street, to which the public could apply for nurses, and advertised the fact in the papers. Naturally there was no political distinction as regards the people we nursed.

Many Jewish families were so grateful for the help given that they not only subscribed to the funds but voted for 'our candidates', as Maureen McGavock put it, afterwards.

Not everybody was quite so well disposed towards Cumann na mBan, however. Maureen recollects an encounter at which feelings ran high. The meeting took place

> on the night of the Armistice, November 11, 1918, when the Sinn Féin Headquarters were attacked by British sympathisers who were mafeking [rioting] in the streets. The windows were broken by the excited mob and things looked ugly for a time, but Harry Boland and Simon Donnelly, who had collected a scratch garrison, restored order by firing over the heads of the crowd.

Seamus Ua Caomhanaigh remembered Armistice Day too:

> I think the most exciting time we had was on the evening of 11 November 1918. We had a quiet day in No. 6 [Harcourt Street], just carrying on the ordinary work of the day. The uproar in the city was, I was told, terrific, but it did not reach as far as Harcourt Street.

But they were not to escape the angry reaction of Trinity loyalists, though luckily they had some warning of the impending raid. A friendly student informed them that No. 6 Harcourt Street was to be attacked at 7 PM by hostile Trinity College scholars, reputed to be expert in the throwing of grenades. Ua Caomhanaigh and his comrades had barely time to prepare to defend themselves. Fortunately for them, it so happened that they had a crucial weapon to hand. The colliery at Wolf Hill had previously supplied some coal to the Sinn Féin Headquarters. They had found

41

it unusable, as the 'coal' turned out to be anthracite, which does not burn readily. It was at last put to use against the Trinity College students. The defence of the building was not as successful as the Harcourt Street staff had expected, however, and Ua Caomhanaigh was grateful when Harry Boland and Simon Donnelly intervened and repelled the attack.

Maureen McGavock and her great friend Josephine Aherne met while they were attending university and living at Dominican Hall on St Stephen's Green. When Aherne, later Mrs Josephine McNeill, left the university, she also left Dublin, moving to County Mayo to teach. Her next job was in Thurles, County Tipperary. It was here that she joined Cumann na mBan and began to move once more in republican circles.

Aherne McNeill's witness statement is one of the very few that even hints at romance – despite the many marriages that resulted from the close contact between young men and women in the republican movement. McNeill, unlike most of the witnesses, takes us into her confidence. She had considered marrying Ginger O'Connell but turned him down, and she gives her reasons:

> By this time things had reached a point between 'Ginger' and myself that we were either to marry or break. Marriage was impossible, as there was nothing to marry on, although Ginger's father was well off. He completely disapproved of Ginger's patriotic activities. Ginger had sometimes very strong personal idiosyncrasies which could be trying to a woman's taste. We agreed amicably to let things drop.

After joining the local branch of Cumann na mBan in Thurles, where she had started her new teaching job, she met the love of her life. His name was Pierce McCann, and he was well placed in the leadership of the movement.

Aherne McNeill remembered him as 'a man of great gaiety and charm. His eyes constantly twinkled. Prison was like death to him.' In McNeill's eyes, McCann was ideal in every way. He was a devout Catholic and loved his country. He had learnt Irish and spoke it at every opportunity. He was determined to fight conscription to the last drop of his blood. They both said they would take to the hills rather than submit.

McCann's family had quite different views, however: McNeill describes 'the people he associated with up to then, who were the well-off landed class and very anglicised'. Moreover, he was a great rider to the hounds, and he bred horses. He entered a particularly good horse for Punchestown. Naturally, the horse was called 'Sinn Féin', and he beat the field with ease; he was disqualified 'on some technical point, by the stewards'.

In the end, McCann did not have to take to the hills to fight conscription. He was one of those who was arrested as a suspect in the German Plot. The Archbishop of Cashel came to the convent where McNeill was teaching to tell her the news. McCann was taken to Gloucester Jail, 'when the bad flu was raging'. McNeill continues:

> In March one evening we got a wire that he had pneumonia and his father and mother and I decided to travel immediately. . . . In the middle of that night a call came to the hotel to come at once. . . . We found him delirious and he did not recognise us again. Ginger O'Connell, Desmond FitzGerald and others were next door listening to his ravings all night.

Pierce McCann died that night.

Almost as the Great War ended, it was announced that the general election was to be held in December. By now, the members of Sinn Féin were old hands at elections, and the women of Cumann na mBan were looking forward to it. Orders were going out to every part of Ireland, even to those constituencies which were uncontested. Eilis Bean Ui Chonaill, in her testimony, writes:

> Our next victory was the general election in 1918. We still helped at the collection and distribution of the moneys of the National Aid Fund. Our organisation fell in with the plans of the Sinn Féin Executive, and soon we were out canvassing in our own areas, collecting money, distributing literature, attending meetings and swelling the audiences at the election speeches. We suspended branch operations during this critical period, as our members wanted to throw all their weight into election work.

The women made it a practice to canvass in pairs and to be 'prepared for any rebuffs'. They were not universally popular, but they were a devoted band, and willing to suffer almost any slight in their efforts to achieve the victory of their party. Eilis Bean Ui Chonaill remembers with great pride:

When our canvassing and collecting were finished we assembled at 44 Parnell Square to prepare meals for the election workers. The polling took place on 14 December and we were busy that day preparing such meals. Leslie Price was in charge of that station. We assembled at our stations at 7.30 on Saturday morning. I remember going to my place of business for 9 o'clock and resuming activities again at 1. We worked there until a late hour, as there was a continual stream of people coming in for meals.

There were certain constituencies where feelings ran very high indeed. Not surprisingly, the most notable of these was Waterford, not only in the lead-up to the general election but, even more so, in the by-election which was held there some months earlier. Waterford was the home ground of John Redmond MP, who became leader of the Irish Parliamentary Party after the death of Parnell. James Daly (Captain of C Company, 5th Battalion, Kerry No. 2 Brigade) was sent to Waterford in 1918 even before the election campaign, on orders from the Battalion officers:

> When we got to Waterford we found we were part of a large party of Volunteers drafted into Waterford to protect Sinn Féin meetings and voters who were being attacked by mobs, who were being used by the Redmondite party.

Liam Walsh, who was an officer in the Volunteers and later in the IRA:

> did a lot of canvassing around the Redmondite quarter. . . . I stopped about fifty people voting in the names of dead people for the Redmondite candidate.

The practice of using the votes of dead people was not unknown on either side. Eilis Bean Ui Chonaill regretted to say that a certain number of dead people were shown to have voted in her constituency. One feels that she would not have approved of a Cumann na mBan member from County Leitrim who, in her statement, after describing the packed lunches she and her companions prepared for the election workers, says:

> We enjoyed ourselves very much that day personating [sic] voters. We voted for dead and absentee voters and also for people whom we knew would be hostile to Sinn Féin.

Even more daring was the action taken by some workers in the post office in Derry. Michael Sheeran, who was Company Officer in the Irish Volunteers from 1917, relates:

> One of the members of the TFP [Ten Foot Pikers, an elite selection of IRB men] Centre, Dan McCandy, was an official in Derry Post Office and had access to the postal votes. He arranged to collect all postal votes he could lay his hands on in the course of his employment and hand these over to the TFP Squad. It was well known that the vast majority of postal voters would record their votes for the Unionist candidate.

In Derry, the Sinn Féin candidate won by a small majority.

Robert Barton, who stood for Sinn Féin in Wicklow, did not remember bothering much about 'the dead votes. All our business was to bring in the living, and we succeeded very well.'

The result of the general election was an overwhelming victory for Sinn Féin. The First Dáil met in Dublin and established themselves as the Government of the Irish Republic. The non-republican deputies did not attend. Seamus Ua Chaomhanaigh was there and, in characteristic fashion, took notes on everything that went on. He was able to record the details for the Bureau when he made his statement:

> The first meeting of the first Dáil was held in the Round Room of the Mansion House, Dublin, on Tuesday, the 21 January, 1919. I give now a list of all the members present at the meeting, together with a list of those absent and the reason for their absence. The list is absolutely correct.

The list of absentees is long and outnumbers the list of those who were present. The great majority were 'under lock and key' in England. A few were in America. One deputy – D. Lynch, the member for Cork South-east – had been deported. Two were absent through illness. The Provisional Constitution of the Dáil was read and passed unanimously. All stood as Ireland's Declaration of Independence was read in Irish and in English; it was then adopted.

Ua Chaomhanaigh says that he could not remember the details of that first meeting, but he had a very clear recollection of its significance:

> Our elected representatives, instead of going away to sit in a foreign parliament, assembled together, as many as were free to do so, in Dublin

and appointed a native government. The various departments of state were formed and ministers appointed.

At first only two Departments functioned: the Department of Defence and the Department of Finance. Michael Collins was appointed Minister for Finance and Cathal Brugha Minister for Defence. Almost the first action of the government was the floating of a Government Loan.

At almost exactly the same time, on the same day as the First Dáil was meeting for the first time, the Soloheadbeg ambush took place in County Tipperary. The reverberations from this operation, in which two constables were killed, were to echo throughout the War of Independence, and far beyond. The operation in itself was a small affair. Members of the Third Tipperary Brigade, led by Seamus Robinson, Dan Breen and Sean Treacy, ambushed two RIC constables as they escorted a cart carrying gelignite to a local quarry.

In his witness statement, Seamus Robinson devotes several pages to the subject. No one, according to Robinson, could speak with more authority than he, the officer commanding the South Tipperary Brigade. The Brigade had been formed just three months before, in October 1918, while Robinson was still in jail in Belfast. Richard Mulcahy, Chief of Staff, had presided at its formation. This was to be the Brigade's first operation.

Robinson had fought in the GPO in 1916, until he literally fell asleep standing up. When he was invited by Eamon Ó Duibhir to Tipperary to help reorganise the Volunteers there, Robinson readily agreed. This was a chance to fight with some hope of success. In 1916, the British had burned them out. He vowed that this would never happen again:

> It became abundantly clear to me that we could hope to survive and win only if we were a ghostly army of sharpshooters operating all over the country combining to deal with small bodies of the enemy. . . . I think I can state that Soloheadbeg was the accidental starting point of what later became known as the 'Tan War'.

Much of Robinson's defence of the action at Soloheadbeg must have been very fresh in his mind when he gave his statement, as he refers to 'a controversy in the *Irish Times* in February 1950'. Robinson's main arguments, as put forward in his witness statement, were that the Volunteer

Executive had full power to agree to peace or to declare war until the First Dáil met, or until they took the Oath of Allegiance to the Dáil. The Executive determined policy and, from October 1917, that policy was one of 'armed struggle'. This policy was carried out by GHQ. Robinson states:

> The passive-resistance policy of old Sinn Féin and the apparent policy of the Dáil was not the policy of GHQ. On 14 October 1918, three months before the first Dáil met, 'Oglach' stated: 'Passive resistance is no resistance at all. Our active military resistance is the only thing that will tell.'

This policy was not changed by any statement of the Dáil when it met on 21 January 1919. As the deputies stood for the Declaration of Independence, they heard that 'The existing state of war between Ireland and England can never be ended unless Ireland is completely evacuated.'

Robinson himself describes some of the reaction when news of the ambush reached Dublin:

> There were some violent condemnations. Arthur Griffith said something like: 'If that sort of thing were allowed to continue we would soon be eating one another'. . . . Others too were equally shocked, the clergy in particular.

At the time that the Bureau of Military History was putting the witness statements together, the name of Soloheadbeg had acquired a status amongst the survivors of the War of Independence which was jealously guarded by the participants in the ambush itself.

As regards the motives which inspired the Tipperary Brigade, Dan Breen's statement largely agrees with Robinson's but, when it comes to acknowledging Robinson's part, he is, to say the least, less than generous. It is clear that this grudging spirit goes further than a wish to praise his dead hero, Sean Treacy. According to Breen:

> Treacy had arranged that Robinson should be appointed Brigade Commander. . . . He wanted a sort of yes-man, or a stooge as we would call it now. . . . We thought that Robinson would serve this purpose.

As far as Breen was concerned, all the credit for Soloheadbeg should go to Sean Treacy and himself.

The disparagement was mutual. Robinson, who makes it clear that he was the OC at Soloheadbeg, found Breen's 'hot-headed tension' difficult to control. At the briefing session before the attack, according to Robinson:

> Breen seemed to have lost control, declaring with grinding teeth and a very high-pitched, excited voice, that he'd go out and face them.

Robinson and Breen might differ on details, but both agree that Treacy and Robinson were called to GHQ soon afterwards. Michael Collins arranged to meet them outside on the street before they reached GHQ. According to Robinson, quoting Collins, it appeared that 'a great many people' there wanted them to flee to America. Robinson and Treacy would have none of it. Robinson records the following exchange:

> 'Then what do you propose to do?' said Collins.
>   'Fight it out of course.'
>   [Collins] suddenly closed his notebook with a snap saying as he strode off, with the faintest of faint smiles on his lips but a big laugh in his eyes, 'That's all right with me.'

Mrs Sean O'Donovan (née Kathleen Boland), who was a sister of Harry Boland, remembered

> an interesting incident that took place in 1919, shortly after the Soloheadbeg affair. . . . Mick Collins wanted to see me. I went to his office in Mary Street, just near Liffey Street. He said there were some very important men from Tipperary, mentioning the name of Sean Treacy, coming up to Dublin, and he was going to send some of them out to me. He also asked me whether I knew any other safe houses.

Collins and the Boland family were close – close enough to be trusted by Collins to mind not only his money but also his guns. The tailoring and outfitting business which Harry had opened at 64 Middle Abbey Street in 1917 'became an important centre for despatches from all places', according to Kathleen. In another part of her statement, Kathleen states:

> Mick Collins gave me to bring to my mother sums of money – notes of £100 each – to mind for him. He used this money for his various purposes, and sent for me to get it from her whenever he wanted it.

The escape of de Valera, Sean McGarry and Sean Milroy was initiated inside Lincoln Prison, but was planned and executed by Collins and Boland. The story is told in great detail by Liam McMahon, the IRB man who lived in Manchester at the time. He appears to have enjoyed the whole affair immensely, as indeed did the 'comrades' back home in Ireland. The details of the escape include the 'nervous little priest' to whom the famous postcards were first sent, who did not understand the cryptic drawings but passed them on all the same; the people in Dublin who were no more successful in deciphering the message; how Collins persevered; how Collins and Boland practically took up residence in Manchester at Boland's aunt's place; the cakes, the files, the keys, the disguises, and above all the network – these all became legendary in a very short time. The Lincoln escape lifted spirits among republicans and reassured many who might have been feeling nervous following the first meeting of the Dáil on 21 January. The escape took place on 3 February, and most of the remaining prisoners were released in March.

The second session of the Dáil took place in early April. It was attended by fifty-two TDs, who elected de Valera as President of the Council of Ministers. At the same session, de Valera chose his Cabinet: Arthur Griffith was appointed President-Substitute as well as Minister for Home Affairs; Count Plunkett was to be Minister for Foreign Affairs; Cathal Brugha was to be Minister for Defence; Michael Collins was selected Minister for Finance, with the immediate task of managing the Dáil Loan. The three remaining members of Cabinet were W. T. Cosgrave (Local Government), Constance Markievicz (Labour) and Eoin McNeill (Industries).

At its next session, the Dáil announced its plans for the sale of bonds and the establishment of embassies. De Valera declared the close association of the Minister for Defence with the 'voluntary military forces which are the foundation of the National Army'. In the same session, the Dáil passed a motion calling on the Irish people to ostracise the RIC.

The stage was set for the conflict. Seamus Robinson's 'ghostly army of sharpshooters' was almost ready.

6

MICHAEL COLLINS, THE CASTLE AND THE SPIES

George Chester Duggan, who was Assistant to the Under Secretary for Ireland from 1919 to 1922, was in a good position to observe the situation in Ireland since he had left 'four and a half years before' 1919. He continues:

> The Rising of 1916 had left its indelible mark, there had been the abortive Irish Convention, the successful anti-conscription campaign, [and] Sinn Féin's sweeping victory at the parliamentary elections of December 1918. A few terrorist shootings had taken place but there was no organised body as yet under arms against British rule.

In 1919, the 'organised body' under arms may not have been noticeable, but it was already in existence. The activities of the young recruits who were joining the post-1916 Volunteers were the old familiar ones of drilling and training. The acquisition of arms occupied a great deal of time and attention. There was one other element which had to be organised: the acquisition of intelligence on every part of British rule, from the Castle down. This was the vital element which had to be centralised at GHQ in Dublin. It came to be associated with the name of one man: Michael Collins.

Tomas Malone, who used the name 'Sean Forde' for much of his IRA activities, in his witness statment refers to a visit from Michael Collins, probably in the spring of 1918:

> I met Mick Collins in Mullingar, to where he had travelled by train. He must have been on the run at this time because he went to a great deal of trouble to hide his movements. He came out to our house and spent the night in it. We discussed organisation generally as to who was any good and who was 'no bloody good', as he would say – a general survey of the local situation. I took a message for him to some house in Horseleap and met a lady who I think was a policeman's wife.

Malone had the feeling that the woman might have been 'a sister of his or a cousin . . . or that the policeman himself was related to him.' Malone was fairly certain that this contact, whatever her connection with Collins, was part of the intelligence system that Collins was organising. Malone continues:

> He was definitely building up an intelligence network and he had somebody there, but it was all hush-hush and I knew nothing about the details.

Collins may have had to seek out suitable agents when he started to put the network together; later, they came to him.

Eamon Broy, who had joined the Dublin Metropolitan Police Depot in January 1911, was probably the most important intelligence agent ever to approach Michael Collins. Born in County Kildare of farming stock of vaguely nationalist leanings, he would not appear to be spy material. His motives for joining the DMP had to do with his long-term ambitions to fulfil his potential as an athlete, and he had already decided to emigrate to the United States when he had completed a few years in the police. He opens his second statement to the Military Bureau with a partial explanation of his reasons for the momentous step of contacting the Volunteers:

> In March 1917, when I commenced sending police documents to the Irish Volunteers, I had conceived the idea partly from what I read about the Russian nihilists, partly from the Arsene Lupin French novels and also from Lady Gregory's play *The Rising of the Moon*.

Broy was interested to learn years later, when he got to know Collins well, that they shared the same taste in reading material.

Broy's first contribution to intelligence, at the early meetings with Collins, was a thorough grounding in the number of people in the RIC. Before he ever met Collins, Broy had made a study of the subject. He had found that the RIC numbers had been falling steadily since the beginning of the century. In 1919, they were probably two thousand less than in 'their heyday in the nineteenth century'. Moreover, there was a policy of non-recruitment from 1914 to 1919, 'except for a small trickle of very inferior recruits'. It would appear 'that the RIC had no members of from one to five years' service'. In 1919, in Broy's opinion, 'the RIC could not adopt the old manoeuvre of transferring members temporarily from a quiet area to a disturbed district'. The strategy that came to be pursued by the Volunteers was to have no quiet areas and to have all districts disturbed.

When Broy was given the job of mess officer, in addition to his other duties, it fell to him to do the shopping. He bought the groceries at Findlaters in Georges Street, and paid for them each week. He was in the habit of discussing national matters with the bookkeeper there. They were of the same opinion: 'that force was the only means of securing national freedom'. The bookkeeper's name was Miss Smart, and it was through her that Broy made contact with Michael Collins:

> Miss Smart put the question up to me straight – would I mind meeting Mick Collins? I told her I would have no hesitation whatever.

Broy met Collins for the first time in January 1919, at 5 Cabra Road. The house belonged to Michael Ó Foghludha, who had married Miss Smart since Broy's initial meeting with her. Broy proved to be an indefatigable and well-placed spy. Broy himself suggests how well placed he was:

> In March 1915, I was allocated to political duty and worked in the clerical section of it at Exchange Court. Up to that time all work there had been done in handwriting, and the authorities wanted to modernise the organisation by means of typewriters, card indexes etc. Otherwise I would not have been put into that office as I was very junior in the service.

The section of the DMP (G Division) in which Broy worked

> had men at all the railway stations and at the boats. Their job was to take a note of any suspects leaving the city, ascertain the station for which they had taken tickets, and send cipher wires to the police at their destinations.

Similarly, close attention was paid to men travelling to Dublin 'about whom cipher wires were received'. On arrival, they were shadowed to their destination in Dublin. Each operation was meticulously recorded in a set of books: each detective kept a book of his own, and in addition there was a large central book into which 'was transferred daily the information contained in each detective's book'.

Daily and weekly reports were made to the government. 'A general review of the state of the complete political activity in the district' was submitted each week. Although the system operated only in the Dublin metropolitan area, 'in practice' writes Broy, 'it turned out to be dealing with about ninety per cent of the activities of the whole country'.

In his position as Director of Intelligence, Michael Collins needed trusted advisers. More often than not, he found them in the ranks of the IRB. Sean Nunan, who was Secretary to President de Valera in 1919 as well as Registrar of the Dáil Eireann Bonds, in the course of giving an account of his experiences to the Bureau of Military History relates that:

> Sometime during this period, I was sworn in as a member of the IRB and used to meet Michael Collins and others at Vaughan's Hotel. One night, when I was there, Collins asked me to stay behind after the others had gone home, and at about 12.30 AM he suggested we go for a walk. After walking around the city for some time, we arrived at Brunswick Street (now Pearse Street) Police Station, where Sergeant Ned Broy was alone on night duty. Michael Collins had explained to me that his plan was to examine the files and reports of the G Division and ascertain precisely who, amongst them, was doing political work. Ned Broy took us up to Inspector McFeely's office, and opened a large steel safe in which the reports were kept. Collins and I stayed in the safe listing the names and activities [of those] on political work, until about 4 AM, when we walked home – Collins to Mountjoy Street and I to Botanic Road.

The rest of Ireland was policed by the RIC, who kept a very close eye on the inhabitants. Broy claimed:

> When Volunteer officers visited Dublin . . . as was frequently the case, minute particulars were transmitted to the G Division political section, either by cipher telegram where speed was thought to be essential, or by voluminous confidential reports. The result was one way or another that about ninety percent of RIC information reached the G Division [the section of the DMP which was engaged in intelligence] (and was transmitted by me to the Irish Volunteers from March 1917, when I got charge of it, until 1921).

Broy continued his nerve-racking double life until suspicion fell on him in January 1921. In his statement, he describes his close calls, his careful arrangement of alibis, and the fact that he always wore rubber gymnastic shoes, in order to be prepared for flight. Throughout his long statement, there shines Broy's great love of Collins, for whom he would have laid down his life. He tells a story towards the end of his statement which helps to illustrate their relationship. Broy was boasting about having been paid by the British government for the time he had spent in prison:

> I told Mick about having 'one up' on all the IRA prisoners. . . . He asked to see the money, which he promptly seized, and announced that I would have to 'wrestle' him for it. So we set to and I won, but I don't believe he did his best. That was one of his tricks, to let the other man win. I still do not know whether I would have been able to beat him in an out-and-out wrestling match. In any case none of us would use full force against him, even in play, as to us all he was a sacred personage, the very embodiment and personification of Irish resistance.

There was another spy in the Castle who pre-dated Collins; in fact, he pre-dated the Rising. It was he who leaked the famous Castle Document in 1916. He was Eugene Smith, who lived in Bird Avenue, Dundrum, Dublin; he was still passing on intelligence in 1918. Towards the end of his statement, he reveals:

> Immediately before the arrests in connection with the German Plot, I learned from a conversation with a police officer that the detective force was to be mobilised at 9 o'clock that night to arrest all the leaders, and I gave the information in outline to Liam O'Flaherty.

Patrick Colgan, who had been a member of the small band of Kildare men that had fought in 1916, was in close touch with Collins. He had shared quarters with Collins in Frongoch and knew him well. In 1920, Colgan received a report of some information which was to prove vital for Intelligence. It concerned a young sergeant in the RIC. Colgan writes:

> Early in 1920 Tom Harris reported to me that he had been approached with a proposition that Sergeant Maher, RIC, who was the clerk to the County Inspector, RIC, and who was stationed at Naas, was prepared to render every assistance to the IRA.

Collins instructed Colgan in the procedure which was used to test would-be intelligence agents. Maher passed the test:

> In due course the reports came through and were compared with reports already in possession of GHQ, and were found to be correct. From then onwards Maher gave us anything of importance.

But what Collins really wanted was the Police Code. 'It would be of great assistance'. Colgan recalls Collins saying: 'By great good fortune, Sergeant Maher was able to copy the code and pass it on first to Harris, who passed it to Colgan, who in turn passed it on to GHQ.' Colgan continues: 'Each month a copy of the code and all secret instructions issued to County Inspectors from Police Headquarters reached us.' Eventually it was decided that the method was too risky, and Harris was given the task of finding a suitable courier, based on his knowledge of Naas. He chose an Irish teacher called Sean Kavanagh, who had to be recruited into the IRA specially. The arrangement was most satisfactory, Colgan relates:

> Towards the end of 1920 the only place where the codes for RIC, military or naval forces could be had was from Maher at Naas.

At the time Colgan made his statement, Maher held the rank of Chief Superintendent in An Garda Síochána, a post he had held since the establishment of the State. Kavanagh was appointed Governor of Mountjoy Jail.

David Neligan, who had joined the DMP in April 1918, was so success-ful in concealing his efforts on behalf of IRA Intelligence that he was not only able to draw his police pension and all his entitlements but 'afterwards', he writes, 'I received a letter from General Tudor thanking me for my "magnificent services in Ireland".' Neligan was very good at his job. Before the Truce, he was promoted to the position of paymaster for his section of British Intelligence in Dublin.

After he had resigned from G Division, Neligan, who had come home to Kerry, was approached by representatives of the Volunteers. He was to go to Dublin immediately: Collins wanted him to go back to the police. There were gaps in the Castle Intelligence service which Collins wanted covered. So, sometime in July 1920, Neligan was sworn in as a member of the DMP. Three other fellow G-men – Eamon Broy, James MacNamara and Joseph Kavanagh – who worked for Michael Collins were not really surprised when they were told that he was to join them. Every week, they met Collins at Tommy Gay's house in Haddon Road, Clontarf. Their job was 'to sift every piece of information we could lay our hands on and convey it to Collins or some of his lieutenants', Neligan recalls.

Collins believed that, in the kind of war which the IRA was waging, the acquisition of information relating to British Intelligence was vital. He also believed that, in the pursuit of the aims of war, the logic of the information must be followed to the point of death. Much of Neligan's testimony consists of recollections of occasions when the information he and his three colleagues passed on led to selected assassinations. Neligan relates the fate of one Redmund, 'a live wire' who had been brought down from Belfast as District Inspector:

> He told the assembled G-men one night (including myself) that it was very strange that they could not catch Michael Collins because a man who was only over from England a couple of days had met him several times.

Collins easily identified this individual as a man called Jameson or Burns, who was masquerading as a representative of the 'British Sailors', Soldiers' and Airmen's Union', a fictitious organisation, and pretending to help the revolution. Burns was shot in Glasnevin after being warned by Collins. As for Redmund, 'he was shot in Harcourt Street by the Volunteers, Collins saying, "If we don't get him, he'll get us."'

Neligan makes a point of recounting his part in drawing the attention of the Volunteers to the danger posed by the activities of Alan Bell, an ex-District Inspector, and ex-Resident Magistrate. Neligan describes him as

> a clever fellow who, to my certain knowledge, was conducting an investigation into Volunteer funds, and . . . was running a kind of star-chamber court in the Castle where he was interrogating bank managers and others as to the finances supporting Sinn Féin.

Volunteer funds were held in numerous accounts held by secret sympathisers and, if the identities of these people were to remain secret, Bell had to be silenced. Bell came in each day on the tram from Dalkey. Neligan writes:

> Collins had him taken out of the tram and shot out in Merrion [Road] and that ended the investigation.

As Neligan notes, Collins met his spies every week. However, he met one of his most valuable spies only once, when she was visiting her cousin Piaras Beaslaoi. Her name was Lily Mernin, and she worked as a shorthand typist in the Garrison Adjutant's office (Dublin District, Lower Castle Yard) from 1914 to 1922. An amazing variety of information crossed Lily Mernin's desk for copying, from reports on the courts martial of Volunteers to the movement of troops. Merlinn describes one duty which she remembered in particular:

> Before the 21 November 1920, it was part of my normal duties to type the names and addresses of British agents who were accommodated at private addresses and living as ordinary citizens in the city. These lists were typed weekly and amended whenever an address was changed. I passed them on each week. . . . The typing of the lists ceased after the 21 November 1920.

As one might expect, a wholly different perspective on life associated with the Castle is presented in the witness statement of George Chester Duggan, the Assistant to the Under Secretary for Ireland. For the most part, the testimony regarding his time in that position is confined to administrative matters, including an intriguing account of the procedures involved in promotion in the civil service in the Castle. In many ways, Duggan's daily life resembled the life of any colonial civil servant in any colony of a far-flung empire. In the course of an analysis of a particular promotion, he describes the likely outcome:

> Watt was an Ulsterman and presumably persona grata with the ultra Tories. Two of my colleagues who might have been regarded as eligible were Roman Catholics and therefore written off. I presumably was thought to have been too long out of touch with Irish affairs.

Duggan draws attention to the intensive lobbying engaged in by certain civil servants against their own government when, for example, Home Rule was the issue. He quotes from the published memoir of Maurice Headlam, a prominent civil servant up to 1920, when he was sidelined by Assistant Under Secretary Sir Alfred Cope:

> I had decided that the ordinary civil service rules about taking part in politics did not apply in the Irish case, which was not politics but flagrant disloyalty to the Crown whose servant I was.

Headlam was in the habit of writing to Members of Parliament expressing strong contrary views whenever, for example, the Home Rule Bill was before Parliament.

57

It fell to Duggan to attend at Green Street Courthouse to furnish evidence of Alan Bell's salary and pension rights. He describes Bell as 'an inoffensive elderly gentleman who had been marked down when it became known that he was attached to the "Crime Special".' Duggan felt uneasy in the Courthouse:

> I had never been in that Courthouse but when I entered it and was waiting my turn to give evidence I felt a sinister atmosphere about me, that there were men in that crowd whose passions were burning fiercely, that there was an underworld whose presence I now realised for the first time.

Duggan continued to work in Dublin Castle until the Truce, never feeling any personal danger, but conscious sometimes of being watched – by whom he could not say. He found that there was a certain air of unreality about his work in those last months. He remembers:

> My heartbeats did once quicken when on my way home I ran into a section of the IRA drilling openly on a country road. I spent a Sunday once in the Dublin mountains with Bernard Gilbert, one of the Treasury officials assisting Waterfield, who later reached high eminence in the Treasury. I knew of course that in the mountains were men 'on the run' in hiding but I lightly put that thought on one side. All the signs of civil war that we saw that beautiful late autumn day were a single scouting aeroplane and in the distance what seemed like the smoke of a bivouac fire.
>
> When we returned to my home, Gilbert – a fine mathematician and a brilliant pianist – sat down at the piano and held my wife and myself entranced with the beauty, the life, the sadness of the music of the Masters that he played for us.

Chester Duggan was soon to leave Dublin, never again to return in the service of his King.

7

SECTIONS, COMPANIES, BATTALIONS AND BRIGADES

When Seamus Robinson returned to Tipperary from his visit to Dublin and his meeting with Michael Collins, he was quite sure that the action at Soloheadbeg had been endorsed by the General Headquarters of the Irish Volunteers (soon to become the Irish Republican Army). His opinion of GHQ was that of the 'man of action':

> GHQ naturally want to sit comfortably in their armchairs organising until they can see the daylight ahead.

Sean Treacy was not so sure that GHQ had endorsed their action, but he and Robinson continued to work together, 'contacting officers and trying to get things going'. Robinson describes the task they had given themselves:

> We were being searched for daily. From two to five thousand soldiers would concentrate on an area, search every house and field, rounding up all the male population of military age . . . and always we were just outside one of the apices of the triangle, with field glasses, enjoying the sight. We had to get men in every Company area to be ready to scout for us.

This was easy enough to manage in 1918, when all the people of Ireland were united in their opposition to conscription, but by 1919 that enthusiasm had faded away. It took men like Treacy to attract recruits into a life that was not only dangerous but also extremely uncomfortable. If they were not shot, new recruits would most likely end up in prison. According to Robinson, however, they increased in numbers. They were in no doubt as to what was required of them: 'The Volunteers were told to "go on the run" rather than lose liberty or their arms, and to be ready to fight for both.'

Seamus Robinson made his statement in 1956. By then he was a member of the Military History Bureau. There are certain discrepancies between his testimony and that of Dan Breen. Fortunately, Michael Davern, who took a prominent part in IRA operations in South Tipperary, also left us his testimony. Davern was a TD for Tipperary South when he made his witness statement to the Bureau. Although not one of the 'famous four' involved in the Soloheadbeg ambush, he was certainly familiar with the operation. As far as Davern was concerned, Robinson was no stooge. Robinson was the elected commanding officer of the South Tipperary Brigade, Sean Treacy was the vice-commandant and Dan Breen was the quartermaster. Where there is a divergence in the accounts given by Breen and Robinson, particularly as to who did what immediately after the ambush, Davern corroborates Robinson in almost every detail. Davern never made a secret of his preference for Robinson over Breen:

> Seamus paid us many visits subsequently with Treacy, [Sean] Hogan and Breen. We did not meet Dan Breen so often after Knocklong, as he was stationed mostly in Dublin doing his important quartermaster work.

The operation carried out at Knocklong was almost as important as the ambush at Soloheadbeg. To Robinson, it was a follow-up to Soloheadbeg, and was intended to convey the message that the participants in that action were still in business. The action which the Volunteers carried out at Knocklong was the rescue of Sean Hogan, who had been one of the ambushers at Soloheadbeg.

Hogan had been captured by the RIC a short time before. Davern knew exactly how Hogan had slipped up, even though he was aware that the RIC dearly wanted to catch him. Davern tells us: 'I had been keeping company with Mary O'Brien of Rossmore . . . and Sean Hogan was in love with Bridie O'Keeffe of Glenough'. They had all been to a dance which had been attended by about seventy or eighty couples. It was planned that Hogan and Davern were to return to Rossmore, but Hogan gave Davern the slip. Davern reports:

> When we got there Hogan asked for the [bicycle] pump again. I handed it to him; he put it in his pocket and said 'Tell the boys I'll be in Glenough about 4 this evening.'

He never arrived. Robinson takes up the story:

> Next morning the three were wakened by Paddy Kinnane, who burst
> into the room and almost indignantly asked 'Do you fellows not know
> that one of your fellows is arrested?'

They immediately set about planning Hogan's escape. It was decided
to attack the train on which Hogan was to be transported to Cork. The
Brigade attacked while the train was at Knocklong station. Two constables were killed in the engagement, and both Dan Breen and Sean Treacy
were wounded. Treacy had been shot 'through the neck, the bullet passing between the windpipe and the jugular vein', Robinson reports.

The four men were now on the run in earnest. They travelled to East
Limerick by pony and trap. 'Dan was in great pain', Robinson notes.
Treacy had prepared their itinerary ahead of the move. Robinson relates:

> Sean had made all the arrangements with the local Volunteers, whom he
> knew, about procuring transport to take us to the Shannon, on our way
> to Clare. There were few motors in those days and fewer still whose
> owners could be trusted.

It took them a few days to reach

> Mick Brennan's Brigade area, where we were comfortable for some
> weeks while Sean Treacy and Breen recuperated. I gave them some les-
> sons in swimming and diving in which I was (relatively) an expert.

Leaders like Robinson and Davern were conscious of the help the
Volunteers received from the civilian population. Robinson in particular
was anxious that their generosity would not be abused. It was one of the
reasons he disliked 'large Columns'. He said: 'To me they seemed to
approximate to small standing armies. . . . Big Columns used eat, almost
out of house and home, a whole townland.'

Robinson recounts in some detail something that must have been
unusual in the War of Independence – the support given to him in the
form of vital intelligence, not to speak of sustenance, by Mrs de Vere
Hunt:

> Mrs Hunt was a very tall, stately and cultured lady. A non-Catholic, she
> was suspected by the locals [of being] anti-national.

Robinson had to take steps to prevent some Volunteers from mid-Tipperary from, as they put it, 'removing' the Hunts in order to get the land 'for division'. Robinson dealt with this threat to the Hunts by approaching the local Battalion OC, only to discover that the matter was well in hand: the officer, Tadhg O'Dwyer, was having the place watched. Robinson says: 'I have already warned those fellows off. It is the most comfortable place in the whole Brigade area. Always we are welcome.'

Robinson gives us the details of how Mrs de Vere Hunt was able to pass on information about the proposed movements of a detachment of the British army whose officer in command stayed overnight at the Hunt residence:

> Mrs Hunt told me afterwards that she approached the Captain and bade them welcome 'in these dreadful days'. It was a pleasure to meet and see them around, and would he and his Lieutenants have dinner with her. He agreed with alacrity. Mrs Hunt gave her maid the evening off 'Because maids are dangerous to have around at times like this, they talk so much!' she told the officers. This gave her the excuse to do the serving herself. They enjoyed the meal and when it was over the Captain dismissed his two Lieutenants and settled down to peruse his diary while Mrs Hunt busied herself clearing the table and chatting, keeping on the move. The Captain's back was mostly towards her. She is a very tall woman and her sight must have been astonishingly keen and she must have had a photographic memory, for, as he turned the leaves slowly, she managed to steal a glance at each and memorised the gist of it. She had the dispatch ready in no time and had it sent to the local officer.

This particular dispatch was found in the sole of a captured Volunteer's shoe by the British army, just as they had moved upwards of a hundred men to the borders of Boherlahan. The captain in charge of this operation had been so careful that 'he didn't let his lieutenants know where he intended to go until they were ready to march', but every detail of the operation was there to be read in the seized dispatch. Its capture was not nearly as significant to the officer as the accuracy of its contents, which were almost clairvoyant. Robinson felt sure that this panicked the captain, who left at once for Clonmel 'on a forced march'.

Michael Hynes, who lived on the borders of Templetuohy parish, gives an unemotional account of the life of a member of the IRA in 1919:

A few days after my brother's release in April 1919 I and five others were arrested for collecting for the Gaelic League without a permit. I was sentenced to two months in Limerick Prison. . . . I was released a few days after the famous Knocklong rescue, and was in Thurles with some of my jail pals when District Inspector Hunt was shot. I was raided for that night, and from then until the Truce I was on the run.

This was not a good time to be on the run. However, it was much worse if you were caught, and worse again if you were suspected of being implicated in the Soloheadbeg ambush or Knocklong – or both, as Michael Davern was. He was apprehended near Ballough and taken to Clonoulty Barracks. Davern describes the encounter:

As I was going in the door of the barracks, I was kicked by Sergeant Maloney. Constable Twomey struck a vicious swiping blow at my head with his rifle and, had I not ducked, the murderous blow would certainly have killed me. Before Twomey had recovered I struck him a few times, only to receive blows and kicks from about a dozen RIC who had come in. They continued to kick and beat while [I was] on the floor with shouts of 'Where is Robinson and Treacy from you now?' [*sic*]

But the RIC men were not all hostile. Murtagh, a young constable, shouted: 'You are only a pack of cowards to beat a young fellow like that; he's only a kid.' The rest of them shouted: 'He's a bloody murderer and we always knew it.'

Three weeks later, Murtagh was shot dead. At the inquiry which followed, the verdict was 'accidental death'. Years later, in 1956, when Davern gave his statement, he made no comment about the young man's death.

Davern and the man Ryan, who was arrested with him, were put into a small cell for the night with their hands cuffed behind their backs. There was about six inches of water on the floor. Next morning Constable Walsh, a policeman who did not agree with brutalising the prisoners, arrived. Davern records:

Walsh went into his own home about fifty yards away and brought back tea. He demanded the removal of the handcuffs while we were having the tea. We were both very wet and he brought us dry socks that morning.

Davern was moved to Cork Prison, court-martialled in January 1920 and sentenced to two years' hard labour for having a bag of ammunition, gelignite and documents in his possession.

Robinson, Breen, Hogan, and Treacy moved towards Dublin. Major Patrick Colgan, who had reorganised the Volunteers in north Kildare in 1917, provided a link for the four as they moved in the direction of Dublin. Colgan was approached by Sean Treacy, who told him that the 'Knocklong boys were staying at Bulfins near Birr, that Eamon Bulfin, while anxious to keep them, was having a bad time lest they should be traced.' Colgan had fought in the GPO and was able to arrange with another Maynooth veteran, Donal O'Buachalla, to keep them for a week. Robinson had been able to arrange accommodation for himself at his wife's family home.

Back in Tipperary, Michael Hynes and others like him continued blocking roads, destroying barracks that had been evacuated by the RIC, and sniping at those that were still occupied. George Plunkett, a brother of Joseph Plunkett (one of the signatories of the 1916 Proclamation), came down from GHQ on a tour of inspection. The first Black and Tans – a special force recruited by the British government to deal with the situation in Ireland – arrived in Ireland in March 1920 and soon became notorious for the brutality with which they dealt with Volunteers and civilians alike.

Michael Hynes describes the changed situation in Tipperary:

> We continued sniping attacks on Templetuohy barracks, and the British established a second post there. The hall which was opposite the barracks was taken over, and about forty Black and Tans and RIC men were stationed there. Their position made it impossible for us to launch a big attack. In addition we were only three miles from Templemore, which was garrisoned by about 1,500 British military, 120 Auxiliaries and 50 RIC men.

Michael Hynes was the local contact man for visiting IRA members. He records:

> The first day (14 August 1920) that the party arrived in Templemore to shoot District Inspector Wilson, I met them and spent the day with them, but he was not to be seen that day. He was shot the following

64

Monday, 16 August, but I was not there, and Templemore was wrecked and looted by British forces that night.

Soon afterwards, Michael Hynes and his family began to be personally targeted. The Black and Tans raided the family farm so frequently that no workman would remain in the house. Hynes writes:

> My father [and] sister and a servant girl had to bear the brunt. On a few occasions, the Black and Tans threatened to shoot my father and sister. During a couple of these raids, turkey, hen and duck were killed and taken away, and the famous – or infamous – Captain Phibbs was in charge and condoned it.

In October, the Black and Tans attempted to burn down the Hynes farmstead. Hynes recalls: 'All our hay, straw and some outhouses were destroyed, but a few of us who were staying in a house nearby rushed to the place and the Tans fled.'

The pressure on Hynes and his Battalion became so intense that he moved operations to the neighbouring county of Laois (then known as Leix) and soon afterwards joined the 1st Battalion Flying Column, staying with it until the Truce. Occasionally he would return to his home area to help out 'whatever was doing', but never engaging in direct attacks.

He remembers two of these operations with the 2nd Battalion Mid-Tipperary Brigade in particular. The first was an attempt to blow up the bridges which crossed the River Suir. The second was the destruction of Lord Carden's residence in Templemore, which the Auxiliaries had used as their headquarters.

The last pages of Hynes's witness statement deals with the Truce and the Civil War. It was 1924 before the war was over for Hynes:

> After my release, I worked at home, but was still active if required.

8

ACTIVE SERVICE

When Michael Collins was setting about establishing an intelligence service in the Munster region, the man he went to see was Tomas Malone. In the index of contributors supplied by the Bureau of Military History, Malone's identity is given as 'Sean Forde, Commandant IRA, Limerick 1921'. In other words, Tomas Malone had two identities – and he needed them both if he was to escape detection in his extraordinarily busy 'active service' life.

Tomas Malone was born in Meadin, Tyrrellpass, County Westmeath, and trained as a teacher at De La Salle in Waterford. His activities on behalf of the national movement ranged well beyond the area in which he grew up. In the months before Easter 1916, he knew that there was to be a rebellion, and had tried to take part in it. Afterwards, he was one of the many who were arrested and imprisoned in Frongoch. Early in 1917, his brother Seamus had brought him down to mid- and south Tipperary to help reorganise the Volunteers there, of whom Seamus Robinson, Sean Treacy and Dan Breen were already well known to him. Soon after Malone arrived in Tipperary, the Volunteers carried out an important raid on a large hardware store in Thurles and seized substantial quantities of gelignite.

Malone was in Tipperary for barely three months when he was arrested in Dundrum. He describes the circumstances of the arrest:

> Countess Markievicz was down there in the area, and we were drilling with wooden guns. The police tried to stop us and I hit one of them.

So it was that he was in Mountjoy during the Ashe hunger strike. There he met many fellow Volunteers but, as he says himself, 'I was so many times in jail that I get confused as to who was with me at any particular time.' He himself went on hunger strike later on, after he was imprisoned in Dundalk. On that occasion, everyone was released eight days after he began his hunger strike.

In the latter part of 1919, Malone was available for a special mission which required tact and diplomacy. A split had arisen in east Limerick between two rival factions of Volunteers: one led by Donnchadha Hannigan; the other by Liam P. Manahan. Both Harry Boland and Michael Collins were worried by the situation, but neither Malone nor the leaders from Dublin were particularly concerned about the reason for the disagreement. What concerned them was that, while the Volunteers were fighting amongst themselves, not much fighting against the enemy was taking place. Malone quotes Collins's instructions:

> The instructions, of course, from Mick Collins were to get these fellows doing something and not be wasting their time disputing among themselves, and that is actually what I did. We got them fighting and they forgot all about their troubles. Both sides came in then and that finished the row.

Malone was certain that Collins wanted a 'fight' started:

> That was his idea. It was, 'Get going! Start a guerrilla war there!' That was the gist of his instructions to me when I was going to Limerick. He might have found fault with us for not consulting him or not notifying Headquarters about proposed actions. He often did things like that, but he was never opposed to a fight anyway.

The upshot of Malone's careful discussion with the more sensible members of both factions (excluding Manahan and Hannigan) was that it was decided that the Brigade should attack the RIC barracks at Ballylanders, with Malone in command. The battle was short and sharp. Malone describes part of it as follows:

> I picked seven or eight fellows to come with me into a house adjoining the barracks. We burst through the slates of the house in which we were and got out on to the roof of the barracks. We burst in the slates of the roof of the barracks. . . . We broke in the roof of the barracks anyway and threw in a few bombs.

Malone and his men called on the RIC to surrender, but they did not immediately do so. Instead, they began a discussion with the Volunteers through the hole that the Volunteers had blown in the roof and ceiling. Under cover of the discussion, one of the policemen stole in to the room underneath and fired upwards, very nearly hitting Malone. The RIC eventually surrendered, and the East Limerick Brigade, as Malone records, 'got everything that was in the barracks: rifles, ammunition, revolvers and a box of bombs'.

Malone stayed on in east Limerick despite the fact that the Volunteers in Offaly had been promised to him. He was in high demand and was the commanding officer for the attack on Kilmallock Barracks. This operation involved a much wider area than east Limerick, so Malone got in touch with 'Clare and Mick Brennan', East Clare Volunteers under the command of Michael Brennan. Because Malone knew that the capture of the barracks at Kilmallock was not going to be easy, he made what he described as

> very elaborate plans in connection with this attack which provided for widespread activities in the surrounding area, including North Cork, Mid Limerick, South Tipperary and all the surrounding areas. The local Volunteer Companies were all engaged with the blocking of roads and the cutting of railway lines. . . . It was, I think, actually the biggest barrack attack that took place during the whole fighting, in order of importance.

The garrison in Kilmallock was large and, according to Malone, included some Black and Tans: it was Malone's first encounter with the Tans. The fight lasted all night, and the Volunteers used so much ammunition in this engagement that Malone was reprimanded by GHQ for 'wasting' it. The most dangerous part of the battle, it would appear from Malone's account, was the danger posed to themselves from the big home-made percussion bombs. (These bombs had a small amount of explosive, contained in metal; the explosive was exploded by striking.) At one point, a fire broke out when Malone and his men were filling bottles with petrol. Malone reports:

> I shouted for a bucket of water and somebody came along with a bucket. I flung it into the blaze but it was paraffin oil was in the bucket.

Malone records the death of a fellow teacher at Kilmallock – Liam Scully:

It was in my car Scully died, the car I was driving. We took him away down to west Limerick and we left him in a house down there. I went on that night to his own place. . . . Ballylongford is the name I think.

Liam Scully was buried next morning in Templeglantine. Part of Malone's duties as the officer in command was to arrange for the decent burial of their casualties. It would seem that Malone concerned himself with recording the men's names and the circumstances of their deaths.

Several witness statements note that, on 27 June 1920, General Lucas, a British army officer, was captured near the Blackwater river in west Limerick while on a fishing holiday. Malone dates the capture from the date of the burial of Liam Scully. His Column got a message from north Cork to go there to take custody of General Lucas, 'as there was great enemy activity in north Cork'. Malone continues:

> We took him over somewhere around . . . Newmarket, County Cork. . . . I know that approaching Abbeyfeale on our way back, with him as a prisoner in the car, we ran out of petrol and that he had to help us to push the car to the tops of the hills when we could let it run down. In this way, we got to Abbeyfeale, where we got petrol.

The Column kept Lucas for a week or so. There was some suggestion that he might be exchanged for a republican prisoner, such as Robert Barton. Lucas scoffed at the idea: he did not think he was that valuable. Lucas was well liked by his captors. Malone explains:

> He was a very keen card player, very fond of bridge, and we of course tried to make everything as pleasant as we could for him. He was a bit of a nuisance while he was around, our attention being concentrated on looking after him. He held up the whole place. Nobody could do anything while he was with us. We did of course what North Cork [the North Cork Brigade] did – passed him along to somebody else.

Malone and his men took Lucas across the Shannon to Clare and handed him over to Mick Brennan, who kept him for a while. Malone continues:

> Then he was transferred to mid-Limerick and he escaped from the mid-Limerick fellows . . . and the suggestion is anyway that his escape was connived at by his guards. I would not be one bit surprised if that was so, because they were all sick of him. He was a nice fellow and

everyone liked him. We would have been very sorry if he should become a subject for execution, as a retaliation or anything like that.

General Lucas was an extraordinarily lucky hostage. After his escape, he managed to flag down a military lorry which was later ambushed in Oola by Sean Treacy and his men – who were unaware that Lucas was on board. Lucas came out unscathed but very impressed by IRA Intelligence, which had, as he thought, discovered his whereabouts so quickly following his escape.

Tomas Malone went on to take part in the attack on Scariff RIC barracks, and the ambushes in Grange and Glenacurrane. At Scariff, he was helping out the 'Clare fellows'; Grange was almost exclusively an east Clare effort; and at Glenacurrane (near the Cork border), Malone and his men collaborated 'with the north Cork fellows'. At Glenacurrane, it was 'the north Cork fellows who had the Vickers gun'. He goes on:

> Only two lorries came along, and they put up no fight at all. . . . We had men extended for about three miles along on either side of the road. It was the biggest number of men I saw together during all the fighting there.

As it was coming up to Christmas, Malone and Hannigan decided that it would be a good idea to disband the Column temporarily and let the men go home for the festive season. Hannigan and Malone took the opportunity of going to Cork, where they had something of a working holiday: they picked up some arms and ammunition from a merchant seaman who happened to be a brother of Hannigan's.

The possession of the ammunition made things awkward for Malone in the hours which followed. His encounter with the Tans was something he would never forget. He recounts:

> it was uppermost in my mind that I must not be caught with the ammunition in my pocket. So I hit the Tan who was holding me up with his fist and, bursting past the two of them, I ran across the bridge.

Some time later, he woke up handcuffed and in custody. He was questioned and re-questioned by the RIC. At one point, 'one of the RIC gave me a kick in the mouth. He broke every tooth I had with the kick.' The RIC were all very drunk.

Malone was removed from the drunken officers by a kind RIC man. Later, the questioning became more formal:

> At about two o'clock in the morning I was taken out and brought along into a sort of sitting room. . . . A fire was lighting, there was an officer sitting at the table, and two other military officers were standing by.

The questioning, which was very thorough, continued, and Malone thought that he was getting on quite well. Not well enough, it seems. The interrogating officer nodded to one of the others. 'All right, Jack,' he said. Malone continues:

> Jack went over very deliberately and, taking up the tongs, put them into the fire. Nobody said anything for an awfully long time. Then they sort of nodded at one another.

They used the red-hot tongs on him, but Malone did not break. Instead, he became more and more angry, and refused to answer any questions at all. They did not use the tongs a second time. They hit him instead and threatened to shoot him. The officers took him to an address they had found on his person but, finding nothing there, put him back in a lorry. Malone remembers:

> I was very cold and very battered. One of the officers asked me if I would like to get into the driver's cab in front, where it was a little warmer. I said I wouldn't mind, and I got in in the front. He took a flask of whiskey out of his pocket and offered me a drink. When I refused this, he said 'It is all right. You need not be afraid. It is not doped or anything and it will do you good. . . . He took a drink out of it anyway and he gave it to me. I took a mouthful and I can say it was very welcome.

Eventually, Malone was court-martialled and imprisoned: first in Cork, and then in Spike Island in Cork, from where he escaped.

Malone's witness statement runs to a hundred pages, each one of which is an adventure. He is always appreciative of the occasional chivalrous enemy, such as the officer in the lorry, or the District Inspector, who had him moved from the Bridewell to the Military Detention Barracks out of the reach of the Tans, or the kind RIC man who had him removed from the hostile officers.

Towards the end of his statement, Malone describes an extraordinary encounter with a member of the opposing forces:

I had a single combat with a British Intelligence Officer, named Captain Brown. Brown was a tough nail. It was just outside Kilmallock. I was driving a motor car. I came out a by-road at the back of Mount Coote, which was Lord Daresbury's place. It was one of the by-roads that we usually travelled, and just as I approached the junction with the main road, Brown passed by the end of it, also driving a car. I kept going and went out on the road. He was the local military intelligence and he was in uniform at this time, but I knew him and he knew me. . . . The car I was driving had been captured from a District Inspector somewhere. He stopped and I stopped. I had an automatic, but he fired first. . . . We fired three or four shots at each other but without effect. We were sixty or seventy yards apart, and to make a hit at that distance with a pistol was an uncertain kind of thing. My engine was running all the time, and I put the car into reverse . . . so as to close the distance somewhat. I was keeping my head down firing an odd shot at him as I moved. His nerve failed as the distance began to close. More than one of my bullets had hit the windscreen of his car and others had hit the back of the car. He had a Webley. It was heavier than my pistol. He skedaddled in the end.

Malone chased him for a bit: 'I gained a little bit on him and fired a few more shots after him.' But Malone was afraid to go too near Kilmallock, so he turned and drove away. The contest did not end there, however, but lasted right up to and after the Truce.

Maurice Meade, who was a member of the East Limerick Flying Column, was greatly entertained by the saga of the motor cars. His interest in the story had far more to do with the cars which Malone and Brown had managed to acquire in the course of their military activities than with the War of Independence. It so happened that the car which Captain Brown was driving during the encounter did not belong to him either, but had been captured from Malone. As Malone says in his statement:

That was half the reason I was so anxious to capture him and [the car], because he had done great boasting about having captured my car and he had been using it himself to drive around since its capture.

Malone was extremely attached to the car, which had originally belonged to DI McKettrick of the RIC. According to Maurice Meade, the car had a special significance:

The registration plates had been painted out on the car and the derisive identification 'DI 303' painted on instead. Malone had become very well known with this car.

Malone had 'lost' the car to the British while he and his party were waiting for tea in Hayes of Kiltealy and Malone was playing the piano. This was a sore point with Malone and his Column. Naturally, Brown was very pleased. Meade takes up the story: 'We all met Brown after the Truce and had drinks with him, but we still felt sore about the car.' Brown had rubbed salt into the wound when he turned up to a coursing match at Mount Coole driving the famous car. An opportunity to even the score now presented itself to the men of east Limerick. Maurice Meade and his comrades decided to take it away from him, 'even though [this] might be taken as a breach of the Truce'.

It was arranged that Malone would ask Brown to have a drink with him so as to keep him occupied. While the two erstwhile enemies were enjoying their drink, Meade and another man drove away in the famous car. Unfortunately, one of the men crashed the car into an old quarry. Neither Malone nor Browne ever got the car as, despite every effort, it could not be repaired.

Malone ends his long account of his adventures on a note of quiet pride. He records the tribute which Ernie O'Malley paid him in his book about the troubles:

> O'Malley mentioned . . . 'I was now in east Limerick, where Tomas Malone was in charge of a Column' . . . . He also said, 'I knew I was in safe hands and I slept for the first time for so many nights' or something like that. He just mentions that.

Malone was happy with the judgement of his peers.

Michael Brennan, who was the East Clare Brigade OC, had close contacts with the West Limerick Brigade. He took part in the well-known attack on Kilmallock RIC barracks, led by his 'old prison comrade' Tomas Malone. Brennan remembers that, on the way back to Clare:

> As we passed through a village from Killmallock, men and women rushed out of their houses and cheered us. They had probably been up all night, as they were within sight and sound of the fight.

On his return to Clare, Brennan plunged himself into various republican activities, including a search of the RIC barracks at Newmarket-on-Fergus. He ends his account of this episode with the remarkable statement: 'We left the garrison tied up, and when the Sergeant was freed he cut his throat.' According to his statement, Brennan was one of those into whose hands Brigadier General Lucas was entrusted to be held as hostage 'for a few days'. The few days turned into several weeks. Brennan complains:

> [Lucas's] presence completely immobilised us, as we daren't do anything which would involve raiding by the British. In addition, he was an expensive luxury as he drank a bottle of whiskey every day, which I hated like hell to pay for.

Lucas, who had a young wife in London, was hugely impressed when Brennan was able to arrange that a daily letter from him could be sent to her and, even stranger, that a letter from her could be delivered unopened to him daily. Such was the control of the Volunteers over the postal system. He was even more impressed when Brennan was able to arrange a night's poaching on the Shannon, in the company of some IRA men, headed by a man called Sean Carroll. Lucas was extremely nervous. Brennan tells the story:

> The boat was held in the strong current for about two hours while Lucas cast for salmon. . . . Every now and then he expressed anxiety as to the possibility of the river bailiffs discovering us, but Carroll reassured him.

Later, Lucas asked Brennan how Carroll could be so certain that there would be no interference from the bailiffs. Brennan goes on:

> I didn't know, but I promised to find out the next day. I got the information and passed it on to Lucas. Sean was the Head Bailiff. This seemed to be about the most astonishing bit of information Lucas ever got.

The East Clare Brigade became desperate in their efforts to rid themselves of Lucas. As a hostage, he was of little use, and the idea of killing him was unthinkable. So, unknown to Lucas, they decided to arrange his escape:

> Up to this we had always left a man on duty outside his bedroom window, and now when the room was on the ground floor we withdrew this man. At first nothing happened . . . but when we got up in the morning our prisoner was gone.

Brennan was able to turn his mind to other things, namely the collection of the rates. The war had spread to the bread-and-butter issues of local government.

Our next witness, Joe Barrett, was the Officer in Command of Operations of the IRA in mid-Clare in the War of Independence, and also a rates collector. At the end of 1918, Clare was divided into three Brigade areas: East Clare, Mid-Clare and West Clare. Soon afterwards, Ernie O'Malley, sent by GHQ, came to Clare to organise and train the members.

Long before the movement for independence took off in Ireland, Clare had a history of 'land trouble', as Barrett calls it. One important legacy of this was a superfluity of special RIC stations, known as 'RIC Huts':

> The result . . . was that, by the commencement of the Black and Tan struggle, our county had perhaps twice as high an 'RIC population' and twice as many 'RIC centres' to contend with.

In addition to this, the Volunteers were so poorly equipped that they were forced to use home-made bombs in their attacks on stone-built barracks. They were not too successful in these attacks, at least in the early stages of the war. When the RIC began to use hand grenades to resist attacks on patrols, the IRA had even less success. In February 1920, the Vice Brigadier of Mid-Clare, Martin Devitt, was killed. Barrett describes their efforts to provide a funeral:

> Devitt was waked that night in the fields outside Inagh village, and next night was buried in a turf stack. There was intense British military activity in the area. The hearse and coffin were followed by them to Inagh, but the Volunteers succeeded in eluding the enemy watchers and brought the corpse across country, on their shoulders, to Cloona, where they carried out the burial. The RIC discovered the body about a week later. An inquest was held at Ennistymon, at which the verdict of the jury was, 'We find that Martin Devitt died on the 24 February from bullet wounds received while fighting for the freedom of his country'.

As time went on, the situation improved for the IRA. Not all the RIC barracks were impregnable, and in October 1920 the Volunteers captured

Ruan barracks. As well as acquiring a respectable amount of arms in that engagement, they also captured thirteen bicycles – essential equipment for any service unit.

Barrett goes into considerable detail in his account of IRA engagements. Major David Joseph Conroy, who was a member of the Union Defence Forces of South Africa when he submitted his witness statement in 1952, gives a much looser account of his experiences in County Clare. To begin with, he was something of a 'part-time' soldier in the movement, being a student at the time, but he

> duly joined the Volunteers and at some time took the usual oath of alle-giance to the Irish Republic and Dáil Éireann. I later administered the same oath to other members.

Conroy does not remember many of the names of his comrades, after an interval of more than thirty years, but he does record that the Volunteers were few in number around Kilkee, and that they 'were piti-fully short of weapons'. He continues:

> I once succeeded in purchasing a German automatic pistol from a returned soldier with fifty rounds of ammunition. Shortly after, Michael Brennan visited, and this was shown to him with pride. . . . His need being the greater, that was the last the Battalion saw of this fine weapon. . . . There was also a rather unfortunate tendency in Kilkee to refrain from any action that might militate against the livelihood of the inhab-itants of the town, who had to depend on this on a short summer hol-iday season.

Conroy fell into poor health before the War of Independence ended and was forced to emigrate to South Africa on medical advice.

Commandant Haugh, who signed his statement on 1 January 1951, records, in the course of a very full account, the fighting in west Clare. His account is remarkable in that it conveys the sense of discouragement which he and his men experienced when the civil population began to be hard pressed. The effect of enemy action on the morale of the popula-tion was undeniable: indeed, the tactics employed by the Black and Tans were designed with this in mind.

Haugh describes a raid by the British:

At 4 PM on April 26 a mixed force of the enemy in twelve lorries drove up to the Brigade adjutants's home in Monmore. . . . Sentries were posted and the work of destruction commenced. Permission to remove anything whatsoever was curtly refused. All articles commending themselves for the use or comfort of the enemy was piled on to the lorries. The sight of a particularly fine bundle of linen being removed to the lorries proved too much for the owner, and a struggle took place which resulted in some being retrieved. A mine was laid underneath the wall in the kitchen fireplace: all unwanted articles were also piled therein.The dwellinghouse, together with the out-offices, were now plentifully sprinkled with petrol. The latter were also mined. But an unusual incident was to delay matters somewhat further. A pet thrush was released from its cage and thrown outside. This was reminiscent of its daily bath, but seeing none at hand [the bird] returned to its cage, now on top of the kitchen pile. When [it was] again removed, a Tommy held it in his hand. A sow with a progeny of fourteen took matters philosophically and, on being evicted from her sty, suckled her brood in the yard. The explosion shook the countryside and brought the sow to her feet with a ferocious snort. The descending avalanche of stones and rubble completed her rout, and she took to the fields in wild stampede. . . . Probably for moral effect, the mines seemed to have been overcharged and a number of the wreckers had narrow escapes. One Tommy was rendered unconscious. . . .This soldier died of his injuries within the week.

The home of the Brigade commandant was looted and burnt out on the same date. Haugh was particularly disappointed when he came back a week later. His dug-out, in which he and other IRA men could shelter in safety, had been destroyed. He concludes:

Alas! The moral effect had materialised. The dug-out had been destroyed by local residents in frenzied panic; two others a distance off had been denuded of their furnishings and left bare.

Worse still, 'the demolition squad was led by the Company lieutenant, no less!'

When the terror was at its height, wanted IRA men were not as welcome as they once had been. Haugh remembers:

The wanted man was in many cases furtively received. The usual procedure was the immediate setting of the tea table. . . . When the tea was finished, holy water was immediately produced, and excuse for further delay there was none.

They couldn't wait for him to go.

The West Clare Column fought on grimly, despite the scourge of scabies, which was an unwelcome hazard of the life they led. All the time, they were looking for a chance to attack. But, as Haugh writes, 'the enemy sat tight in secret outposts in the fringe [*sic*] of the town.' Haugh concludes his statement:

Stalemate had set in and continued until the Truce on July 11, 1920.

9

The Rebel County

When Ernest Blythe was sent down to Cork before the Easter Rising by the Volunteer Executive to re-organise some Companies there, he found little to encourage him. The numbers of what he called 'McNeillites' were small.

In Cork city, he met both Tomas MacCurtain and Terence McSweeney. 'I went with Tomas MacCurtain one night . . . the local Company did not number above twenty', Blythe tells us. Mallow had very few potential recruits, though Mitchelstown was better. In Kinsale, he found nobody. Blythe went on to Bandon and walked out to Ballinadee, where he met the Hales family. Tom Hales had, it seems, already taken steps to get a Company of Volunteers established. Blythe went to many other places in Cork, and his verdict on the county before the Rising was that 'Generally speaking, the position . . . was nearly as bad as it could be.'

During the War of Independence, Blythe was to meet many Corkmen, most of them in jail: one of them would die on hunger strike; another would be shot in front of his wife and family. The Hales, whom Blythe met in Ballinadee, would be known far and wide for their courage and dogged persistence. The most famous Corkman of all was Michael Collins – whom Blythe did not meet until the general release of prisoners after 1916, as they were detained in different prisons in England. That other famous son of Cork, Tom Barry, refused to submit a witness statement to the Bureau of Military History. He did, however, ask that his reasons for refusing to do so, as given in his letter, be included in the files of the Bureau:

> In any event I have always held that the whole set-up is wrong in so far as all the statements are confidential. As far as I understand, there will

be no records until a quarter of a century at least will have elapsed. Any individual is entitled to make any claim he likes and defame any officers he likes, and it must be recorded by your Bureau. In my opinion no history is a real history unless all statements are subjected to the light of publicity during the lifetime of those who took part in the events being recorded.

Tom Barry joined the British army in 1915 when he was seventeen years old. As he writes in his book *Guerrilla Days in Ireland*, he did not join up on the

> advice of John Redmond or any other politician. . . . I went to the war for no other reason than I wanted to see what war was like, to get a gun, to see new countries and to feel a grown man.

He arrived back in Cork in February 1919, after a four-year absence, and settled down to an intensive course of reading Irish history. In addition, he read 'all the daily papers, weekly papers, periodicals and every available republican' sheet. Having 'read himself' into the republican movement, Barry approached Sean Buckley from Bandon, seeking admission to join the IRA. He was taken on as an Intelligence Officer. Barry was a comparative latecomer to the West Cork Brigade. It was the middle of 1920 before he became active.

Oddly, the witness statement of William Hales would appear to be a chapter from his book *Ballinadee: The 3rd Cork Brigade – The War of Independence*. Both his witness statement and the book are an account of the German Plot and its impact on the Hales family.

The German Plot and its consequences feature in many of the witness statements, including Eugene Smith's, the civil servant in the Castle who had passed on the information that the Castle authorities intended to swoop on the leaders of the republican movement and intern them. This did indeed happen. The most prominent leaders were imprisoned, with the startling exception of Michael Collins. There are hints in Hales's statement that this omission was not an accident. According to Hales:

> In Dublin, Michael Collins escaped the raiding party set to capture him; his timely warning caused the escape of his great comrade, Harry Boland; Michael Collins's escape at that time and [the escape of] the other physical-force leaders of the Irish Volunteers throughout Ireland

was destined to affect the whole course of events as far as the destiny of the fighting forces was concerned.

Hales remarks that those who were seized for imprisonment went 'without a struggle, and in silence'.

Not so the Hales family: William Hales provides us with a dramatic account of the struggle that was put up by his family when a force of armed police motored out to their farmhouse 'to effect the arrest of John Hales'. Hales notes that the incident was reported in the *Independent* and the *Cork Examiner*: he was clearly proud of his role in the event. He goes on:

Ten police constables (under Srgt. Brennan, a native of Clare), sturdy and regular in their tread, moving out silently in the grey mist of a May morning, there is scarcely daylight to see their polished carbines as they move along the lonely roads and approach the farmhouse – no need to fear scout or sentry, for the Viceroy's proclamation is not yet out. Silently they approach, [there is] the barking of a faithful sheepdog, and they have the house surrounded.

Hales describes the struggle in colourful detail. Almost everyone in the house, including Madge Hales, his sister, and their cousins, joined in the mêlée. Hales escaped and went on the run. From the Hales point of view, and indeed from that of others too, the episode ended happily. Two of the constables resigned, and a third followed their example a few days later. Hales ends his testimony:

Sean and his father now sleep side by side in Innishannon Churchyard under the shade of the old ivied tower.

The other well-known actively republican family in the Bandon area was the Deasy family. Jeremiah Deasy was an officer in the Innishannon Company, Bandon Battalion, Cork 3rd Brigade, IRA. He was a brother of Liam Deasy, who was the Adjutant of the same Brigade.

In Deasy's witness statement, he describes the organisation of the Volunteers from the Companies around his area into the Bandon Battalion. He traces the development of the Volunteers through the conscription crisis in 1918 and the general election which followed the Armistice in November. Deasy identifies the significance of the training that was given to the men:

Normal training continued throughout 1918. Public parades, often in Battalion strength, were now a feature of our activities. During the summer, manoeuvres, in which three or four adjoining Companies took part, were held at weekends. These operations were usually carried out under a Battalion officer. On these occasions we learned to move across country in extended order, making the best use of the available cover. Selected men were now being trained as scouts and despatch riders, and these manoeuvres were used to test their efficiency.

When the First Dáil met in Dublin and established the Republican Government, there was only one Brigade in Cork. The county area was very large, and it possessed at least twenty Battalions. It was decided, therefore, to divide the county into three areas, each of which had a Brigade. The area which included Bandon had six Battalions and was known as 'Cork No. 3'. At this point, too, the Volunteers formally tendered their allegiance to the government of the Irish Republic and came under the control of the Department of Defence. As Deasy put it: 'We became the army of the Irish Republic – [the] IRA.'

Much of the activity of the Bandon Battalion entailed selecting an enemy target (usually based on information acquired in various ways), getting into ambush position, and sometimes waiting for hours. For example, Deasy describes a fairly typical day:

> All positions were occupied [by] about 8 AM. There was no activity until about midday, when one of our scouts reported that a local British loyalist – Stennings – had been talking to some men working. . . . We moved with the remainder of the party to Kilpatrick, where we again took up ambush positions. We remained here until darkness set in, but there was no appearance by the enemy.

The training camps made a welcome change:

> About mid-September 1920, a training camp for the officers of the Companies south of Bandon river in the Bandon Battalion was established at Clonbulg in Kilbrittain Company area.

The Brigade Training Officer was Tom Barry, who drilled the officers for about a week. After a short break, they were recalled to duty. This time, after drawing a few blanks, they managed an engagement which was partially successful. Another week's training was arranged for the Companies north of the Bandon, again with Tom Barry in charge.

82

Jeremiah Deasy and his comrades had another duty which was not easy. They were obliged to collect for the IRA's Arms Fund from people who were willing to pay – and also from those who were not. People who were not willing were liable to have their cattle seized.

Deasy had one special responsibility because of his special knowledge of the Bandon river. His father was a pilot on the Bandon river at Kilmacsimon Quay. As a result, Deasy knew about the comings and goings of boats on the river, as well as the best crossing places. When preparations were being put in place for the establishment of the nucleus of a Flying Column, both the training of the men at the camps and Deasy's special knowledge of the river were vitally important. Deasy explains:

> There being no road crossing between Innishannon and the sea at Kinsale – it was most important that a number of crossing places should be arranged in this span. As I had lived on the river bank all my life and had a detailed knowledge of the river, I was instructed at this stage to select a number of crossing places at which boats and men to man them would always be available to ferry IRA Columns or officers across the river in this area.

His brother's witness statement is very short, and the contents are confined to one issue: the matter of the Italian arms which never arrived. Liam Deasy was able to date his first involvement with 'this matter'. He remembers:

> It must have been about Saturday, the 11 December 1920, for I remember the ruins of the burnt portion of the city were still smouldering. I travelled to Dublin by train along with Florrie O'Donoghue.

They attended a meeting at Barry's Hotel with Michael Collins, Cathal Brugha and Liam Mellows, amongst others. Detailed plans were laid for the purchase and transportation of arms from Italy. Negotiations with the Italians, they were told, were almost complete. Michael Leahy, from the Cork No. 1 Brigade, was chosen to go to Italy and return with the ship to guide it to a selected landing place. Cork Brigade No. 3 was to have ready plenty of places to dump the weapons in case the British authorities intervened. How seriously the leaders took the enterprise is hard to gauge. Liam Deasy remembers: 'When the meeting was over, Collins told us of the intervention by Archbishop Clune of Perth, Australia, to bring about an end to the fighting.'

West Cork and the Irish Republic had a contact in Italy: Donal Hales, one of the Hales brothers from Knockacurra. He set about acquiring arms and ammunition as soon as the messengers arrived from Ireland, which was, he thinks, 'about three or four months before the Truce. . . . We could get as many rifles as we wished. . . . we could also get ammunition.' But when he wanted further instructions, no word came from Ireland. 'No money was sent and [the rifles which had been stashed in Rome] were never removed.' In his testimony, Hales speculates on what might have motivated Collins in trying to acquire the arms only to abandon the plan (to Hales's embarrassment).

Michael Leahy (Vice OC Cork No. 1 Brigade), whose witness statement corroborates that of Hales, was more than embarrassed: he was furious. It took a little time for him to realise that he had been sent out to Genoa, where Hales lived, on a fool's errand. He had been coached in every aspect of the mission. Worst of all, the money he had been given for expenses soon ran out. Eventually, he returned to Cork 'only a fortnight before the Truce'. He concludes: 'From that day to this I never heard just how or why the purchase of the arms in Italy was not pursued.'

Most unusually, Leahy appends a note to his statement, which foreshadows the fierce debates on the Treaty:

> As Collins and some of those closely associated with him were continually engaged in overtures with 'peace' representatives of the British government from the autumn of 1920 up to the Truce of 11 July 1921, it is possible that he (Collins) was simply playing for time so that, with the people tired of war and the IRA unable to procure any arms and ammunition from Headquarters, the way would then be clear to settle with Britain for something much less than a Republic.

It is interesting that another witness statement, that of Florence O'Donoghue, corroborates the others in most details. He was as much in the dark on the reasons behind whatever decisions had been made for the abandonment of the project as they were: 'My recollection is that we did not have any definite information about the complete failure of the project at the Italian end until after the Truce.' Florence O'Donoghue was Adjutant, Cork No. 1 Brigade. He was also a member of the Advisory Committee attached to the Bureau of Military History.

The witness statement made by James Hurley, from Kilkerrimore, Clonakilty, County Cork, is a more significant document than it appears to be at first reading. It deals with the routine – almost boring – activities of a typical member of the movement. Hurley joined the Volunteers in 1913 and had achieved the rank of OC Transport and Supply by the time of the Truce in 1921. Two passages in his statement clearly indicate the changes which were taking place in places like west Cork during those years. The first passage refers to the early years:

> I well remember the day of this parade because only one civilian followed the parade to Ardfield. He was a man of about fifty years of age at the time – a tailor by trade.

The second passage is taken from the last pages of the statement:

> The seizure of four farms in the area from Loyalists – some of whom had been shot as spies – threw a lot of responsibility on my shoulders. I was responsible for removing the stock, implements and household goods from these farms to the lands of friendly farmers as an inventory of all stock and goods had to be furnished to the Brigade OC.

In contrast to the many full and detailed accounts submitted by the people of west Cork, the statement submitted by four members of the Cork No. 1 Brigade working on the document together is almost laconic, but nonetheless highly informative. It lists the members of the Company staff and its activities and area of operation. The statement reflects the larger events that were taking place in Cork city at that time. For example: 'On several occasions, armed guards were provided by the Company to escort Brigade Commandant Lord Mayor MacSwiney to the various places in which he resided at night', and then 'In October 1920, guards of honour were provided at the lying-in-state of Brigade Commandant Lord Mayor Terence MacSwiney.'

The four who put this careful record together were: Mark Wickham from Curragh Road; John J. Lucy of York Terrace, Summerhill; Patrick J. Deasy of South Main Street; Maurice FitzGerald of Endaleigh Park, Douglas Road, all from Cork.

One entire witness statement is devoted to the terrible events of 11 December 1920. We are indebted to Sean Healy for the narrative. He belonged to A Company, 1st Battalion, No. 1 Cork Brigade:

> It began with the targeting of the occupants of Victoria Barracks by the IRA. The barracks was the headquarters of the Auxiliary Police, who had made themselves highly unpopular in the area. The ambush was first put in place on 10 December, a Friday night, at a position inside the boundary wall at Dillons Cross. But the Auxiliaries did not show and the whole operation was postponed until the following night, Saturday, December 11, 1920. Positions were occupied by the attacking party, who were armed with revolvers and Mills bombs. . . . a short shrill whistle sounded in the night air, quickly followed by a second blast, to the accompaniment of the drones of Crossley motor engines and the boisterous voices of the Auxiliaries. . . . immediately bombs were hurled at the lorries, followed by revolver shots. When the smoke had cleared away, wrecked lorries and wounded auxiliaries could be seen on the roadway.

The attacking party then withdrew, disappearing without a trace. Healy describes what followed:

> Then followed the crowning act of frightfulness: the whole force of Auxiliaries, accompanied by Black and Tans and soldiers, were let loose in the city. Utterly out of control, the military and so-called police sacked, plundered and burned the principal shops, the City Hall and several public buildings. The doors of numerous private dwellings were smashed in, their occupants dragged out and beaten. Neither old nor young were spared. Children were squealing in terror while their parents were being brutally beaten and their homes given over to flames. . . . the Black and Tans broke into a dwelling house in Dublin Hill and murdered two brothers named Delaney.

The story of the burning of Cork is well known. Not so well known is the engagement in Clonmult near Cobh, an account of which was submitted by another member of Cork No. 1 Brigade: Patrick J. Higgins, Captain Aghada Company, 4th Battalion. His account deals with the attack on Sunday, 20 February 1920 on the East Cork Flying Column, of which he was a member. The IRA were occupying a one-storied, thatched farmhouse with mud walls when they were surrounded by the military. They did not realise this until two of their members were shot dead as they went to the well to get some water for their tea. Higgins describes the shoot-out:

Jack O'Connell now decided that we should make a rush from the house and fight it out in the open. He led the way, carrying a rifle and fixed bayonet, and got safely across the yard under heavy fire.

Three IRA men were shot in quick succession. The survivors retreated into the house but the military outside kept up continuous heavy fire. When they began to throw bombs on to the thatched roof, the position became hopeless. They had to surrender or be burned alive. Higgins remembers what happened next:

> We were lined up alongside an outhouse with our hands up. The Tans came along and shot every man, with the exception of three . . . who were saved from the Tans by the officer in charge of the military party.
>
> A Tan put his revolver to my mouth and fired. I felt as if I was falling through a bottomless pit. Then I thought I heard a voice saying, 'This fellow is not dead, we will finish him off.' Only for the military officer coming along, I, too, would be gone.

But Higgins survived and was taken to the military hospital:

> After some days in hospital, the bullet which had lodged in my jaw fell out. (It was a lead bullet, not a nickel one.)

Higgins made a good enough recovery to be tried and sentenced to death on 21 June 1921. Before the sentence could be carried out, the Truce was declared on 11 July 1921.

Each of the three Cork Brigades took an active part in the short, bitter war which followed the Declaration of Independence by the First Dáil. Many of the witness statements simply list the names of those men who took part, interspersed with accounts of routine engagements. Richard Willis and John Bolster from Mallow, who submitted a joint statement, gave one such account. Their statement also records the capture of General Lucas, the Commanding Officer of the British troops, at Fermoy.

As the War of Independence progressed, the use of Flying Columns became more and more commonplace. Robinson had noticed certain drawbacks to their increased use. There was one he did not mention: the problem of discipline. It was sometimes difficult for the leaders to maintain discipline where many of the men were out of their own areas and not known to the local people. Superintendent Philip Chambers's testimony casts a new light on this problem, and how Tom Barry dealt with it:

> In June 1921, two men were found guilty of breaking into the house of the late Canon Haynes, the Protestant Rector of Kenneigh. The punishment decreed was to have them tied to the railings of the local Parish Church on a Sunday morning. It was my job to have this job carried out. I look back on it now with extreme disgust, for I consider that it was a degrading and most inhuman procedure. It happened on that morning that the mother of one of them actually passed by on her way to Mass – one can very easily picture the poor woman's feelings. This was, in my honest opinion, a rotten method of enforcing the law, and I would have much preferred to take these men out and shoot them rather than [carry out] the procedure [that was] adopted.

10

KERRY

By the time the Bureau of Military History was taking statements from participants in the War of Independence, Austin Stack, a key figure in the development of the movement in County Kerry, was dead. Unusually, the Bureau included the testimony of his widow Mrs Stack, who lived in Dublin at the time. This testimony includes an account in Austin Stack's own words of the peace negotiations in London and the events that led up to them. They are reproduced verbatim in Mrs Stack's witness statement. Stack had intended to write all that he could remember of the years since 1913 and the involvement of Kerry with the Volunteers before 1916. He had intended to trace events through the reorganisation of Sinn Féin and the Volunteers in 1917, the elections in the following two years, the establishment of the Government of the Republic, and its working up to the Truce. He was prevented from doing this because:

> As I am on the twelfth day of a hunger strike and as it is impossible to calculate how long more I may be fit for writing, I am, for the moment anyway, abandoning my idea of a life story.

It fell to his widow to summarise the main events of his life. Mrs Stack concentrates her account on events in Kerry in 1916, particularly the complications regarding the capture of Casement and the expected arrival of arms from Germany. Mrs Stack clearly felt that it was important that her husband's part in these events be recorded in the Bureau's Archives. In the first place, she establishes his credentials:

> The first Kerry conference of the Volunteers elected him as delegate to the Central Council, and he was representative for Kerry at the first National Convention on the 25th October 1915. . . . After the split in September 1914 . . . he remained with the Irish Volunteers . . . [and]

attended a camp for training Volunteers. . . . Instruction was given by J. J. O'Connell. . . . with him were Pierce McCann, who was afterwards elected TD for Tipperary and who died of flu in March 1919.

In March 1916, Austin Stack had been summoned to Dublin to make final arrangements for the Rising in Kerry. He was told that a German ship would land arms in Kerry, near Tralee, on Easter Sunday night or early Monday morning. Mrs Stack goes on to emphasise Stack's position:

> Austin had received strict instructions from Pearse on the occasion of the latter's visit to Tralee three or four weeks before the Rising, that a shot should not be fired [on] Easter Sunday when the general hostilities would start, and nobody expected the arms to be landed before that. The *Aud* did not come into view of Tralee, and Austin did not expect the landing of Casement. . . . Austin was blamed by some for not trying to organise a rescue of Sir Roger Casement and I know he felt sore about it, but [he] always said his orders were definite that no shot should be fired before the start of general hostilities on Easter Sunday, and he knew well that any fracas that might take place in Tralee would frustrate all the plans for the Rising.

But Casement's fate remained a sensitive subject for years to come. It was still a raw memory when Patrick Walsh from Annascaul, tells us that, in 1917, he and his Company 'attended a parade in the sports field in Tralee and marched to Banna Strand for the Casement anniversary.'

The whole question of Kerry's part in 1916, and the landing of Casement and Robert Monteith, caused a great deal of unease among many of those Volunteers who had been prominent in republican activities locally before the Easter Rising. They felt fairly happy about the way things had gone under their direction up to that fatal Holy Week before the Rising.

Joseph Melinn had joined the IRB in Dublin in 1905 and had moved to Tralee to take the post of manager at Slattery's Bacon Factory in 1909. Sean McDermott had given him a letter of introduction to Austin Stack, and he set about recruiting members for the IRB in a careful and methodical manner. The membership was small to begin with. He informs us:

> There was no IRB district organisation in the county before 1916. We had periodic visits from representatives of the Supreme Council, Cathal

Brugha in 1911, Major McBride in 1914, and Diarmuid Lynch in 1915. These men did not visit Circles, they saw only the officers.

The IRB took a keen interest in the formation of the Volunteers in Tralee. According to Melinn:

> The IRB was quite satisfied to let the organisation develop in a natural way; we were well represented and felt that if the necessity arose we could direct and influence the national policy of the new body.

Melinn took an active part in the reorganisation of the IRA in 1917, when many of the pre-1916 Volunteers, including James Houlihan (who, at the time he made his witness statement, was living at Benmore, Ballyduff, Tralee), rejoined the Volunteers. In 1918, when the strength of the Volunteers/IRA in Kerry increased, as Joseph Melinn records:

> three Brigades, in place of one, were formed. At a meeting of Battalion officers, presided over by the Chief of Staff from headquarters (Richard Mulcahy), I was appointed Vice Commandant, Kerry No 1. Brigade, Irish Republican Army.

All officers and men took the oath of allegiance to Dáil Éireann when it was established.

For the next few years, Melinn was in and out of jail. He does not go into any great detail about the ambushes and raids which were a feature of the war in Kerry but describes the final step in the organisation of the Irish Republican Army: the formation of the 1st Southern Division. When he met the officers from Cork, Waterford and other southern Brigades, he realised 'the necessity of keeping in touch with Cork Brigades'.

William Mullins, from Moyderwell, Tralee, County Kerry, was Quartermaster of Kerry No 1. Brigade. He too spent a great deal of time in prison. Between the Rising and 1918, Mullins had spent time in Frongoch in Wales, Tralee Jail, Wetherby in England, Cork Prison, and Dundalk, where he went on hunger strike. Some of the enmity between men like Mullins and members of the RIC began to develop at this early stage:

> The local RIC men were the witnesses against us, swearing they saw us parading in Volunteer uniform on such a date. Each prisoner in turn naturally refused to recognise their Court. Some days after this, we

decided to go on hunger strike. The strike started at midday on Monday but that morning a large number of us were transferred to Dundalk Gaol to serve our two-year sentence

Kerry was unusual in the variety and number of connections which some Kerry people, including members of the IRA, were able to form in the most unlikely quarters. Tadhg Kennedy, who lived at Ardrinnane, Ardfert, County Kerry, remembered:

> When I was a boy, I think it was before the Boer War, a number of artists [and] painters used to come each year to Annascaul, doing what they called sketching. I remember some of their names: Yeats, Addy, Miss Lloyd, Miss Brownrigg. They roamed the hills about the district painting the scenery, and I became friends with them.

Kennedy used to help the artists carry their painting paraphernalia on their expeditions. One of the visiting group was more interested in the stories told by the local seanchaí, Sean Kennington, who lived in a 'one-roomed house at the end of the village next the river'. Kennedy remembered: 'He went to every wake, and I often stayed out all night at a wake listening to Sean relate his tales and adventures, all in Irish of course, and some made up by himself.' Kennedy was bi-cultural, however, and was particularly friendly with a son of Sean Kennington's, who kept him well supplied with Wild West and mystery books, 'which I used to read like other young lads, with great gusto'.

As well as the artists' group from Dublin, Kennedy tells us that 'in those days there came to Moriarty's Hotel at Annascaul a good many "big" people to fish and to shoot'. Tadgh Kennedy was a relative of the Moriartys and 'was constantly at Moriartys' and saw there 'British generals, colonels and majors. I remember General Buller, General French, Major Kigell and a host of others'.

Kennedy went to the Christian Brothers school in Dingle. His two great friends there were Richard Hudson, a Protestant, and Paddy Sullivan, a son of Lord Ventry's head bailiff. When Richard Hudson went to boarding school at Portora Royal School at Enniskillen, Kennedy kept up a correspondence with him. The friendship continued when Richard Hudson returned to Tralee as a solicitor. Kennedy tells us that 'when I was in the IRA . . . he gave me the safety of his home in Strand Street, Tralee, with his mother'.

Kennedy's witness statement goes far beyond the events of the War of Independence. Throughout the conflict, he was in close touch with Michael Collins and GHQ in Dublin. Kennedy had first met Collins in Ballybunion in the summer of 1914 or 1915: 'He was there on holidays from London with Sam Maguire, Brigade OC, London'. He himself, Kennedy tells us, was invited by Collins to accompany him to London for the negotiations at the end of 1921. But Kennedy declined. It appears that infighting in the ranks of the IRA required his diplomatic skills in Kerry rather than in London.

Kennedy found it necessary to refer two episodes in particular to GHQ. The first of these involved a Dominican priest in Tralee. According to Kennedy:

> Complaints had reached me in 1920 that Father — (name abstracted) was making all-too-frequent visits to the RIC barracks and made no secret of his sympathy with the Tans and the RIC. I have no doubt that his service in the British army during the war had given him a false idea of his duty to his own people and his country.

Kennedy, who was kept well informed about everything that happened in the barracks, complained to the Prior, Father Ayres, who happened to be a republican. Things became worse after a British officer was shot on the golf links in Tralee. A member of the congregation, who condoned the killing, was condemned from the altar by the Dominican sympathiser. The Prior, Father Ayres, took the unusual step of removing the priest from the altar.

Kennedy felt that he had to report the full circumstances to Michael Collins:

> After long deliberation he decided to send me to the Superior-General, who was then Father Finbar Ryan. . . . I went to see him and I never went through such an ordeal in my life. I was received by Father Ryan, with whom was a very old Dominican priest who, I was told, had been a Fenian in his young days – a Father Headley. I spent some time telling Father Ryan, who sat at the head of the table, what I knew and had learnt through my intelligence system. . . . Father Ryan was very visibly moved. . . . And Father Headley, when I was finished, asked me what I would do if he weren't a priest. I told him and he said: 'You are a brave man.'

The whole affair necessitated a second interview. In the end, the ex-British army chaplain was transferred to 'a safer place' and it was decided that Father Ryan should send for him and give him some fatherly advice.

The second situation which caused problems for Kennedy was the nature of the war itself. Much of it was carried on by undercover officers. This gave rise to difficulties with the rank and file, who could not be told what was going on. Three or four men, of whom Kennedy was one, were members of the Active Service Unit which carried out secret operations in the Tralee area. He speaks of one OC in particular:

> I think I should pay tribute here to the efficiency and courage of John Joe and the members of his Column, who had a very difficult and dangerous period of service in 1921. He was in charge of many unpleasant jobs which were, to say the least of them, dangerous and difficult, and he carried them out with the utmost efficiency. Amongst them were the executions of Major McKinnon, Boxer Mahony, Cosey FitzGerald and [name omitted] in Knightly's pub.

Two priests in particular grew tired of the apparent lack of activity in the area. They blamed this situation on Paddy Cahill, the Brigade OC. Between them, they drew up a petition for GHQ demanding Cahill's removal, citing his age and his poor state of health. They got the petition signed by members of the IRA, who seem not to have understood the serious implications of their actions. Kennedy was aghast when the OC of the 1st Battalion came to him with an order from the Chief of Staff, Dick Mulcahy, for the execution of the IRA men who had signed the petition. Kennedy records the procedure:

> That was the first I heard of it, and I went to Dublin to Mick Collins, who of course was my superior officer. He sent me to Cathal Brugha, GOC and Minister for Defence, to whom I explained the position and protested against any such action being taken without consulting me. He sent me to Dick Mulcahy, whom I met in a house at the top of Harcourt Street. I reported to him and, as a result, the order was cancelled.

Paddy Cahill resigned soon afterwards, but the difficulties lasted up to the Truce and beyond.

Two members of the Kerry No. 2 Brigade, Michael Spillane and Michael J. O'Sullivan, both living in Killarney, provided the Bureau of Military History with two joint witness statements. As well as recording the activities of their own Battalion, they comment on the political situation in Kerry at the time. Their perspective on a local election is expressed as follows: 'In the local elections, the elements that had represented jobbery and graft for years had to be fought.' They also remembered the social and cultural activities of those years:

> Concerts and dances were organised by the Volunteers and Cumann na mBan and were a great success. Prices of admission to the dances were small and so these functions were decidedly popular.

By 1920, the two witnesses noted that

> friction with the Crown Forces was increasing. The Volunteers of the Killarney Battalion cut and blocked roads to impede their movements and to facilitate the attacks on . . . RIC barracks.

In contrast to the overall view given by Spillane and O'Sullivan, Thomas McEllistrim gives a detailed account of the many engagements in which he personally took part.

McEllistrim, who was a TD at the time he made his witness statement, had been arrested after the Rising in 1916 and duly imprisoned in Frongoch. On his release, he immediately reorganised his old Company at Ballymacelligot. In the next few years, he followed the pattern that had been so well established by the Volunteers in their guerrilla war. The first attack was on the RIC barracks at Gortatlea, where McEllistrim lost two men. The object then was to shoot the two RIC men who were responsible for the deaths of McEllistrim's two men:

> In June 1918, I got word that an inquest on Browne and Laide [the two IRA men] . . . would be held in Tralee on the 29th June, and that the two RIC men, Boyle and Fallon, who did the shooting, would be in Tralee.

McEllistrim and his men hid out in a felt hut in Ballymacelligot, where they slept and sometimes cooked. They were never discovered.

In between engagements, McEllistrim and his colleague, named Cronin, drilled and trained their Volunteers, collected shotguns where they could, and, in 1920, went up to Dublin to buy rifles. They made another attack on Gortatlea RIC; this time it was successful. 'After [the] Gortatlea barrack surrender there was no enemy post left in Ballyelligott', McEllistrim writes.

The Company broadened its repertoire to include making mine traps in felled trees, combined with digging trenches across roads. By the middle of 1920, the Black and Tans in their large convoys of lorries had become the Volunteers' main target. In June, an Active Service Unit was formed with McEllistrim as the OC. 'The unit provided itself with a motor car and two horses with springs', which, according to McEllistrim, greatly improved its effectiveness:

> We travelled over a big area with this equipment and never had to bother much about road trenches as we just lifted our cars across trenches on our shoulders.

The conflict worsened, and it was decided to form a Flying Column selected from Kerry No 2. Brigade. Ambush followed ambush, and comrades were killed and wounded. McEllistrim was still intent on vigorously prosecuting the war. In June, he received word that a party of soldiers was to travel by train to Castleisland. McEllistrim decided that he would intercept the train by removing a rail from the railway track. The Column had time to remove the rail at a curve of the track and crouched on either side of the railway 'ready for action'. McEllistrim continues:

> To our amazement, that train travelled along that railway line on one track. The wheels on the other side of the train rolled on the line without a track. It travelled a distance of thirty feet in that way and jumped on to the railway track at the other end of where the railway had been discontinued by us.

James Daly, who in between jobs slept in a dug-out under a barn, kept his Company active by blocking roads. He describes his experience of attempts to capture enemy posts. An attack on Rathmore RIC barracks was planned by his Company. According to Daly, there was no agreed method for carrying out an attack.

> Con Morley . . . was banking on spraying the barracks with paraffin, using a line of hose and setting the barracks alight with lighted torches.

Another line of attack is described by Daly:

> [Michael] Dennehy . . . had prepared four hods with long handles in which large bombs had been placed, and his idea was to tip the bombs out of the hods through an opening in the barrack windows between the windows and the shutters.

The witness statement given by Patrick McElligott is very different from that of Tadhg Kennedy. There were no trips to Dublin to see Collins, and little relief from the hard world of the guerrilla fighter.

In 1919, when the IRA was in the process of reorganising, McElligott's Company took part in collecting shotguns from farmers and others in the area. This was in preparation for the attack on the barracks in Ballybunion, which was not a success – but it was early days. In May 1920, the IRA attacked three RIC men in Listowel. In the engagement which followed, the RIC sergeant was killed. Shortly after this, the Tans arrived in Listowel. McElligott writes:

> After this we had to be very careful. Our numbers were dwindling through arrests. Many of our men had received beatings in the streets by the Tans, the result being that it was not easy to find members to attend meetings. A young student named John Lawlor, home on leave at this time, was beaten to death in the street by the Tans with the butts of their rifles.

At the end of 1920, the Flying Column for Kerry No. 1 was formed, mostly composed of men on the run. In early January of the following year, an order was received that District Inspector Sullivan, RIC, was to be executed as a reprisal for the killing of Liam Scully at Kilmallock while under the command of Tomas Malone in the East Limerick Brigade. Patrick McElligott's brother, Robert, who was the Battalion OC, was involved in the shooting of the District Inspector. According to Patrick McElligott:

> My brother planned the execution. . . . He was there to see that the job was done, or to carry out the job himself if for any reason the men appointed for the job failed.

A month or so afterwards, Robert McElligott was himself shot by 'a cycle corps of military' in an unconnected operation. McElligott continues:

> At the funeral, which I could not attend, the people attending were rounded up, abused, searched and beaten. The wreaths, numbering forty, which had been placed on the grave were taken out on the public road and broken up by the Tans.

After the death of his brother, Patrick McElligott was appointed Battalion OC.

McElligott and his Company soldiered on from one engagement to another, attacking the British patrols where they could, and retreating when they could not.

In the spring of 1921, McElligott

> received information that Sir Arthur Vickers was a spy and that his house – known locally as the 'Great House' – was to be taken over by the military as a 'Block House'. If this happened, Abbeyfeale and the surrounding areas . . . would have been in danger. . . . I issued an order to Jim Costello. . . .for the execution of Vickers and the burning down of the 'Great House'.

The Bureau of Military History holds in its archives a witness statement which recounts the events of the morning of Vickers's shooting from a very different viewpoint. Michael Murphy was born at Kilmorna near the 'Great House'. He joined the RIC in 1906 and in 1914 enlisted in the British army. When he was discharged, he returned to Kilmorna, where he was employed as companion and valet to Sir Arthur Vicars, Knight Commander Victorian Order, and a step-brother of Pierce O'Mahony. Vicars had been in charge of the Crown Jewels at Dublin Castle when they went missing, never to be recovered. As a consequence, Vicars was dismissed from his post as Ulster King-at-Arms, and in 1910 retreated to Kerry in some disgrace.

McElligott appends the details of the information which led to the shooting of Vicars. According to this account, Vicars made enquiries from his land stewards and tenants in regard to the movements of the Flying Column. British officers were constantly being entertained at the 'Great House'. Kilmorna House commanded an excellent view of the area of operation of the Flying Column.

On the other hand, Michael Murphy protested: 'I could not understand why Vicars was shot. He was a thorough gentleman who mixed freely with the tenants on the estate.' Murphy had discovered that the house was on fire and roused Vicars and his wife. He describes the fatal scene:

> Vicars went downstairs and left the house by the main entrance. He had come about 150 yards from the door when he ran into a second party of the IRA who held him up and shot him dead on the spot. I had followed him close on his heels. He was not questioned in any way.

McElligott's version is at complete variance:

> Our intention was to arrest Vicars and have him tried. He refused to come out, and was running from room to room, armed with a revolver. The house was then set on fire; he rushed out through a side window.

McElligott was not the only witness to attempt to deal with the difficult issue of the execution of spies. Tadhg Kennedy describes the distress of his own family when a relative was executed:

> To us, his friends, it was a terrible tragedy and I was very upset about it, more so than my own brother's death at the hands of the British.

Patrick Walsh from Annascaul gives a chilling description of a similar event involving an unnamed man. Walsh writes:

> On the night he was held in a shed near Glenmore School and was then passed on to the Camp Company. A court martial was held that night. The Court examined all the evidence, including the documents found in his possession, and it was clear that he was a spy. He was sentenced to death. The execution took place on the 15th April 1920. The job was done at Camp and the body was left in the creamery yard at Dealis, near Camp.

11

THE RIC, NED BROY AND OTHERS

Colonel Eamon Broy signed his witness statement on 31 October 1955. It began:

> I was born and reared at Ballinure near Rathangan, County Kildare, on the borders of Offaly, where my people were farmers. This district was far off the beaten tracks, beside the Bog of Allen, and so the people retained most of the ancient Irish characteristics.

A generation or so before Broy's time, there was much resentment amongst farmers towards the landlords who owned the land, which the farmers worked. Moreover, as Broy put it:

> As practically all landlords were magistrates, they had complete and despotic control over their tenants. They were protected by the Royal Irish Constabulary, and the British army was near at hand at the Curragh, whence in the past 'regiments' had been despatched to protect the landlords' interests.

Despite the farmers' 'almost helpless position', there was a rich folk history in the area dating back to the 1641 Rebellion. The ordinary people felt that, sooner or later, they would be freed. Some looked back to the Geraldines, 'who would, one day, return to drive the English out of Ireland. . . . Some believed that it would be through the Irish Party winning Home Rule.'

About the time of the centenary of the 1798 rebellion, Broy listened to

> stories of the Battle of Rathangan . . . . the rebels defeated the British forces with sanguinary losses. Here an ancestor [of mine], John Broy, took part in the battle.

Broy held strongly to the belief that with

> all these memories it is not surprising that deep down in the people's hearts burned strongly a bitter hatred of English rule with its soldiers, police, informers, landlords and followers, who composed 'England's faithful garrison'.

In Broy's opinion, the greatest ally of 'England's faithful garrison' was the RIC:

> The people felt that the local RIC knew all about them and there was no use in doing anything illegal and secret because the police were certain to find out.

Broy was inclined to think that they were quite right.

Broy decided to join the Dublin Metropolitan Police when he finished school. He had a much higher opinion of this force:

> The members of the DMP were considered in the country as being 'decent' men and more liberal and national-minded than the RIC, who were regarded as both military and police enemies of their country.

Broy points out that two members of the DMP refused to disarm the Volunteers who were returning from the landing of arms at Howth in 1914. Broy does mention a somewhat discriminatory reference to secret societies which was part of the oath administered to DMP recruits on completion of their training. It included, according to Broy, the following:

> I swear that I do not now belong to and that whilst serving I shall not belong to any secret society whatsoever, the Society of Freemasons excepted.

According to Broy, police practices in Dublin were much the same as in London. The men were armed with batons and were trained in the use of revolvers but not in rifles. Stringent regulations regarding the use of firearms were laid down.

Politics was a common topic of conversation in the DMP depot when Broy was a young constable. Most of the young men favoured Home Rule, but not the senior officers, some of whom were members of the Orange Order. Events such as the Curragh Mutiny further divided a force which was already split along sectarian lines.

The rest of Ireland was policed by the Royal Irish Constabulary – a very different force from the DMP, according to Broy. His main contention was that:

> Whilst acting as police, the force was based on military organisation and wherever possible military terms were used, for example forces sent to protect evictors or even to take part in eviction were referred to as detachments.

The Royal Irish Constabulary was set up in 1836. The force had got its title of 'Royal' from its activities against the Fenians in 1867. Broy goes on:

> Over 90 percent of the officers were recruited by the cadet system from wealthy and anti-national sections of the population and from England. The RIC was avowedly a military force armed with rifle, bayonet and revolver and [was] trained to act as an army up to Battalion strength, being carefully taught skirmishing, volley firing up to 1,500 yards, defence against cavalry etc., exactly like an infantry Battalion.

To drive his point home, Broy quotes in detail from the drill book used by the RIC.

Judging by some of the extracts which Broy cites, the RIC should have been well prepared for the onslaught of ambushes and gun raids which awaited them:

> Drill and fire action should be combined on all parades. Thus after a change of position or direction or when marching in fours the Company commander should point out some objective . . . and order the Company . . . to open fire. . . . The Company should also be exercised in meeting sudden rushes.

There are detailed instructions on how to maximise the results of firing weapons. For example:

> Fire is only effective when the mark can be seen.
> It is useless to fire merely for the sake of firing.

Ten in all are given. The last one is:

> Well concealed, a few bold men extended at wide intervals can, by rapid fire, deceive the opponent as to the strength of the force by which he is opposed [and] may delay him for a considerable time.

102

But it was the RIC's methods of obtaining intelligence which most interested Broy, who was of course an intelligence agent himself. It would be only fair to say that every area possessed people who, for whatever reason, were willing to give as much help as they could to their local force. These were what Broy described as 'loyal citizens'. They not only supplied information to their local barracks but also regularly wrote to the Castle 'if they considered members of the local force not sufficiently energetic'.

The police found other ways of gathering information in the process of carrying out their duties. Collecting particulars for the census, or statistics relating to agricultural production, provided opportunities for collecting all sorts of information. They were also adept at extracting information from children in the course of friendly chats and were not above pumping their own children about what other schoolchildren were talking about amongst themselves.

A constable was expected to use every opportunity to win the trust of the local people. He would, for example, engage in helping the blacksmith in striking the iron with a sledgehammer and, in the relaxed and congratulatory atmosphere that was thus engendered, gradually collected all the local gossip.

Broy goes into detail regarding what might be called the punctured-bicycle-wheel method:

> When it was thought that members of a family had information which the RIC needed, a constable would be sent on a bicycle to their house. When nearing the house, he would deliberately puncture one of his tyres with a pin. Then he would call on the house for a basin of water to locate the puncture and, whilst carrying out the repairs, would enter into conversation with members of the family and gradually lead up to the subject in which he was interested. Members of the family would thus, quite innocently, supply the Constable with all the local gossip, and when the repairs were finished the Constable would have the information he needed in order to supply a very valuable report to Dublin Castle and perhaps also to supply the police with clues as to where to institute further enquiries.

Broy's witness statement leaves us in no doubt as to the important obstacle the police force presented to the aims of the republican movement. The force was held in the highest esteem by the Lord Lieutenant and other representatives of the Crown, and was constantly praised by them. Broy is careful to state that by and large the members of the RIC were personally honest and decent men, with discipline and self-respect, and in peaceful times were influences for good in small communities. This applied particularly to Sergeants, who were often the most exemplary citizens in these communities.

This, in Broy's opinion, made the task of 'national resurgence' all the more difficult: 'It took some time . . . to convince local people that the RIC were their enemies.' Broy reminds us that:

It is, of course, well known that many of the children of RIC men were active members of Sinn Féin and the IRA and that members of the RIC resigned in 1920 and joined the IRA Flying Columns.

Broy is adamant, however, that, apart from the exceptions indicated by him, the 'RIC machine remained an apparatus of oppression to the very end'. He points out:

The top storey was completely loyal to England; about 25 percent were nationalist in outlook and desired Home Rule, and the remainder believed in their divine right to rule Ireland and were proud of all the adjectives of praise the force had received from Ireland's oppressors for a whole century.

The witness statements submitted by members of the RIC to the Bureau of Military History many years after the conflict bear out the substance of Broy's evidence. The most important of these was that of Jeremiah Mee, who in 1919 was posted to Listowel, County Kerry. Mee found his new posting undemanding:

There was no crime in the district apart from the usual minor offences. . . . Listowel was the District Headquarters and comprised one acting County Inspector, one District Inspector, three Sergeants and fourteen Constables.

Mee could look forward confidently to a pleasant station in Listowel where 'people went about their business and did not show any active animosity towards the police'.

It is true that a Company of military had stationed themselves close to the town in May 1920, but this Company did not interfere with either the police or the people. The change came on 16 June 1920 when an 'important despatch' was delivered to the barracks:

The despatch contained transfers for all the policemen at Listowel Barracks, with the exception of one Constable and three Sergeants.

Beyond the fact that they had to remove themselves to various outposts around the county, the policemen knew nothing. They called a meeting, which Mee addressed. His summary of their situation was masterly:

> I pointed out that a war had been declared on the Irish people and that, looking at the case from the most selfish point of view, we had to consider our own position. We were asked evidently to take part with the military in beating our own people. I might find myself shooting the mother of one of my comrades, while he would be shooting my mother in Galway. I pointed out that, in a war, one of two things must happen. We had either to win or lose. I assumed that we would win the war with the assistance of the British military. When we had defeated our own people, the British military would return to their own country and we would remain with our own people whom we had, with the assistance of the British government, crushed and defeated. That would be the best side of our case. If we lost the war, the position would be still worse.

There and then, Mee proposed a mutiny:

> I suggested that instead of going on transfer, we would hold the barracks and refuse to hand [it] over to the British military. . . . To this I got a rousing cheer from each and every man.

This was the beginning of the mutiny of the RIC in Listowel. At the confrontation with the County Inspector the next day, fourteen constables resigned. The County Inspector opened negotiations with the men but they did not go too well. One objection the men made to working with the British military incensed the Inspector: they described the British military as 'men of low moral character who frequented bad houses [and] kept the company of prostitutes'. Worse was to come:

> At ten o'clock on the night of 18th June, a phone message came from the County Inspector to the District Inspector to have the men ready . . . to meet Colonel Smyth at ten o'clock next morning, 19th June.

Colonel Smyth was the new Divisional Commander for Munster, recently appointed directly by the British Cabinet. Nobody at Listowel

Barracks knew anything about him. They waited for his arrival with some foreboding:

> About 10.30 AM General Tudor, Inspector General, RIC, arrived from Dublin in a Crossley tender and [was] escorted by a large force of RIC men, including at least three officers. They were all in full war dress.

Next came the County Inspector, then the British military with their captain, all suitably escorted. Last of all came Colonel Smyth. Mee felt that

> this display of force was no doubt intended to terrorise and overawe our little garrison within, and I will admit that I never felt less cheerful in my life.

Mee and the other RIC men assembled in the day room, where Colonel Smyth made a most astonishing speech, which Mee reproduces word for word in his witness statement. He was able to do this because, the first chance he got in this extraordinarily busy day, he went up to his bedroom and wrote out 'as near as I could, word for word, Colonel Smyth's speech'. He signed this paper and had it co-signed by three others. He then set about getting it delivered to Republican Headquarters for publication.

Smyth's opening sentence was bound to grab the attention of the little garrison. Mee quotes: 'Well, men, I have something of interest to tell you, something that I am sure you would not wish your wives to hear.' He continued in this vein as he laid before them the new policy which he expected the RIC to operate. It was a long speech, and Mee summarises it for us as follows:

> 'I am getting seven thousand police from England'
> 'If a barracks is burned, the best house in the locality is to be
> commandeered'
> 'The police are to lie in ambush and shoot suspects'
> 'No policeman will get into trouble for shooting any man'
> 'Hunger strikers will be allowed to die in jail'
> 'We want your assistance in wiping out Sinn Féin'

The dramatic events immediately following Colonel Smyth's speech are best told by Mee himself:

Colonel Smyth then, pointing to the first man in the ranks, said 'Are you prepared to co-operate?' The man . . . replied, 'Constable Mee speaks for us.' Smyth pointed to each man in turn, asking the same question and getting the same reply, until he reached myself. I was about the seventh man he addressed, and by the time he reached me I was so horrified . . . In desperation, I stepped forward and said, 'By your accent I take it you are an Englishman. You forget you are addressing Irishmen.' He checked me there and said he was a North of Ireland man from Banbridge in the County Down. I said, 'I am an Irishman and very proud of it.' Taking off my uniform cap, I laid it on the table in front of Colonel Smyth and said, 'This too is English; you may have it as a present from me.' Having done this, I completely lost my temper and, taking my belt and sword, clapped them down on the table, saying, 'These too are English and you may have them. To hell with you, you are a murderer.'

At that point, Mee was removed from the room to the kitchen, somewhat shaken by what he had just said. The men were highly excited, one or two suggesting that Smyth should be shot. It was in this highly charged atmosphere that their senior officers decided to parley.

When Smyth and his party left Listowel, Mee and his men rang the other police barracks in Kerry: 'The police cheered us over the phone and promised to stand by us. Smyth tried to address the RIC but was met by opposition from the police.' Having tried Killarney as well with no success, the tour was abandoned.

On 6 July, Mee records that 'five of us, Thomas Hughes, John Donovan, Michael Fitzgerald, Patrick Sheeran and myself, left the force without either resigning or being dismissed.' Then, on 10 July, Smyth's speech was published in full in the *Freeman's Journal*. It was distributed at an International Labour Conference in London, and was raised in the House of Commons by T. P. O'Connor. Mee comments:

Colonel Smyth's address to the police at Listowel got the widest publicity, both in Great Britain and America, and caused quite a sensation as it was taken that Smyth was acting as spokesman [for] the British government; and there was a general outcry and demand for a full investigation.

Mee regarded the whole Listowel 'incident' as highly important. The publicity following it 'helped to expose the hidden policy of the British government', he said. And Mee was anxious to prove that 'the orders given to the Listowel police were the same orders given by the Prime Minister himself to Colonel Smyth before he left London two weeks earlier'. No investigation was ever held into the Listowel incident. Smyth was recalled to London by Lloyd George but, according to Mee, 'was sent back again to Cork by Lloyd George [as] a "marked man".' Mee points out:

> Once Colonel Smyth's instruction to 'shoot at sight' was published, it must have been clear . . . that Smyth was a marked man. Yet when he was shot dead in the Cork County Club a few days later, he had no bodyguard and not even a private soldier or policeman in the vicinity of the Club.

Smyth's death was altogether too convenient for Lloyd George, in Mee's opinion, and Mee devotes a considerable part of his testimony to this topic. He was clearly proud of his part in the Listowel incident. He records:

> Similar instructions had been issued to the officers of all other counties. The police co-operated with the military, but Listowel was the only barracks which had refused to co-operate.

John Duffy from County Galway worked within the RIC for the IRA from 1917 until 1921. While stationed at Athlone, he had the distinction of having been recruited as an intelligence agent by Michael Collins himself through a Dr McDonnell, who obviously had connections in General Headquarters in Dublin. Duffy describes what was probably his most important contribution: his success in acquiring the police cipher, as well as a list of known IRA men from the County Inspector's office in Roscommon. His observations on the Black and Tans and on their impact on the RIC are notable. He sheds new light on this situation:

> As I am on the subject of loot, I feel that it should be recorded that the Black and Tans in Roscommon did not confine themselves to looting of Jackson's shop for jewellery, blankets and other articles of wearing apparel. It was a common practice for them when they went out the country in their lorries to shoot down fowl and other poultry, the property of poor people, and bring them back to the mess, where some of them were cooked for their own use, and those that were not required were dispatched to their families in England.

No wonder then that 'the old RIC hated the Tans to the end'.

There was at least one other RIC man who was moved to taking extreme measures when he found himself torn between loyalty to the Force and love of his country. Tim Brennan was a member of the RIC stationed at Tullamore from 1918 to 1920. He was an ardent opponent of conscription. When this was no longer a threat, he campaigned amongst members of the RIC against the establishment of an armed police force. He writes:

> Continuing my activity, I issued a second circular from Carlow dated 6th July 1920, three copies of which I am handing in. From that date I refused to carry arms when on duty, although I went with men who were armed.

In the end, Brennan's efforts to strive for 'the welfare of the Force' and to be true to his country at the same time were not acceptable to his superiors. He was dismissed from the force in 1920 and cautioned that, if he interfered further with the discipline of the Force, 'he would be charged under the Defence of the Realm Regulations'.

Eugene Bratton's membership of the RIC went back to 15 June 1898. When the Rebellion broke out on Easter Monday 1916, he was on duty at Fairyhouse Races. He was a witness to the Battle of Ashbourne and brought the body of the District Inspector back to his home after that bloody encounter.

His account of the capture of Trim RIC barracks corroborates Superintendent Patrick Meehan's account of the same event almost exactly. Meehan's witness statement is particularly authoritative on this subject – perhaps not surprisingly, as it was thanks to the close co-operation of Meehan that the IRA was able to capture the barracks so easily. Some days before, the Tans were expected to come to Trim. The IRA leader, Mick Hynes, called to Meehan's house to impress on him the urgency of taking some action. Meehan recounts the details of their plan:

> I told him the best time for the attempt would be on a Sunday morning during first Mass in the local Chapel. Half of the garrison would be at this Mass, whilst most of the remainder would be still in bed. Things

were always slack in the barracks on a Sunday morning. I drew a plan of the barracks for Hynes, marking out all the rooms, including the ammunition store. I also gave him an impression of the keys of the front and back doors, which I took in soap at a later date.

Meehan wisely resigned from the RIC on the Wednesday before the Sunday of the raid. He left Trim with his wife on Sunday morning to stay with her people at Ballymore-Eustace, County Kildare. He was not forgiven by his RIC colleagues.

In his witness statement, Eugene Bratton records what was planned for Meehan by the County Inspector:

> Meehan was suspect for his part in the raid on the barracks and had a narrow escape from being shot. County Inspector Egan, DI Egan and a Tan from Gormanston took Meehan out of his lodgings one night and, only for the County Inspector's bodyguard intervening, he would have been shot.

Bratton's statement is a mine of information on the murky deeds of some officers in the RIC. He was in a good position to know about this subject: he looked after the cars of the Egan brothers, as well as driving them. Included in his witness statement is what amounts to an account of the murder of a Postmaster in Navan:

> There was a serious leakage of police messages from the Post Office in Navan. Paddy Dunne worked in the Post Office and he was able to decipher all messages going through. . . . To counteract this, Head Constable Queenan's daughter was put into the Post Office without any entrance examination or anything else. One day the Postmaster, Mr Hodgett, pulled her up for something she was doing. She became impertinent and said she would tell her daddy. A couple of nights afterwards, Mr Hodgett was taken from his house by three armed men in civilian clothes and shot and thrown into the river. The three men who shot him were the County Inspector Egan, his brother DI Egan, and a Tan from Gormanston.

Bratton investigated the affair, 'secretly, of course', and was quite sure that he was right in his suspicions.

Word was passed to Bratton that the Egan brothers and a third officer had held a court martial in Bratton's absence, at which he was condemned to death. Bratton recounts the course of subsequent events:

110

From that [time] on, I always carried a small revolver in my sleeve as well as my service Webley in my belt. A week passed by, and one night the County Inspector Egan brought a few of the Tans into the canteen and [got] them drunk. I was in a bedroom over the canteen. I could hear the voices underneath me and hear my name being mentioned. After a few minutes, I heard footsteps coming up the passage to my room. I took up my revolver and fully cocked it. One of the Tans opened the door and just entered the room with his Webley revolver in his hand swinging by his thigh. I had my gun up and covering him. When the Tan saw this, he turned away. They did not try it again.

Near the beginning of his witness statement, Eugene Bratton records his part in the Ashbourne encounter in 1916. He found the memory of that occasion distasteful. He writes:

Subsequent to the Battle of Ashbourne, I was brought to Buckingham Palace and decorated by the King for my actions. I resented this, but I had no alternative.

There was a select group in the RIC whose presence in Dublin became particularly noticeable during the last year of the bitter conflict. They were known as the Igoe Squad, after the police officer who was their leader. In many ways, they modelled themselves on the other Squad – the Intelligence Squad – forever associated with Michael Collins. Not surprisingly, the members of the Igoe Squad feature in the testimony of the leaders of the fight in Dublin. Vincent Byrne, who was a member of the 2nd Battalion, Dublin Brigade, as well as a member of the Squad, devotes several pages of his testimony to Igoe and the efforts of the IRA to assassinate him:

Igoe was an RIC man who hailed from the west of Ireland. Around him, the Castle authorities formed a group of RIC men who were selected from different parts of the country – especially those who had a good knowledge of the active members of the IRA, wanted by the British.

Charles Dalton, also a former member of the 2nd Battalion of the Dublin Brigade and a member of the Squad, remembered how the IRA first heard of this new RIC enterprise:

A report was received to the effect that several country members of the RIC were living in the Depot, in Phoenix Park, and were moving around the city in civilian clothes. We had no lead to begin inquiries until I was instructed to interview a lady who ran a tea-room and who was a member of Cumann na mBan. I made the acquaintance of this lady, Miss Maire Gleeson. . . . Miss Gleeson informed me that . . . several plain-clothes RIC men dropped in shortly before supper fairly frequently.

In Dalton's opinion, these men were invaluable to the Auxiliary Division of the RIC, 'for identification purposes'. Dalton held that, in addition:

they were ideally situated to carry out the task allotted to them, which was evidently the tracking down of country Volunteers visiting the city, and summarily shooting them.

No longer could men from the country who had fled the attentions of their local RIC men feel safe in Dublin. Igoe's men were likely to visit the railway termini as trains were arriving or departing, 'to see if any "wanted men" were travelling', as Byrne put it. Byrne noticed that the Igoe Squad

adopted the same procedure as we did in the Squad. They moved along in pairs, on each side of the street or road, with a distance of a yard or two between each pair. So you will understand that it was going to be a very heavy operation to get the lot of them.

The task was made all the more difficult by the fact that, at the beginning, they didn't know what Igoe or his men looked like. But, even when they became more familiar with him, Igoe managed to elude them. Time after time, using all their street skills, they failed to get him or his men.

Oscar Traynor, who before the Truce achieved the rank of Brigadier of the Dublin Brigade, and could never be described as being of a nervous disposition, remembered vividly almost running into the Igoe Squad. He was coming from a meeting and was in the company of Gearoid O'Sullivan, another of the leaders of the Volunteers. Traynor describes the experience:

We left the meeting carrying with us the usual papers which it was necessary to have, and were crossing the road to enter St Stephen's Green when we were both almost frozen stiff by seeing Igoe and his gang advancing towards us on foot. They were in their usual formation of twos, some little distance apart. As they approached, they stared at us, but we continued walking on into the Green. They passed us, but we felt that we were still not safe.

James Short (First Lieutenant, Armagh Company (IRA), 1921), who survived an assassination attempt on him at his home on the night before the general election of 1921, was certain that Igoe was involved in the attack. Short records:

I was at home, and on my way upstairs going to bed I looked out of a window and saw a man wearing civilian clothes and a soft hat on a wall outside the back of our house, holding a revolver in his hand. He was getting down from the wall when I noticed him. I then went into a front room and, looking out on Irish Street, I found that a man was at the front of the house. As a rap came on the front street door, I threw up the upstairs window a few inches. The man then asked me was I James Short. I said I was not James Short. He then asked me to come down to the door as he would like to see me in connection with the election. I said I would not come near the door. During this conversation the man outside was speaking to me in a low tone of voice and I was answering him in a loud, penetrating voice. He requested me to speak easy. He then opened fire on the window. I dropped to the floor. He emptied his revolver into the room and then withdrew. After he withdrew, I got out of the house at the rere. Shortly after the shooting, a patrol of RIC [men] came to our house to make enquiries into the circumstances of the shooting.

Shortly before this occurrence, a man named Igoe, who was in charge of a murder gang in Dublin, came to Armagh with a few others and put up in the Beresford Arms Hotel. Warning notices were posted all over the town, warning the IRA that, if any further operations were carried out, serious reprisals would be made, and the notice ended with the slogan: 'God Save the King'.

The Dublin Brigade were never able to establish fully the names of those members of the RIC who were part of Igoe's group. Charles Dalton was certain that it contained 'members from all the "hot spots" in the country':

113

They were all Irishmen who had considerable service in the RIC, with the exception of a Scotsman who was known as Jock. He may have become associated through his membership of the Black and Tans.

As far as Oscar Traynor could remember, 'they survived the struggle in the city and eventually got away to England at the end of the war'.

12

THE WAR IN THE WEST

Mr Igoe was well known in the west of Ireland, particularly in Galway. By the end of 1920, he was based in Dublin, but his notoriety did not deter him from visiting Galway. Mr J. Togher from Francis Street, Galway, who was IRA Intelligence Officer in the city from 1917 to 1921, noted his appearance there in early 1921:

> About this time Igoe arrived in Galway on a visit. He was well guarded. We decided to shoot Igoe as I had been told in GHQ [that] he was badly wanted. I sent out immediately to Castlegar, the nearest unit with arms, asking for revolvers and bombs. Unfortunately they were not in the spot, and when the messenger returned Igoe had left.

Togher had joined the Volunteers in 1917. He worked undercover as far as possible, right up to the Truce in 1921. As an employee of the Post Office, he was well placed for his Volunteer work as Intelligence Officer. He not only copied enemy ciphers but also 'nearly always' deciphered them. Part of his work involved intercepting correspondence addressed to the police and military authorities.

Togher was arrested in November 1920. By then, practically all known officers and Volunteers were 'on the run'. On his release, Togher felt that 'in the circumstances' he had to form a new Unit. He describes the problems of his group:

> We were badly hampered at first as the men who knew where arms were dumped could not be contacted and our own supply was negligible. Further, our training in arms and military work in general was scanty.

He was, however, able to carry out valuable work. He continues:

> We kept up intelligence work, burned military stores, spread false information, e.g. impending attacks by IRA, strangers seen in town, etc., all

for the purpose of using enemy force in town, while the Columns outside (Mayo and Clare) were getting on with the real war.

Sometime in the autumn of 1920 or the spring of 1921, Togher went to the IRA Headquarters in Dublin, looking for arms. There were none. He 'got all the advice and assistance they could give, but arms and ammunition were not available'.

In Galway city, it was difficult for the IRA to be overtly active: the city and surrounding areas were heavily garrisoned. Various posts were occupied by the British. Sean Broderick, who was OC, 4th Battalion, Galway Brigade, lists the posts that he could remember which were occupied at the time of the Truce:

> Renmore Barracks, the Headquarters of the Connaught Rangers . . . was occupied by the Sherwood Foresters . . . a portion of this Battalion in Oranmore Camp, a distance of about four or five miles from Galway.
> Earls Island, University Road – a large detachment of Lancers.
> Eglinton Barracks together with two more in Dominick Street – and many private houses . . . 400 to 500 men.
> The Auxiliary RIC had a Company in Lenaboy Castle at Taylors Hill.
> Together with the above, there were at varying periods a number of troops encamped near Galway.

It seemed that all Sean Broderick could do was to mount limited operations in the city which might serve as a distraction from the real activity taking place in the county. At the end of 1919, his Company attacked the Lough George RIC barracks but, despite an all-night onslaught and with the roof ablaze, the garrison refused to surrender, and Broderick and his comrades were obliged to withdraw. Broderick continued and, 'following an order from GHQ, took charge of the burning of all Custom House books and documents, also any evacuated RIC Barracks.' Having disposed of the Custom House, which was a substantial three-storeyed building, with twenty rooms, Broderick went on to ambush a party of RIC men at Merlin Park.

When a member of the Black and Tans called Krum was shot dead in the course of an IRA attack at the railway station, Broderick was arrested by the Tans. He describes his ordeal:

> They pulled me down the stairs in my shirt and trousers, without boots, and brought me towards the station, poking me with their rifles and

revolvers and accompanied by choice language. I saw several patrols of military on our way and when we got to the station, I shouted to a British army officer that as an officer of the IRA I demanded a fair trial. The reply from several was: 'You bloody b—s didn't give much trial to the policeman last night.' I was brought further up and put against a wooden railway door and a party of about seven or eight RIC and Tans took up a position as a firing party some short distance away. I heard the words of command: 'Present', 'Fire', closed my eyes and prayed to the Blessed Virgin, who undoubtedly saved my life. I felt a sharp sensation on top of my head and fell to the ground.

Broderick survived: the bullet had barely grazed the top of his head. Like so many other IRA men, Sean Broderick now had to go 'on the run'.

His sister too attracted the attention of the Black and Tans. He records:

The following night, my sister Peg was taken out by the Black and Tans, who cut off her hair to the scalp and attempted to burn down our home after doing a considerable amount of damage.

His sister, Margaret Broderick-Nicholson, who was Section Commander of Cumann na mBan in Galway, gave her own testimony to the Bureau.

The Broderick parents were strongly nationalist in outlook, and when Liam Mellows was sent to organise the Volunteers in County Galway in 1915 he stayed in the Broderick household.

The organisation of the Volunteers in west Galway fell mainly to Peter McDonnell, who was OC of the West Connemara Brigade from 1920 up to the Truce. It was not an easy task. McDonnell details some of the problems:

It was practically impossible for me to supervise the Battalion properly. I had no means of travel except cycling; the area was very scattered, and I had to give some attention to my business, which was left more or less to run itself for weeks at a time. After the first flush of reorganisation had worn off, attendances at drills and parades started to fall away again.

As happened all over Ireland when the fear of conscription hit the country, membership of the Volunteers increased dramatically. McDonnell notes:

Some Companies swelled to twice their original size and drills were held at least three times weekly, after Mass on Sundays and after supper on weekdays.

But when the conscription scare was over, attendance dwindled again. The 'hardy few' remained, however, and their training and discipline proved to be invaluable in the 1918 election campaign. McDonnell records:

> It was the Volunteer training that consolidated the Sinn Féin movement, and without it the 1918 election could not have been the success it was. Even when the votes were cast, the Volunteers never left the ballot boxes out of their sight until they were opened and counted.

In 1917, one of the main problems facing the reorganised Volunteers was the difficulty in procuring arms. Despite raiding 'some fishing and shooting lodges belonging to absentee English industrialists', they were desperately short of arms. Increasingly, too, McDonnell's Volunteers were short of money. 'The merchant and well-to-do farmer class gave us a wide berth', he noted.

Even more serious for the organisation and for McDonnell were the difficulties he began to have with the Brigade council when he proposed perfectly feasible plans of action. Martin Conneely, who became the adjutant of the West Connemara Brigade, corroborates McDonnell's account. Conneely explains the situation:

> Early in 1920, all small RIC barracks were closed and the men transferred to other areas. All barracks vacated were burned by the Volunteers. Of the two remaining, Clifden held about twenty-five men and Maam eight or nine men.
>
> As I mentioned earlier, our Battalion was under Galway Brigade. Our OC went to the Brigade staff with plans for the capture of Maam barracks. They did not agree with his proposal and also refused his request for material. . . . The Brigade staff also vetoed an arrangement he made with Westport Battalion for an attack on a barrack in that area.

Fortunately for everyone, the situation was saved by Dick Mulcahy, Chief of Staff. It so happened that Mulcahy had 'come to stay in Tommie O'Malley's house in Kilmilken (four miles from Leenane) to recuperate from an illness'.

Mulcahy's enforced rest cure had important consequences for the area. Conneely goes on:

> The OC discussed all his problems with him (Mulcahy) and made various suggestions for reorganising Connemara. When Mulcahy got back to Dublin he brought the matter before GHQ. The effect of this was that Connemara was to be divided into two Brigades – West Connemara and East Connemara.

Later:

> Battalion OCs were instructed to appoint their officers, organise their areas, get the Companies active, raid for arms, and most important of all get money collected so that we would be able to purchase arms to enable us to get a Flying Column started as quickly as possible.

According to McDonnell, it was vital to get an active Column in the field:

> or else look forward to being picked up singly and imprisoned, or shot trying to escape. Furthermore, it would help in some small measure to ease the strain on areas that had been carrying on the fight for some time and were being overrun by troops.

They collected £120, which McDonnell took to Dublin. According to Conneely, he was only able to get two rifles and some ammunition. Some time later, they acquired another small consignment of arms. The arms situation was very tight. When McDonnell checked up on it, 'it was seen that the most we could hope to arm would be about twenty men, and most of these would have only shotguns'.

There was another disadvantage which McDonnell pointed out:

> The roads in Connemara are like the country, 'bare and bleak' with no sheltering walls where shotguns would get within range of the enemy.

They spent a considerable amount of time looking for suitable ambush spots. John Feehan, who was Quartermaster, 4th Western Division, makes this clear when describing preparations for an ambush on the RIC coming from Maam Cross:

> There was only one position which was of any use, and this was on rising ground when coming from Maam Cross – on a small hillock of

granite rock on the east side of the road was a small Protestant Church partly hidden by a grove of trees. RIC coming from the Maam Cross direction could see us in this position two miles off, unless every man lay under cover completely and remained under that cover for a long time, a hard thing to do.

Similar problems presented themselves a month earlier when McDonnell examined the countryside within reach of 'an old deserted shepherd's house in a place called Aille na Veagh, in the Twelve Bens', where the Brigade was to assemble. McDonnell writes:

We found no suitable place until we arrived at Derrylea lake, within three miles of Clifden. Just at the end of the lake there is a sharp turn and there is a cliff to the hillside rising to a height of thirty to fifty feet over the road, with deep clefts and shelves running through the face, and the lake is coming right up to the roadway on the left. We decided that this would suit all right, for it gave [us] a chance to bring the shot-guns into play, and the home-made grenades could be used with effect against the lorry.

McDonnell, Feehan and Conneely all had very clear memories of their engagements with the patrols of RIC and Black and Tans which began to traverse the roads of west Connemara from 1920 onwards. The Volunteers were severely handicapped by their shortage of ammunition. As McDonnell remarked: 'no matter how carefully it is handled, when you start with much less than a hundred rounds, over twelve hours exchanging shots in an engagement will eventually find bottom'.

Moreover, McDonnell wrote that, as time went on, enemy forces learned

never (to come) in less than two lorries, well separated, more often four; and seven miscellaneous rifles with inadequate ammunition and a sup-ply of shotguns would make little impression on them.

As befits a Flying Column, the Active Service Unit moved around a great deal on foot, generally over difficult terrain and usually at night. McDonnell describes the kind of life a member of the Flying Column could expect:

We rested another day here and sent word of our movements, and for J. Connolly to have the tent delivered to Wallaces and to make arrange-ments with them to be prepared to ferry us across the channel the

120

following night. The channel meant was the narrow neck of the Killary just north of Leenane village. We arrived there all right, crossed the channel, and had a feed in Wallaces and then across the shoulder of the hill into a little valley, nestling at the back of Bengorm. We collected the tent canvass and took it with us, but could not erect it that night because we had no poles for it.

It turned out that the tent had not been used for years, so nobody knew where the poles were. Next day McDonnell crossed the channel again to Leenane. He was able to get to his workshop there and make some poles and pegs. McDonnell was a carpenter who shared a workshop with John Feehan, the quartermaster. McDonnell slept that night in a little dug-out on the hillside over Wallace's house:

> We were up again at daylight, and when we looked over towards Leenane we saw a great cloud of smoke over the village. We thought at first that the whole village had been burned out, but when it cleared daylight and I could use the glasses I found that my own house and workshops were all they had done.

Despite a 'massive round-up' by the British forces in the spring of 1921, the members of the IRA in west Galway escaped capture. McDonnell judged that the area would have a quiet time for a while – giving him the opportunity to get married. His best man was, unsurprisingly, his old friend and quartermaster, John Feehan. Immediately after the short wedding festivities, as Feehan and McDonnell were making their way to Derrylahan after dark, they heard 'the sound of marching feet and we stopped dead'. Feehan remembers:

> We were five feet above the ground and the field was rising behind us without any cover, and, to make matters worse, the moon at that moment appeared from [behind] a dark cloud. We flattened ourselves against a depression a few feet from us and held our breaths. The police came in pairs, ten paces between each pair. They halted and we were then in the middle of them. Suddenly they took up position across the wall on the other side of the road to us. . . . they were lying in ambush for some of the Newport IRA. . . . the moon kindly went behind a dark black cloud and, creeping on our bellies, we slid thirty yards to a low hedge, where we were able to get away.

Feehan and McDonnell were not in their own territory. The wedding had brought them to Mayo.

Thomas Kettrick, who was living in Howth when he recounted the events of the Mayo war, had been quartermaster of the West Mayo Brigade from the time of its establishment. It appears that the men of Mayo were enterprising enough to go to England themselves to import arms; Kettrick went there twice. When they met their contacts: 'we arranged for them to pick up arms or explosives from the various mines in which they were working'. This practice was not encouraged by GHQ. When Kettrick began to make arrangements for the transport of the arms back to Mayo, Collins heard of it. Kettrick reports:

> Collins was enraged at our going independently to England without per-
> mission from Headquarters, as he maintained this would upset the mar-
> ket. . . . However he promised that I should get some of the stuff, but
> I never did.

Patrick Joseph Cannon, who came from Islandeady in County Mayo, remembered that it was 1920 before his Company engaged in any signif-icant activity, although on Easter Sunday his Company had burned down an old police barracks which had been abandoned some years before. He notes:

> This burning of evacuated barracks was a countrywide operation and
> gave a good insight into the extent of the organisation of the IRA.

The RIC may have taken the same view. Cannon writes: 'The RIC now started raiding and searching houses of prominent members of Sinn Féin and the IRA', and Cannon himself was forced to go on the run – a familiar sequence of events. In 1921, an Active Service Unit was estab-lished and, as was the practice, would combine with other units for par-ticularly challenging operations. As in Galway, the country presented some difficulties when it came to the blocking of roads necessary for a successful ambush. Cannon records:

> There were no trees available for felling at this point, but on each side
> of the road there were substantial dry stone wall fences, and it was
> decided to use these by throwing them on to the road and so obstruct-
> ing it.

As it turned out, that particular ambush 'at the Big Wall, on the Westport side of the Half-Way House on the road between Castlebar and Westport', was not a great success. Two men from Islandeady were killed.

Other ambushes followed. The IRA continued to engage with the RIC and the Black and Tans, with varying success. They were mostly involved in retreats, and desperately tried to escape the 'round-up' which was clearly imminent. Cannon describes their plight:

> We moved back some distance and took up a position of hiding on the flank. From here we watched the enemy advance. They numbered about forty and had one or two Lewis guns. They advanced up through Glenlara valley.

Much reduced in number, the Volunteers moved by night. Cannon continues: 'Our Commanding Officer, Michael Kilroy, had a map of the area, and he and Dr Madden were studying it to see if they could get out of a possible round-up in the area.' They decided on a particular cross-roads which would, they thought, be outside any round-up area. This spot became the target for their night march. It was a terrible march. They could not leave the road, as the land on either side was boggy, but when the headlights of a lorry 'swept around the bend in the road', they had no choice. Six of them found cover, but Dr Madden 'got stuck in the drain and had to remain there'. When he joined them later, 'he was covered with mud up to his shoulders'. On the third night of the journey, they met their comrades from the Westport Column and, later, some of the men from Newport. They were now 'about thirty-one strong'.

Astonishingly, this battered group of men, under the command of Michael Kilroy, were able to snatch a victory of sorts out of a slow and debilitating retreat. Cannon described the turning point:

> On the side of the enemy lorry there was a white circle painted. One of our fellows, Walsh, fired at this white circle, as he could see nothing else to fire at. At this time four or five others of our men had crept down by a wall to try and bomb the enemy. Immediately Walsh fired at the cir-cle, a bomb exploded inside the lorry. A white flag was now hoisted from the lorry.

A short time later, the rest of the RIC and the Tans came out of the thatched house, which was their base, throwing down their arms as they left. A number of police were killed, and four or five were wounded. The West Mayo Brigade had no casualties.

According to the witness statement given by Patrick Cassidy, who was commandant of the East Mayo Brigade, the war in his area was much more low key. This was not Cassidy's fault: he did his best to stir things up. He recounts:

> About February 1920, I decided to raid the gunshops. . . . We raided three gunshops . . . and collected shotguns [and] cartridges . . . but no enemy force showed up. We raided the local Post Office and fired shots, and got a man to go to the barracks and report us as being in the area, to try and get them out, to no avail – they would not oblige.

Senator Sean T. Ruane's witness statement bears out Cassidy's view of the war in east Mayo. Not everyone was an enthusiastic supporter of the war but, 'though not in sympathy with us, they certainly would not assist the enemy forces against us', Cassidy said. Some were frankly opportunistic. For example, through information given to a brother of Ruane's, a party of Volunteers was able to take a supply of petrol into their possession off a train which was on its way from Sligo to Claremorris. The petrol was intended for the use of a hackney firm whose owners always made their cars available for Volunteer work. But the petrol went astray. Ruane recounts events:

> The Volunteers who captured the petrol were incensed and instituted a search. Late that night they came across the petrol being distributed to a hackney-car owner who never did duty for the movement.

Senator Ruane had trained as a teacher and had taught in Dublin for some years, which made him eminently suitable as a messenger for Michael Collins, to whom he was well known. He brought 'five important communications' from Michael Collins to the west in 1917. He performed a similar mission in August 1919.

But the part played by the East Mayo Brigade must not be underrated. Martin Mooney, who was vice-commandant of the East Mayo Brigade, reminds us in the last paragraph of his short statement that

> While Kilroy's Column was being severely pressed, we carried out many actions to prevent the military from travelling between Swinford and Castlebar.

One engagement, the Tourmakeady Ambush, which took place in south Mayo on 3 May 1921, was still exercising the minds of many people at the time the Bureau of Military History was assembling its archives.

Lieutenant Geoffrey Ibberson (of Parsonage Mead, Winterbourne Earls, Salisbury, England), thought this engagement important enough for him to submit his account of events in 1955. He had been contacted by the son of one of the RIC men who had been stationed in Ballinrobe – a Mr J. R. W. Goulden, who also provided a witness statement for the Military Archives.

They were both concerned about inaccuracies which had appeared in print in two recently published books. Ibberson's account of his ordeal crossing the rough country around Tourmakeady, while he was quite seriously wounded, makes interesting reading. Goulden's account is a meticulous reconstruction of the events of 3 May 1921. The last sentence of Goulden's statement reflects the crisis of the times:

> My father was ordered, some time later, to take a party to burn the house belonging to O'Brien's mother in Cross. He refused to obey the order, and resigned.

125

13

ESTABLISHING THE THREADS OF GOVERNMENT

Among the more informative witness statements in the Military History
Archives are those submitted by Robert Brennan in the early 1950s.
Brennan had been 'Acting Commandant, Wexford Brigade, Irish
Volunteers 1916; Under Secretary Foreign Affairs, Dáil Eireann, 1921–22;
and Irish Minister at Washington, 1938–47'. Brennan's accounts are particularly valuable because, by 1953, the historians and archivists at the
Bureau had identified some gaps in the record of events. A copy of a letter from the Director of the Bureau of Military History to Brennan is
included in the file. It opens:

> Whilst the evidence which is being collected by the Bureau is of great
> historical value, there are still some important points in which historians
> of the future will be keenly interested on which information is very
> meagre or altogether lacking.

The Bureau supplied a list of questions with their letter; much of
Brennan's testimony is in the form of answers to these questions.

The signed typescript of Brennan's book, *Allegiance*, is attached to the
witness statement No. 779 submitted by Brennan. The statement provides explanatory notes on the text of his book; among other things,
these notes discuss the different strands of opinion within the Sinn Féin
movement after 1916. According to Brennan, there were three different
approaches to the future of Ireland. First there was Arthur Griffith's,
which envisaged a King, Lords and Commons of Ireland. The second
was that of those who had taken part in the 1916 Rising, who felt that
Ireland should be 'remoulded along Republican lines', and the third was
an organisation called the Liberty League, set up by Count Plunkett.
According to Brennan, Éamon de Valera worked on these groups and

finally succeeded in getting them all to accept a formula that the aim of the organisation was the independence of Ireland and that a plebiscite would be held as soon as that independence was attained, so that the Irish people could decide the form of government they wanted.

Thus united in policy, it still came as a surprise when, as Brennan records of the Ard Fheis in 1917:

Griffith proposed de Valera for the presidency. I do not know a thing about a meeting beforehand at which Griffith was asked to give way to de Valera.

The Sinn Féin manifesto for the general election of 1918 was drawn up by Brennan – a fact of which he was very proud. He argues that it was this manifesto on which the people made their judgement in the 1918 election, leading to the setting up of Dáil Éireann, the national parliament, 'by the establishment of a Constituent Assembly comprising persons chosen by Irish Constituencies as the Supreme National authority to speak and act in the name of the Irish people'. Brennan continues: 'These words could only mean the setting up of some such institution as Dáil Éireann, though these words were not used.'

The Bureau of Military History also used the questionnaire method of collecting evidence from at least one other witness, who was of equal importance to Robert Brennan in the founding of the State. Robert Barton – who lived at Glendalough House, Annamoe, County Wicklow, when he signed his witness statement for the Bureau of Military History, on 27 July 1954 – was appointed Director of Agriculture in early April 1919, in the Mansion House, during the second session of Dáil Éireann. He was eminently suited to this position. He was a member of the Dáil and a landlord in a small way, and was extremely interested in the economic development of Ireland. He had joined the British army in 1915. As for his background, he tells the story of the lady who scribbled a note on the back of one of his election leaflets: ' "What would your father, Charles William Barton, say about you!" My father was a loyal supporter of the British administration here.' Barton's nationalist credentials were impeccable, however: he had his prison record to show for it, taken from an official document which he reproduces in his statement:

Arrested Feb. 21 1919 outside Mansion House
Held in Mountjoy
Escaped night of 16/17 March 1919

Re-arrested 4 AM January 31st 1920
Tried by courtmartial 10.30 Thursday, Feb. 12 in Ship Street Barracks
Moved to Portland Convict Prison, Dorsetshire, England, Feb. 15th 1920

He was not released until the first peace talks, leading up to the Truce, began in June 1921. Barton had little time to carry out his duties. He explains:

> I was on the run. My office was in Mrs Ceannt's house. I immediately set to work at the Land Bank and subsequently I had an office in the Land Bank premises in Leeson Street. Because I was on the run, it was difficult for me to get about freely. Three members of the RIC, who knew me by sight, were sent up to Dublin from Laragh Barracks to watch for and locate me. I employed a secretary who could act for me at some of my interviews and obtain supplies for me. . . . I had no typist. I think that if I particularly wanted something typed, Lily O'Brennan would have done it for me, but she was away by day in connection with her work with Cumann na mBan at the time. All my ordinary correspondence was done in duplicating books in my own handwriting. In view of the circumstances obtaining, Ministers and Directors had to devise their own means of carrying on their work.

On the relationship of Sinn Féin to the Dáil, he is very clear:

> The Sinn Féin organisation was a separate organisation from the Government of Dáil Éireann. It had its own office. It was the political organisation of the Republican party and functioned as such. We were a Government Department.

Though, like Ernest Blythe, he was not a member of the Cabinet, also like Blythe, he 'was present at a number of Cabinet meetings'. Barton continues:

> We held some in Miss Patricia Hoey's premises in Mespil Road; Michael Collins was using her premises as one of his offices. In it he passed under the name of 'Mr O'Brien'. We also held meetings in the house of a lady in Fitzwilliam Street – Mrs McGarry. I don't remember the number.

Barton recalled one meeting of the Dáil in particular:

> I can remember one meeting at which the floating of the Republican Loan was discussed. It was held in the Oak Room at the Mansion House. Michael Collins adumbrated proposals and received formal sanction.

Two of those early projects of Dáil Éireann were extremely dear to Barton's heart: the promotion of a Forestry Section in the Department of Agriculture and the establishment of the Land Bank.

Mr Edward M. Stephens, Barrister at Law, was the organiser of the National Bank, a project initiated by Barton. It was an anxious time in Ireland. Denis Cogan, who was assistant manager of the National City Bank at the time he made his statement, had been a member of the Land Bank staff and was able to provide the Bureau of Military History with details of the importance of the bank not only during the War of Independence but also in the history of Ireland as a whole. It seems that the land-purchase scheme in operation hitherto was in almost complete abeyance due to fluctuating interest rates. The scheme had ceased to operate, causing serious agitation amongst the landless. Barton writes:

> Persons . . . were in some cases making quite drastic proposals and seeking my support. Lest the campaign should get out of hand, I promoted the Land Bank as a means of enabling landless people to get access to land by purchase and to use it.

According to Denis Cogan, Sinn Féin was most concerned that the republican movement would be subsumed into an agrarian conflict if something was not done about the situation. Cogan describes the first meeting of the Land Bank:

> During the opening months of the year 1919, a group of men met at 38 Upper Leeson Street, Dublin, the private residence of Edward Millington Stephens. This group consisted of Robert Childers Barton, James McNeill, Sir Henry Grattan-Bellew, Bart. [Baronet], Batt O'Connor, Lionel Smith Gordon, Robert Erskine Childers and Laurence Casey, who, together with their host, had met to discuss the cessation of land purchase in Ireland.

They decided to form a land bank. The working capital was provided by the First Dáil out of funds acquired from the Dáil Loan, which had been raised in the United States. Lionel Smith Gordon was appointed manager of the bank. According to Barton:

> Before he took up work in the Land Bank, he had holidays due to him, and it was suggested that he should study co-operative banks abroad with a view to putting them into operation here. I sent him to Switzerland and Italy.

Despite the fact that, as Barton put it, 'the Land Bank was framed and registered under British laws . . . [and] its objectives and activities were entirely legal', its premises were constantly raided by the military. These raids were a source of constant irritation for the staff but, more seriously, Barton notes:

> I found it very difficult for my staff in the Bank to perform normal banking functions without admission to the banker's clearing house. I sought the assistance of Michael Collins to bring pressure to bear on the Banks Standing Committee to admit our bank to privileges enjoyed by others. Collins, exasperated by repeated refusals, at length sent a messenger to advise the members of the Standing Committee that, unless the Land Bank was afforded full clearing-house facilities, its members would be regarded as being in the same category as the Black and Tans. The Land Bank was immediately admitted to full membership.

Eamon Morkan, the prominent Volunteer, and a bank official with the National Bank, resigned from his post in order to take up his duties with the Land Bank, which had its headquarters at 62 Lower Leeson Street. He it was who recruited suitable staff for the fledgling bank. He comments:

> The National Land Bank was set up to give effect to the development of the Dáil programme in regard to the utilisation to the utmost of the natural resources of the country, particularly land, agriculture and fishery.

It was felt that the ordinary joint-stock banks were too tied up with the existing administration to have any freedom in regard to undertaking the developments that the Land Bank envisaged.

In 1919, shortly after Barton's appointment, a Commission of Inquiry was set up by Dáil Eireann The first meeting was held on 2 December. Its purpose was to inquire into 'the total resources of the country, which covered every phase of its productivity, minerals, agriculture and industries'.

We are indebted to Robert N. Tweedy for his account. At the time he made his Statement, he still had copies of the printed reports of the Commission and was 'prepared to give them to the Bureau'. He describes some of the work he did as a member of the Commission:

[I] . . . travelled over the whole country with various sub-
committees investigating peat, fisheries, dairying and coal mining. I went
into every rabbit burrow that was called a coal mine, as well as two good
coal mines. We investigated everything, including water power and stock
breeding.

The members of the First Dáil were well aware of the implications
of its decisions for the day-to-day administration of the country. The
most serious consequence was the cutting off of all revenue used to fund
the many services administered by the local authorities. The Dáil tackled
this area of government comparatively early. The first Minister for Local
Government was W. T. Cosgrave. When Seamus Ua Caomhanaigh
became Secretary of the Department of Local Government, Kevin
O'Higgins was acting as a substitute minister in place of W. T. Cosgrave,
who was in prison in Wormwood Scrubs. Ua Caomhanaigh describes
those early days: 'When I went over, the staff of the department consisted only of myself and a shorthand typist, Miss O'Hegarty, with Kevin
O'Higgins the acting minister on top.'

They decided that the first thing to do was 'to contact all the local
authorities and get them to pass a resolution of allegiance to Dáil
Eireann'. The difficult part of this operation was contacting the local
authorities. It was impossible to use the ordinary post: all letters would be
seized and opened. 'So a system was evolved by which we would direct an
envelope to some person who was unsuspected of being friendly to us.'
Ua Caomhanaigh goes on:

> The address to which the letter was sent through the post was called a
> covering address. Through my long connection with the Gaelic League,
> the Volunteers and Sinn Féin, there was hardly a parish in the country
> in which I did not know of someone who would act as cover. These
> people were prepared to help us secretly.

The response was most satisfactory. 'The system of receiving correspondence was the same as that used for sending it out. . . . a number of
the addresses in Dublin were business firms.' Essential for this method of
communication was the loyalty and dedication of the messengers in all
the Dáil departments. They were all members of Fianna Éireann. Ua
Caomhanaigh pays tribute to these young men:

131

I never heard of a traitor amongst them, nor of any one them breathing a word of what he knew to anyone but the person to whom it was his duty to report.

The witness statement recorded by John Quinn, who was a senior officer with Clare County Council from 1912 to 1942, gives a valuable insight into how the machinery of local government was enabled to carry on, in what was a truly revolutionary situation. Quinn was a member of the Volunteers and, as well as carrying dispatches on his way to work in Ennis, 'on numerous occasions . . . he carried ammunition and dispatches through the villages of Newmarket, Clarecastle and the town of Ennis, which places were well supplied with enemy forces'. He continues:

In September 1920, a definite break with the British Local Government took place in County Clare by the various local authorities, comprising the County Council, eight Boards of Guardians, nine Rural District Councils and two Urban Councils.

When inspectors or auditors came to the offices, they were informed of the situation. The local authorities were under new orders. They did not produce records for inspection. Instead:

Minutes of Proceedings of Meetings were sent to a special address in Dublin for consideration by Dáil Éireann's Minister. All correspondence was similarly dealt with.

Financial arrangements were more difficult, but the local authorities were able to take some measures. Funds which the local authorities had received as loans were transferred to Trustees appointed by the County Council. Other funds were collected by specially appointed collectors and deposited at several centres for payment in cash by 'the various Clerks of Unions and responsible officials of other Local Authorities' to use as cash payments. All accounts for goods supplied to institutions, salaries and wages were now paid in cash. Not unexpectedly:

Councils and Boards were financially embarrassed as the ordinary system of collection of rates had to be abandoned and grants previously obtained from the British Local Government were withheld. Local officials and employees were unpaid for months, and then received a percentage of monies due to them. Contractors were in the same position, but all were anxious to assist and did not press for payment. As many members of the Councils and Boards were 'on the run' from the British forces, only those who were not known as 'active' could attend meetings.

The chairman, Michael Brennan, was a much-wanted man.

In his witness statement, William T. Cosgrave describes the difficulties of the local authorities during the War of Independence. He had personal experience of the situation in Dublin:

> The British Local Government Department was making it extremely difficult for local bodies to finance the many services for which they were responsible, and the local bodies throughout the country were looking to the Dublin Corporation for a lead in all these matters. It was obvious that if the Dublin Corporation failed to maintain the public services, I, as Minister for Local Government, would find great difficulties in supervising County Councils and other Corporations in their administration and financial problems. It became necessary for the Corporation to obtain money, and for this purpose I approached the Munster and Leinster Bank, which was regarded as the most National of all these institutions, although their colour of green could never have been described as [being as] pronounced as ours was at the time. I was met with a blank refusal by the Bank.

This was a rebuff which Cosgrave never forgot. Similarly, he never forgot the 'accommodation so urgently required by the Corporation' which the Bank of Ireland gave him a short time later after he interviewed two of the directors, H. S. Guinness and Andrew Jameson. He was introduced to the two by the City Treasurer. Cosgrave records in his statement: 'It was for this reason that when President of the Executive Council at a later stage, I nominated these two gentlemen as senators.'

The Department of Local Government and the arrangements which it made for the many local authorities were extremely important for the survival of the emergent State – as indeed was the establishment of the Land Bank for the stability of the country.

None of these developments and adjustments would have been possible without the existence of the Dáil Loan. In the first half of 1919, Dáil Éireann made arrangements for the floating of the Dáil Loan at home in Ireland and in America. Barton describes how it was planned:

> As far as I remember, de Valera went to America to co-ordinate all the Irish interests in that country, to weld them into one organisation and promote the Loan. The authority to float the National Loan was given to Michael Collins by Dáil Éireann; it then devolved on him to perfect the collection machinery. Receipts were issued by the Department of Finance with Collins's signature. In all the Departments of Government the machinery to make them effective had to be devised and operated by the minister responsible.

The task of those Volunteers chosen by Collins to organise the Dáil Loan was far from being purely clerical. As recounted by James Hunt (OC Gurteen Battalion, County Sligo):

> Paddy Hegarty came into [the] Gurteen Battalion area to organise the Dáil Loan. The RIC made a few attempts while he was in the Sligo area. One attempt was made on him in Ballymote and the police had him in custody when Josie Hanson . . . and Hanson's sister and some others rescued him.

On the following Sunday, Hegarty came to Cloonloo, under the protection of the local Volunteers. From there, he went to Kilaraght Church to address an after-Mass meeting, and on to Breedogue in County Roscommon, where he addressed another meeting. The attack from the RIC came on the return journey. Hunt describes what happened: 'About thirty RIC, under Head Constable Sullivan of Boyle, had thrown a cordon across the road to intercept us.' They drove through at speed; the police opened fire. Hunt continues:

> About half a mile further on we met two other RIC, who attempted to stop us by holding bikes in front of the car. During all this excitement Hegarty was the only person in the car who had arms and he blazed away with his revolver at the police at the various points they tried to stop us, with unknown effect. Dr Doyle sustained a few slight flesh wounds. The car was riddled with bullets.
>
> Subsequently I rowed Hegarty across Lough Gara into the Monasteraden area. . . . I came home for a change of clothes and on the following morning I was arrested and later sentenced to three months.

As regards the Dáil Loan and the bond drive in America, Sean Nunan, who joined President de Valera's party in America, was made Registrar of the bond certificates issued. He reports in his witness statement:

> The success of the bond drive is common knowledge. Approximately $6,000,000 [was] subscribed. Every dollar was accounted for, and the bond certificates issued for the subscriptions were repaid at the rate of $1.25 for every $1 subscribed.

Just before he finishes his account by placing on record his assessment of 'the outstanding services rendered to Ireland by President de Valera during his year and a half in America', Nunan records an account of the 'Russian Jewels'. It appears that

> Harry Boland brought with him to Ireland the 'Russian Jewels' which Mr James O'Mara had accepted, with the approval of the President, as collateral for a loan made to the representatives of the Russian government in New York some time previously. On our arrival in Dublin about a week later we reported to the Dáil, which was in session at Earlsfort Terrace, debating the Treaty, and I accompanied Harry Boland to Michael Collins, to whom the jewels were given.

Kathleen Boland, who later married Sean O'Donovan, takes up the story of the jewels in her statement:

> I should have mentioned that a day or two after Harry's return from America, he went to meet Mick Collins in the Gresham Hotel with the intention of handing over the jewels. This was of course during the recess of the Treaty debate. Evidently, there was a row between Mick and Harry, I believe because Harry refused the side of the Treaty, and this was the end of their friendship. In the course of the row, Mick took the jewels out of his pocket and threw them at Harry, saying, 'Take these back, they are bloodstained'. Harry, who had already obtained Mick's receipt for them, put them in his pocket and walked out.

They never spoke again.

14

Legal Adjustments

According to Conor A. Maguire, the Chief Justice, who tells the story of his work in connection with the Republican Courts in 1920–21, the possibility of striking at the British Court system had often been talked of in Sinn Féin circles. In the spring of 1920, formal approval was given from Dublin for the setting up of arbitration courts. The success of these courts was immediate. Once there was an alternative, litigants were easily persuaded to withdraw from the courts and submit their dispute to arbitration instead. The arbitration courts later became Parish Courts.

A system of District Courts was devised in Mayo. This was particularly successful in that county partly because, in each area, the Sinn Féin organisation had a solicitor amongst the leading men. A solicitor always presided at these courts. In Maguire's experience:

> After a very short time , the list of cases for disposal became formidable, while business in the Petty Sessions and County Courts dwindled almost to vanishing point. Solicitors, even those who had no sympathy with Sinn Féin, found it necessary, if they were to retain their business, to practise in the Courts.

It was in the area of disputes about land that the new Republican Courts unexpectedly provided welcome solutions. In the spring of 1920, when land agitation suddenly became widespread in Mayo, landlords and tenants, landowners and landless men all resorted to the Republican courts. Maguire notes that 'the courts thus quietly assumed a jurisdiction for which there was no counterpart in the British system'.

In those early months, the system was subjected to 'a searching test', as Maguire described it. This test came to be known as the

Kilmaine Land Case. In south Mayo, two tenants of an estate under the control of the Chancery Court in Dublin held lands up to between fifty and sixty acres in size. Neighbouring tenants had holdings which were far smaller. The smallholders, in order to force the division of the larger holdings between them, organised an agitation including intimidation and a boycott. After some initial hesitation, both parties agreed that the matter be submitted to the Sinn Féin District Court. The case attracted widespread attention, especially when it became known that Arthur Griffith was sending observers. The hearing was held in the Town Hall in Ballinrobe before a packed hall. Maguire describes the scene:

> It was an exciting day. The proceedings were watched from a distance by members of the RIC, who did not, however, interfere. . . . Judgement was given in favour of the two owners who had been attacked.

Despite all legal advice, the losers refused to accept the decision. It was at this point that the IRA intervened. As Maguire records:

> The IRA police, however, under the orders of Commandant Thomas Maguire, seized the sons of some of the most defiant and at night took them to an unknown destination, which was in fact an island in Lough Corrib. After a week's imprisonment . . . on promises being given that no further agitation would take place in the locality, they were allowed to go home. Thenceforward the Courts were firmly established.

The lowest rung of the judicial edifice was the Parish Court. The Bureau of Military History is indebted to J. J. Bradley for the detailed records of the activities of the Parish Court at Monkstown in County Cork, as well as a graphic description of how he preserved these records.

Bradley, who lived in Rathcoole, County Dublin, when he signed his witness statement in 1949, had been Registrar of Monkstown Parish Court from 1920 to 1923. Like most Registrars, he was a member of both the IRA and Sinn Féin. Bradley worked at Fordes in Cork. His only chance of holding a Republican Court at this period was on Saturday evenings. The sessions often went on until late in the evening. Bradley remembers:

> On two occasions at least, cases at hearing were not finished until nearly midnight. . . . I had then to walk three and a half miles home, no other means being available. I preserved records, correspondence etc. . . . by

the following means: I had constructed at Haulbowline a steel box . . . equipped with a watertight lid. My late father possessed a little farm of three small fields near to the dwellinghouse at Raheens. In the fence of the second field a few furze bushes grew, and I carefully dug a hole in the ground, immediately under one bush, to contain the box.

People like Bradley were vitally important for the success of the whole independence movement. They were usually less active and less well known than the fighting men. Michael J. Cronin, who lived at Kiskeam in County Cork when he submitted his witness statement in 1955, describes his role:

> Beyond the normal training, I did not have much active service with the militant side. When Columns or Brigades officers were billeted in the area, I always took my turn of guard duty or scouting as required.
>
> When the Republican Courts were established in June 1920 I was appointed Clerk to the Kiskeam Parish Court.

When this court was amalgamated with the neighbouring one in Boherbue in the spring of 1921, Cronin worked as clerk of both – a post he held until June 1922.

Members of Cumann na mBan also worked in the courts. Both Aine Heron and Aine Ceannt (the widow of Eamonn Ceannt) were co-trustees of the moneys of the Pembroke and Rathmines Courts. According to her own statement, Aine Heron was 'selected by the Pembroke Comhairle Ceanntair to act as Justice in the Sinn Féin Courts.' In County Galway, Alice Cashel, an organiser for Cumann na mBan, was appointed a County Justice in the Galway Sinn Féin court. She describes how a particularly stubborn land dispute was settled, by using her knowledge of and contacts with the Land Bank:

> I received a telegram asking me whether I would act as Trustee. . . . I accepted. . . . The next step was to acquire the money for the purchase of the lands. About this time the Land Bank had been started in Dublin for just this purpose. I went to Dublin, met the Manager of the Bank, put my case before him, and obtained the necessary thousands to buy the land from Joyce. We bought the estate, stripped the land and transferred the land to the tenants.

As demonstrated in south Mayo, the credibility of the new courts and their success lay in the belief that their decisions could be enforced by the militant wing of the republican movement. Cronin describes a particularly significant operation which was carried out immediately after the hearing of a case 'relating to the ownership of a field adjacent to the village'. Cronin goes on:

> In order to convince the public that the authority of the Courts would be upheld, the Battalion OC (Sean Moylan) paraded a strong force of IRA outside the parish church on the Sunday morning following the hearing of the above-mentioned case when the people were leaving after Mass. The congregation were held up by the IRA and were addressed by Sean Moylan regarding the authority of the courts and the outcome of the proceedings in the particular case under review. He told those present that the decision of the court would be upheld by the IRA and that anybody taking the law into their own hands would be punished.

There was no further trouble.

Mr Justice Cahir Davitt, who was a son of Michael Davitt, was no activist in the independence movement. As for the Rising in 1916, he writes:

> The whole thing appeared to me to be tragically insane. After a severe examination of conscience, I did not feel myself bound to participate and [had] no inclination to do so. At the same time I felt like a deserter and was miserably unhappy. During the course of the week, wonder at their insanity gave way to admiration for their courage and pride in the fight they made. Then came anxiety and apprehension as to their fate upon the surrender, and eventually grief and futile indignation at the executions.

For the next few years, Davitt was busy building a practice at the Bar. He found time to help out the National Aid Association, which had been formed to provide help for the families of imprisoned volunteers.

In 1920, Davitt , according to his own witness statement, 'was beginning to enjoy a reasonably remunerative practice' on the Connaught Circuit. Cahir Davitt remembers that

> As the year 1920 wore on, the amount of litigation in these courts was affected more and more by the work of the Republican Arbitration Courts. These had been functioning for some time and had made great progress. I had no contact with them.

While Austin Stack was Minister for Home Affairs, the First Dáil provided:

1   That Courts of Justice and Equity be established.
2   That the Ministry be empowered, when they deem fit, to establish Courts having criminal jurisdiction.

Davitt remembered the opening day of the Swinford Sessions:

> The usual quantum of counsel and solicitors, together with the customary complement of court officers and police, were assembled before Judge Charles Doyle. There was however nobody else. . . . . This was in fact the last occasion upon which I appeared in the County Court.

In late July, while he was in the Bar Library, Davitt was approached by Arthur Cleary (Professor of the Law of Property, UCD), who told him

> that Austin Stack had authorised him to ask me would I accept a Judgeship in the Dáil Courts. As I was then only twenty-six years of age, and of only four years' standing at the Bar, I was more than surprised at this offer.

There was an explanation, however: 'As one might well imagine', Davitt writes, 'these judgeships were not keenly sought after.' In fact, the new State was short of judges throughout the War of Independence. Davitt now had his chance to make a contribution: he accepted the appointment. He was required to keep the matter secret – to the extent of keeping up his attendances at the Law Library. Davitt remembered that he was paid by cheque each month. The cheques were signed by Michael Collins. Although Davitt had another account, he records:

> I opened an account in the National Land Bank in Leeson Street and lodged [the cheques] there. I was somewhat shy about lodging them in the National Bank in College Green, where I also had an account.

Davitt had a busy time in those early months:

> After I returned from a short holiday in England during late August or early September, we four judges met on many occasions, usually in Meredith's house in Herbert Place, to draft and settle the constitution of the courts in detail, and the Rules of Procedure and Forms for the

Parish and District Courts. We all did our share of drafting, and eventually produced a Provisional Constitution, and Provisional Rules and Forms, which were in due course approved and enacted by the Minister for Home Affairs. They were issued by his authority in booklet form, consisting of some forty pages of type, and bear the date 1921. I believe they became generally available in January of that year.

Davitt appeared to have enjoyed his years as a Sinn Féin judge, despite the fact that many of the venues were bizarre. In Cork city and county, for example, they were lucky to have anywhere to hold the courts at all. Davitt writes:

On occasions when a court had been arranged for a certain date in particular premises, we would have to cancel it because, before the date had arrived, the place would have been raided and wrecked by Crown Forces. . . . They were, I was told, systematically eliminating every place which had been used as a Sinn Féin Club.

In particular, he relished the memory of an encounter 'in the dusk of a lovely evening in Ballyvourney'. He goes on:

As we topped a rise in the mountain road we were walking, we came suddenly in view of a party of riflemen, clad in trench coats and steel helmets, coming against us at a distance of about fifty yards. My guide rapped out an oath and leaped into the ditch at the side of the road, where I followed him a split-second later. . . . they were not, as we feared, a party of British soldiers, but a section of the West Cork Flying Column wearing captured material. They were transporting their impedimenta, I remember, including a Lewis machine gun, in a handcart.

All in all, Cahir Davitt did not regret his time as a Judge of the Irish Republican Courts.

15

AT THE INTERFACE

Alec McCabe was a member of both the Irish Volunteers and the IRB.
He was Chief Organiser and Centre of the IRB in Connaught and a
member of the Supreme Council. In his witness statement, he is careful
to record that, as far as the Rising in 1916 was concerned, he had obeyed
orders to the letter. He had even gone to Dublin and tried to have the situation clarified. He had talked to both Pearse and McDermott. His orders
were clear: he was to go back to Sligo. By the time he set out for Sligo, it
was time to mobilise his men and await instructions. No instructions
came. McCabe records:

> Eventually I heard of the surrender in Dublin and I went on the run in
> the locality. I managed to evade arrest. I kept in contact with the IRB
> and did an amount of propaganda work and kept in contact with the
> various units.

He was ready for the resurgence of the movement in 1917 when the
prisoners who had been detained after 1916 were released. In 1919, the
whole Battalion area in the Sligo area was reorganised. According to the
joint witness statement made by Thady McGowan and Tom Brehony,
McCabe's plan for the reorganisation was to ensure that 'all Volunteer
officers elected on the Battalion and Company staffs were also members
of the IRB'.

John P. Brennan, who came from Tubbercurry, was not a member of
the IRB 'up to about the Truce period and [I] cannot now state why I did-
n't join earlier'. He thought that 'it may have been that I had an early distaste for secret organisations'.

There was a Fenian tradition in Tubbercurry, however, and Brennan
is careful to record the names of four local elderly men who went so far

as to buy six Martini rifles for the Battalion when they heard that the men had no arms at all. Brennan writes:

> The four old men whose names I mentioned had been bred in the Fenian tradition, so that when an opportunity to purchase rifles came, although [they were] men of over sixty years of age, they availed of the chance . . . in the hope that other younger men would be available to use them.

The burning of Tubbercurry Courthouse was one of the more memorable actions of the Third Battalion of Sligo Brigade. Brennan notes 'the favourable impression it made on the civilian population' because:

> the job was carried out in an efficient manner and all records of the court, such as decrees and fines imposed and papers dealing with dog licences etc., were destroyed. This operation had a fine moral effect on the Volunteers.

Martin Bernard McGowan was quartermaster of the 2nd Battalion and as such had a special duty to procure arms, by whatever means – mainly collecting shotguns. Gamekeepers were good sources of shotguns, but they were loath to part with them. Near Ballintrillick, McGowan tells us:

> The Volunteers called on a gamekeeper named Rooney and ordered him to hand up his gun. This he refused to do. He barricaded himself in his home and opened fire on our men, wounding the Company Captain.

Gamekeepers were not popular with the Volunteers for a variety of reasons. McGowan relished a story he heard about a gamekeeper after another raid carried out by the IRA:

> By way of a practical joke, these men, at a later date, sent an anonymous letter to the British forces that Mitchell was armed and had strong Sinn Féin sympathies. Acting on this information, two lorry-loads of British forces surrounded his house some nights later. Mitchell, who was pro-British, thinking that it was the Volunteers who had come to raid, opened fire on the party, wounding two British soldiers. Intermittent fire was kept up on both sides throughout the night. When morning broke, Mitchell realised his mistake. He still refused to surrender until his employer was brought to the scene. He was then taken into custody and got a short term of imprisonment. The whole story was hushed up and got no publicity.

143

The rescue of Frank Carty, Brigade OC, from Sligo Jail in June 1920, had a most uplifting effect on the Volunteers. McGowan was one of the party engaged in that operation, and recalls in his statement that it was 'carried out quietly and in a short time'.

By the end of 1920, the pattern of IRA attacks on RIC detachments and barracks, followed by reprisals against the population by British forces, was well established. It was a pattern that Carty, as Brigade OC, had to take account of when planning an ambush on an RIC cycle patrol which regularly travelled on the main road between Cliffoney and Grange. It was decided that, should an ambush take place, the most likely target for a reprisal would be the Ballintrillick Creamery. It was arranged that a special detachment would protect the creamery. McGowan writes:

> The ambush was carried out as planned, on the 25th October 1920. . . . One sergeant and four constables were killed and two constables were wounded.

Not surprisingly, in spite of all the efforts on the part of the IRA to protect the creamery:

> the British forces from Sligo and Finner Camp came out and burned the creamery in daylight by way of reprisal. A number of houses were burned in Grange and Cliffoney areas.

It was not a lucky encounter for the Volunteers either. The rifles which they managed to acquire in the ambush were all 'captured by British forces outside Sligo town', as McGowan records. Moreover, it so happened that the occupants of the car in which the rifles were being carried were all captured and taken away to Belfast Jail to await trial; among the occupants was Nurse Linda Kearns. McGowan found it necessary to go to Belfast to do what he could to assist the prisoners. By the time he returned to Sligo, the British forces had made a large scale 'round-up' in the Glenada and Ballintrillick mountains. McGowan notes that

> British forces converged on the area from Sligo, Manorhamilton and Finner Camp. A large number of men – some of them were Volunteers – were arrested and badly beaten up. Four were detained and later interned until after the Truce.

But McGowan and his Battalion fought on. He had been appointed OC when Seamus Devine, one of the occupants of the ill-fated car carrying the rifles, was stopped on the Sligo road. He ends his statement:

> Plans were made for a further attack on the RIC stationed in Cliffoney a few days before the Truce on 11 July. The Brigade OC sent on instructions to withdraw our men and not engage in any further activities pending definite orders from him.

James Hunt, who had given such a good account of himself in affording protection to the representatives of the Dáil as they attempted to sell the Dáil Loan to possible subscribers in County Sligo, describes an encounter with the enemy which may be unique in the history of the battles of the War of Independence. It took place in the months leading up to the Truce. Hunt was OC of the Gurteen Battalion. He writes:

> We then got on to the engine of a train going to Ballaghdereen, and one of our men was an engine driver named McGough from Tuam. He took charge of the engine when we approached Ballaghdereen and stopped it on the railway bridge which was situated about thirty yards from the RIC barracks. Two RIC men, who were on the streets when we commenced shooting, disappeared and took up positions from which they replied to our fire. This exchange of fire lasted for about ten minutes. We then drove the train backwards in the direction of Kilfree. When we were about three hundred yards from Ballaghderreen, we saw six RIC coming from Frenchpark towards Ballaghderreen. We moved the train up again to our original position on the bridge and opened fire on these police.

But when the police had dealt with the element of surprise, they were able to make use of the loopholes in the upper storey of the barracks, and rained down heavy fire on the Volunteers in the train. Hunt remembers the moment:

> When we tried to retreat, McGough [the train driver] failed to start the engine; it then appeared that we had run out of steam and we made an attempt to get up steam by shovelling coal into the furnace, without result. We then abandoned the engine . . . and retreated along a half-mile of low-lying land without any cover, under continuous fire from the police. We succeeded in getting safely to the mountains towards evening.

But the retreat was not over for Hunt. The police caught up with him and his comrades when they took a chance and went in for a drink in 'Peter Finn's public house'. Hunt managed to escape and took to his heels. He writes:

> After half an hour's running, pursued by the Tans, I was able to keep them at a safe distance. I was in perfect physical condition at the time and was a good long-distance runner. After this race was on for some time I noticed that there was one man keeping very close to me. I was able to keep him at a safe distance by firing an odd shot whenever he came near me. He was an Englishman named Little.

As it turned out, Little was a better runner than Hunt, and caught up with him when the latter's ammunition ran out. When the rest of the Tans arrived, they wanted to shoot Hunt 'and commenced to belabour me with their rifle butts. Little then drew his gun and came to my protection; but for him, I would not have survived', Hunt remembered. Hunt had been a member of the RIC but resigned in 1916 'when the Rising took place'.

In neighbouring County Leitrim, according to Bernard Sweeney, who had been quartermaster of the 2nd Battalion of the South Leitrim Brigade, the RIC were the main target of Volunteer activity. He describes their first effort in 1919:

> In the latter end of 1919 a boycott of the RIC was instituted by GHQ. Business houses were instructed not to supply them with foodstuffs or other materials and it was taboo to speak to the members of this force or associate with them.

Sweeney did not think that this action was very effective if the intention was to force members of the RIC to resign:

> Only one man resigned in this area. . . . It did however cause a wide gulf between the people and the RIC, and this was all to the good. It was well known by everyone that the RIC were the principal tool used by the British government to keep the country in subjugation.

Sweeney notes that:

> Towards the end of 1919 and in early 1920, a number of small RIC barracks throughout the country had been attacked by the Volunteers and

in some places captured, with the consequent loss of arms and prestige. Their headquarters realised that they could not hope to hold those small stations.

As they pulled their forces into the larger stations, Volunteers like Sweeney felt that

> this was the first loosening of [the RIC's] grip on the country, and their function of being the eyes and ears of the British government was being contracted.

Hugh Brady, who was Brigade Ordnance Officer, South Leitrim, noted that

> the Volunteers now assumed responsibility for the effective policing of the country. The RIC, even when they remained in the towns, now took little interest in this duty and more or less left it to the Volunteers and became more of a military garrison. By this time, the RIC had lost the co-operation which they had received from the people, and were non-effective as a police force. The Volunteers carried out the duties very effectively and kept the peace wonderfully well, although they were only spare-time policemen. A place of detention for individuals whom it was necessary to arrest was established at Scotch Hill, in an unoccupied house. Such places were called 'unknown destinations' as they were secret to the general public.

At the same time, Sinn Féin Courts were being set up. They were so popular with litigants that 'the British courts were left almost idle'. Brady continues: 'The courts were held in a local disused granary on the mountainside and continued to function effectively well into 1921.'

By 1920, the Volunteers began to concentrate on discouraging prospective recruits to the RIC, despite the many inducements that were being held out to them. There were sometimes sad results. Sweeney records one such case:

> One night as McCabe was going home, he was taken off his cycle by the Volunteers and questioned about his joining the RIC. One of the men who was armed fired a shot accidentally, hitting McCabe in the leg. As a result of this, he had to have his leg amputated, and that finished his attempt to join.

By December 1920, as related in Sweeney's witness statement, the Active Service Unit or Flying Column could be said to have come into existence:

A number of the lads who were on the 'run' had come together for companionship and also for safety reasons and were staying in the one district. . . . We lived on the hospitality of the people and as long as they had any food we had it also. In fact, they would do without it themselves to give it to us.

It was towards the end of 1920 also that 'the Tans and Auxies' arrived in County Leitrim, according to Brady. He describes the situation:

[The Tans and the Auxiliaries] established themselves in the centres where the RIC and military were. Strong garrisons were established in Ballinamore, Mohill and Carrick-on- Shannon. They took over private dwellings and such premises and fortified them with steel shutters, sandbags and barbed wire, turning them into veritable forts; and it looked as if they were preparing for an extended stay and that we were in for a bad time.

The newcomers immediately started into raiding houses and holding up people, beating them up, and threatening them with guns. Brady continues:

In this way, I think they planned to frighten the people and the IRA. . . . Their actions . . . turned people who, if not openly hostile to, had no sympathy with, Sinn Féin, or who were lukewarm, into enthusiastic Sinn Féiners.

The IRA responded by building larger and larger bombs, not all of which had yet been perfected. For example, Brady records:

The road mines were made of concrete, eighteen inches square, with a hollow cavity, twelve inches by six inches, to take explosive, fuse and detonator. . . . When the explosive was filled, the open end of the cavity was rammed with dry, hard clay. . . . We made about twelve or fourteen road mines and they were distributed throughout the Brigade area.

Towards the end of his statement, Hugh Brady describes the IRA's further efforts at manufacturing their own ammunition:

In addition to the bombs and mines we made, we also filled a large amount of shotgun cartridges with slugs, after having first removed the ordinary shot from them. We made our own slugs or buckshot from scrap lead, which we melted down and ran through a mould.

Brady was glad of the Truce when it came, but he says that

we set about putting our armourer's shop on a sound basis. We installed a lathe and purchased several tools, and we would have been in a much better position to produce material and do repairs if the fighting resumed.

Sweeney's memories of the bombs and mines were not good. In February 1921, Sean Connolly, formerly OC of the North Longford Brigade and a high-ranking officer at GHQ, took over the reorganisation of the Flying Column. Before embarking on the offensive, Connolly had a number of road bombs constructed. Sweeney remembers: 'We put bombs . . . on the streets but we never had any luck, as the enemy never obliged us by turning up.' On a subsequent trial run, a large bomb simply disintegrated.

But when disaster finally hit Connolly and his comrades, neither bombs or mines could be of any help. They were caught in a house in Garvagh which Connolly had selected as a place where the men could have a rest. Connolly ordered everyone to go to the rear of the house. Sweeney was one of those trapped, although he survived the encounter. He writes:

Enemy machine guns immediately opened up a barrage of fire on our position. Each of our sections concentrated on the direction from where the machine-gun fire was coming and opened fire in that direc-tion. The enemy were well informed of the position of the place. . . . We had not a chance from the start. . . . Five of our men were killed almost immediately. Connolly was wounded and captured, and died that night in Carrick-on-Shannon Military Barracks.

Sweeney himself was badly wounded. He lay in a drain, his body cov-ered by water:

The cold water probably helped to stem the haemorrhage from my wounds. . . . I could see the enemy as they swarmed over the place, pounding our dead or dying on the ground with the butts of their rifles. . . . They did not find me.

At last, after he had heard the lorries pulling away, he began to cry for help. His cries were heard. 'I was then taken to Fenagh in a pony and trap.' It took him a long time to recover. The encounter happened on 11 March, but Sweeney did not rejoin his Column until 'the early days of May'.

After Connolly's death, GHQ sent Paddy Morrissey to replace him, and the Brigade began to build up its strength again. But Sweeney remembered that

> during all this time the enemy kept hammering away without let-up. Raid after raid and round-up after round-up. Just prior to the Truce, the enemy carried out a big round-up between the border and Mohill. They combed the mountains for us, even using aircraft extensively. We got to know about this round-up in time and succeeded in getting away into the County Cavan to a place called Glann which was outside the area of search.

When the Truce came, Sweeney

> could not understand the Truce and it took some time to realise the change it brought about – to be able to go home and walk about freely. None of us thought it would last long.

16

THE ULSTER CONTEXT

At the time of the Rising in 1916, Monsignor M. J. Curran was Secretary to the Catholic Archbishop of Dublin. In a long, considered witness statement, he directs our attention to three aspects of Irish politics which exercised the minds of many in the second decade of the twentieth century: Home Rule, the Irish Party and the idea of partition (or 'exclusion', as he preferred to describe it). According to Curran, the idea had been floated as early as 1912. In a carefully argued submission, he outlines the steps whereby an unpalatable solution gradually became acceptable to most unionists in the North. Moreover, the question was not faced up to by the Irish Party, who are heavily criticised by Curran. Much of Curran's witness statement was based on his diaries, which were contemporary with the political events he analyses:

> I am convinced that the party leaders knew that some form of exclusion was settled on by the Liberal Cabinet as early as 1912 and, although they knew so, they kept the people in the dark. They were not only guilty of silence, of incorrect statements and of misleading implications, but they resented all criticism and any reflections on the Liberals; they followed a spineless policy.

Curran was certain that the politicians did not set out the full facts of the case. He writes:

> The whole question of partition was for a long time very vague – partition or exclusion. It was vague firstly as to whether it was temporary or permanent. It was vague secondly as regards the area affected, whether it covered four, five, six or nine counties. . . . [The question] . . . was under the surface since the Home Rule Bill was introduced.

Unionists in Belfast did not wish to discuss the subject lest it appear that they were ready to abandon the unionists of Donegal, Cavan and Monaghan.

In January 1913, when Carson for the first time formally proposed the exclusion of all of Ulster, the proposal was rejected, but Curran writes: 'It now became known that some of the Liberal leaders were willing or anxious to compromise on the basis of separate treatment for Ulster.' A month later, Augustine Birrell, Chief Secretary for Ireland, hinted as much, but still no notice seems to have been taken in nationalist quarters.

In June 1913, the reintroduced Home Rule Bill was again rejected, but the forces of unionism consolidated their position in the northern part of the island. 'An English Lieutenant General, Sir George Richardson, was appointed Commander-in-Chief of the Ulster Volunteers', Curran records.

This paramilitary step was followed by numerous parades in the Province, most of which were attended by Carson and Craig. On 24 September 1913, Carson announced the formation of an Ulster Provisional Government in Belfast. Step by step, the Irish Party gave way to pressure. Exclusion was on the table. Worse still, once exclusion had been conceded temporarily, Curran argues that there was 'a moral certainty [that] a general election would oust the Liberals and return a Tory government, which would make exclusion permanent'.

On 19 March 1913, John Dillon MP, a prominent member of the Irish Parliamentary Party, made an honest assessment of the situation, which Curran quotes:

> We recognise and accept, though not very happily, that if Ulster – the four counties and the city of Belfast – vote themselves out of the Bill, it will be open to this Parliament if the Tory Party should come into power – not an unlikely contingency in the next six years – by a one-clause Bill to make it permanent. . . . That is the concession we have made . . . and we did it with our eyes open.

Curran continues:

> Three days before Home Rule was put on the Statute Book, it was suspended indefinitely and an amending bill was guaranteed that would exclude an unknown number of Ulster counties for an indefinite time.

Curran notes with some bitterness that

> the only spark of public interest in Ireland at this period was a popular Dublin demonstration in the Phoenix Park on 2 May 1915 against a Beer and Whiskey Tax.

From March 1914, according to Curran, 'partition swamped the political field'. He felt that Devlin, the Ulster MP, was a most unreliable representative and that it was not just the populace that was responsible for having brought politics to an all-time low.

Devlin maintained in a speech at Longford that the Carsonite campaign was just bluff: 'Let the soldiers and the police make a ring and we will wipe the streets of Belfast with these bluffers before twenty-four hours.'

In the years since then, the Great War, the 1916 Rising and a suspended Home Rule Act had intervened. The War of Independence was being fought in Ulster, as in every other part of Ireland. The Very Reverend James Canon O'Daly, from Clogher, County Tyrone, and a member of the IRB, speaks for many nationalists in the North when at the end of his witness statement he states:

> Considering the hostility of a large unionist population in the areas where they lived, the Volunteers deserve great credit for the sacrifices of time and effort made.

Seamus Dobbyn, a member of the Supreme Council of the IRB in the middle of 1920, as things were beginning to 'hot up' in the South, had received some very disquieting intelligence. The organisation of the IRB in Ulster was tight, and Dobbyn was the intelligence officer for the Belfast Brigade:

> Through our espionage system we had learned that the Orange section were being prepared by the Masonic pro-British junta to attack the Catholic population in Belfast, but such an attack, while previously planned, was going to be made as a result of some action on our part either against them or against the British authorities. The impression to be given was that the Orange section was rising in just wrath against some action we had taken, as indicated above. We investigated thoroughly, over a period of a month or more, the genuineness of this

report of the coming pogrom and satisfied ourselves that it was gen-
uine. The Brigade Council decided that I should go to Dublin and
report to Headquarters. . . . I decided to explain the case to the Supreme
Council. . . . Michael Collins pooh-poohed the idea of the Orangemen,
as he said, wrecking their own city, and suggested that we in the North
were more inclined to fight against the Orangemen than against the
Tans. He said that under no circumstances would we be supplied with
any more guns.

Dobbyn was so worried by this decision that he went to see the Chief
of Staff, Dick Mulcahy. He spent most of a day explaining the particular
circumstances of the province: 'Masonry, Orangeism, Hibernianism, and
all the other factors.' Mulcahy was persuaded that Dobbyn might be right
and that the IRA in the North should postpone any military action. One
of the projects that was postponed was the assassination of the British
officer Oswald Swanzy, who had just been transferred from Cork. The
IRA held Swanzy responsible for the shooting dead of Tomas
MacCurtain. Because the Belfast men delayed their action, two Corkmen
were sent to carry out the assassination instead. Dobbyn asserts:

The result of that operation was that the pogrom began in Lisburn
instead of Belfast. Two days later the pogrom was in full swing in
Belfast and continued intermittently from then until the middle of 1922.

As a member of the Irish Republican Brotherhood, Dobbyn could perhaps have expected more understanding on the Northern situation than
he received from Collins.

John Shields was Head Centre of the IRB in County Tyrone from
1917 up to 1921 and was consistently engaged in national activities for the
organisation up to 1924. He had attended the meeting in Dublin in 1917
which had been arranged for the purpose of reorganising the Volunteers.
Later on in the year, another meeting was held in Carrickmore, County
Tyrone, to draw up plans for the establishment of a local Brigade of the
Volunteers. But Shields writes:

In addition to Volunteers attending this meeting, all the Tyrone Circles
of the IRB were summoned to attend and many did. . . . The IRB had
been very well organised in all parts of Tyrone and it was felt in republican circles by the men who were responsible for the reorganising of
the Volunteers that this work could best be done through IRB channels.

. . . It was decided that the IRB be instructed to take over the organising of Volunteer Companies.

The pattern of involvement of the IRB was repeated in other parts of the North and in Belfast. Shields records a meeting held in Belfast in connection with the reorganising of republican forces

in a private house in Belfast. Liam Gaynor was also present at this meeting. A representative from General Headquarters in Dublin named Murphy presided at the meeting. There were also present representatives from the counties of Armagh, Tyrone, Derry and Belfast city. Jim McCullough of Armagh travelled with me to it. At this meeting, both Irish Volunteer and IRB matters were dealt with.

Shields later attended meetings of the Ulster Council of the IRB. He remembers in particular meetings held

on the matter of arranging safe lines of communication from Belfast through the various north-eastern and north-western areas. The dispatch routes which were organised at these meetings and the various depots for dispatches then arranged worked satisfactorily and safely all through the period of the Tan war and on after the Truce of 1921. Dispatch routes were opened from Belfast through Lurgan, Armagh South, Blackwaterstown, Dungannon, and Sixmilecross on to Omagh, and Derry City, taking in Strabane and Newtownstewart.

The route we organised for Dublin dispatches went by Clogher, Monaghan, Carrickmacross etc.

Shields is emphatic on the subject of the part played by the IRB up to the end of 1918. He notes that 'the whole directional policy of the Volunteer movement was carried out through IRB channels.' However, Shields recalls that, in early 1919:

a set of instructions were issued by the IRB and sanctioned by the Irish Volunteer Executive for the reorganisation of the Irish Army under Dáil Éireann, which was then established.

Documents were sent to Shields which dealt with the necessary adjustments which could be expected on the appointment by Dáil Éireann of a Minister for Defence. Who was to control the Army of the Republic?

At this point, Shields began his long periods in jail, and he never saw the documents again. His activities as an active republican caught up with him. He recounts:

> During the latter months of 1920, the Benburb Company carried out various raids for arms on unionists' houses. . . . One of the houses raided was occupied by the gamekeeper on the Caledon estate. Attached to the gamekeeper's house was the local Orange Lodge.

In another encounter, Shields tells us:

> We had information that a quantity of arms was kept in a particular house which was situated quite close to an Orange Hall. . . . This hall had been used as a mobilisation centre by the B men and it appears that a number of B men were actually in the hall when we arrived to raid the nearby house.

In the ensuing short battle, Shields and his men managed to escape. Their raids on unionist houses and Orange Halls, with the occasional attack on mail trains, were bound to lead to them being captured, and 'on the night of 7 July 1921 a party of RIC and Special Constabulary forces in two or three motor tenders began to search all the likely houses in the Benburb area.' They found Shields in a less likely house, he says:

> I was staying in a house belonging to people who were Catholics but unfriendly to the Republican Movement. . . . I was found in the search and arrested.

The B Specials knew everything that was happening in the Benburb area.

Manus O'Boyle, who had been a member of the Irish Volunteers from 1913 and was a personal friend of Seamus Dobbyn and his brothers, describes some features of the conflict:

> In Harland and Wolff's shipyard there were always murmurings about clearing out the Catholic workmen. I remember the day the attack started there, it started in the east yard. The Orange workmen started throwing rivets, bolts and all sorts of missiles at the Catholic workmen, who were hopelessly outnumbered. . . . The Catholic workers who had to leave the yard retaliated by throwing stones. The Protestant workers

burned out the homes of the Catholics. I know that the heaviest fighting took place in the Ballymacarratt area, where there were about seven
thousand Catholic families.

O'Boyle was detailed by his superiors in the Volunteer Brigade to
organise a Company to defend the Ballymacarratt area. He relates:

> It was a continuous street fight in Ballymacarratt. Our opponents were
> heavily armed and had the assistance of the police and military. During
> all the fighting our headquarters were in the Cross and Passion Convent
> in Bryson Street. The nuns were magnificent. Mother Teresa, Sister
> Ethna, Sister Peter Paul and Sister Bridget.

O'Boyle had some other well-placed allies in this defensive war,
notably certain members of the RIC. One was his brother-in-law, who
was stationed in the Shankill Road and was 'one of our chief intelligence
officers'. Another was an inspector of the RIC, J. J. McDonnell.

O'Boyle records: 'Mother Teresa could always present us with hun-
dreds of rounds of .45 ammunition which she received from him.'

James J. Smyth, who was Battalion Adjutant of the Lisnaskea Battalion,
describes in outline the activities undertaken by the Volunteers in the
Fermanagh area. The real author of the history which Smyth records in
his witness statement was Mr Thomas Cox, who had been an officer of
the Fermanagh Brigade. The activities included the burning of vacated
police barracks and income-tax offices, as well as raids for arms, which
were 'an every-night occurrence'. Something of the hostility encountered
by the Volunteers is clear from Smyth's witness statement:

> Also in this month an unsuccessful attempt was made to burn Lisbellew
> Courthouse and Barracks – while preparations were being made, an out-
> post fired on an onlooker and in a minute the village was in arms. The
> Volunteers . . . had their work cut out to carry out a successful retreat.
> This they did with only one casualty. . . . This village was ninety-nine
> percent hostile.

The capture of Belleek barracks was carried out by Enniskillen
Volunteers in September 1920. This achievement 'was very highly praised
by the late General Collins', according to Smyth's statement. Several more

risky operations were planned and executed by the Volunteers; according to the statement, there would have been a lot more if they had been given permission for 'major stunts'.

The statement is careful to record the difficulties under which the IRA operated in County Fermanagh:

> They were constantly very great and often indeed were insurmountable. Company areas were isolated from each other and their Battalion HQs. Battalion areas were in the same position as regards their Brigades. It must also be remembered that the majority of those who were opposed to the IRA were fully armed and constantly on the lookout for any movement on the part of the IRA. This was clearly illustrated by the manner in which the pro-British element turned out to attack the IRA both in Tempo and Lisbellew.

John T. Connolly, who was Captain of the Roslea (County Fermanagh) Company, describes a sequence of events that begins with Sinn Féin's Belfast trade boycott and culminates in the burning of Roslea. This sequence includes several shoot-outs and attempted assassinations. Connolly writes:

> When I got back to my own house, which was about one and a half miles from Roslea, I harnessed two horses and went to plough with a neighbour named Cassidy. I heard at dinner hour that RIC Specials and military forces were in Roslea and that a threat was used to burn the village that night. Later on that evening from the field in which I was working I saw different families getting out their furniture and belongings in preparation to evacuate their houses. I saw Sean Connolly . . . with his wife passing on a byroad leaving the village. There was an exodus from the village in all directions.

That night nearly all the Catholic houses in the village were burned. Police came into the village and took over Flynn's public house and the market house: the two largest buildings in the village.

The Volunteers arranged that, on a date 'exactly one month after the night the nationalist houses were burned, a number of unionists' houses would be attacked and burned.' Connolly did not know how many houses were destroyed, but he had a clear recollection of a particular raid for arms on a unionist house:

We called first at a house belonging to people named Warrington, about 11.30 PM on a summer night. The inmates of the house were the father, two sons and two daughters, and all were praying in the dwelling house. Our walking in on them came as a complete surprise and the two boys made an attempt to get outside when we arrived. In preventing the boys going out, we explained to the inmates of the house that we were calling to get their firearms. They then took us out to the barn loft where all the household beds were arranged, and we found that each member of the family had arms at their bedsides – girls included.

In County Monaghan, there was no special constabulary, according to Eugene Sherry, who was a member of the Clontibret Volunteers, and

therefore no B Special patrols. The RIC and Tans were keeping mostly within the defences of their barracks. We made several efforts to carry out operations by crossing the border in County Armagh and attempting to ambush B Special patrols.

The difficulty in finding an opportunity of engaging with the Crown forces in County Monaghan may have led to a curious development in that part of the War of Independence, in which the IRA was under the direction of General Eoin O'Duffy. The account is to be found in the witness statement submitted by Lieutenant Colonel Tummon, who was a member of the Irish Volunteers in County Monaghan from 1918:

Towards the end of the dance, one of the Clones Volunteers reported that some poteen was offered for sale by a certain gentleman. On investigation, it was further learned that a small quantity had been actually made by this man. General O'Duffy, to whom the matter was reported, decided to hold him prisoner and use him as a guide to find the remainder of the stock. . . . O'Duffy took charge personally and off we started on bicycles, taking our prisoner along. En route it was learned that the poteen was under the control of a Protestant who would possibly resist us by force. Plans were accordingly made to use surprise as the chief weapon. A large pole was secured from a hedgerow, and on arrival at the 'still house', it was used as a battering ram on the front door

When the attackers found a four-gallon crockery jar, O'Duffy smashed it on the laneway leading to the house and ordered his men to search for the still apparatus. Oddly enough for men engaged in a war:

a shotgun seized in the house where the poteen was found was ordered
to be returned to the owner by General O'Duffy, who stated it was a
poteen raid he was conducting not an arms one.

Although it carried out several other poteen raids, the Company also
engaged in more orthodox paramilitary activities. For instance, they managed to destroy a boat used by the RIC at Newtownbutler. The boat was
loaded with stones and its sides punched in with a crowbar, 'and in less
than five minutes it went down', never to be seen again. The main activity was that associated with the boycott of Belfast goods. This involved
the disruption of the delivery of bread in that particular area, and was
largely engaged in as a reprisal for the Belfast pogroms. Tummon records:

> A firm of bakers conducted a bread trade in my area and regularly deliv-
> ered to retail shops. The Company Commander . . . decided . . . to noti-
> fy the driver of one of the horse-driven vehicles to cease delivery.

The driver took no notice whatever and continued to deliver the
bread, 'generally at the same time and day of each week'. It was decided
that the van should be destroyed by burning, 'as this action would have
the best chance of bringing the matter to notice'.

This action drew a sharp response from the Crown forces. Gunfire
was used on both sides as the Volunteers attempted to remove the horse
from the bread van's traces before setting the van alight. Tummon records
that 'an exchange of shots with revolvers took place and one of the
police, Constable Farrelly, was hit and wounded. . . . This stopped the
chase.'

The police turned up the heat and 'very frequent and searching raids
followed this activity. Practically every house was raided several times.'
Tummon took to sleeping out at night. He remembers:

> With a few other Volunteers, including our Company Commander, I
> moved off with a load of bedclothes and slept in a cow-byre in the
> townland of Derryelvin. It was quite warm there at night with the heat
> generated by the cattle. . . . On several occasions during the autumn of
> this year (1920) I slept in hay cocks quite soundly.

Another witness, James Sullivan of County Monaghan (member of
the Irish Volunteers, 1913–21, Brigade Adjutant, June 1921, member of
the IRA, 1919–21 – and a member of the IRB), had very few happy

The funeral of Thomas Ashe, Glasnevin, 30 September 1917
(BMH CD 227/35/3 Mr Fintan Murphy/Military Archives)

An Auxiliary raid on Liberty Hall, 22 November 1920. Among those arrested were Thomas Johnson and Thomas Ferren (third and fourth from left, respectively).
(BMH P 37 Mr Frank Robbins/Military Archives)

The Clonmult IRA unit, which was active in the Midleton, County Cork, area during the War of Independence

West Mayo Brigade Flying Column, 1920–21

Arrested in a raid on the Dáil office at 76 Harcourt Street, Dublin, in 1920 were (left to right) Daniel J. O'Donovan, Sean O'Mahoney and Dick McKee

(BMH CD6/29/1 Mr Erskine Childers/Military Archives)

Captain Stephen Donnelly in Volunteer uniform, . 1915. Donnelly was a leading member of the North Mayo Brigade during the War of Independence.

(from *Hard Fighting in Poor Times: A History of the Troubles in North Mayo and West Sligo*)

Arthur Griffith and Michael Collins

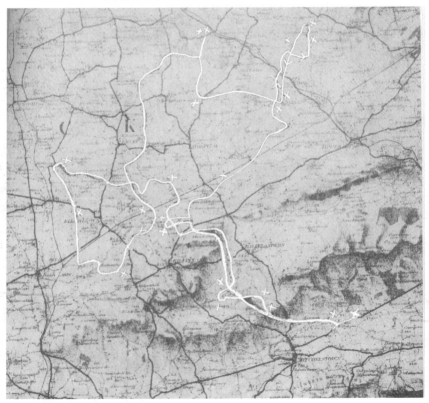

Map indicating the day-to-day routes followed by the East Limerick Flying Column and the places where the unit was billeted

(BMH WS 883 Lt Col John McCarthy/Military Archive

A unit of the Volunteers of the North Mayo Flying Column, *c.* 1921
(from *Hard Fighting in Poor Times: A History of the Troubles in North Mayo and West Sligo*)

An active-service unit of the North Mayo Flying Column
(from *Hard Fighting in Poor Times: A History of the Troubles in North Mayo and West Sligo*)

William T. Cosgrave making a speech from the Courthouse balcony after his election in the Kilkenny by-election

Michael and Brigid Hynes on their wedding day. Brigid Hynes (née Whelan), born in Carlow in 1898, was a founder member of the Cumann na mBan in three areas in her native county. She and other members of her family were involved in the War of Independence, and her sisters Peg and Betty were later imprisoned in Kilmainham Jail. Brigid subsequently became a National School teacher in Castleiney, County Tipperary, where she met her husband Michael in 1926.

A group of IRA prisoners on board a British Admiralty tender docked in Portland Harbour, prior to their transfer to Portland Prison, *c.* 1921

(BMH P 29 Lt Col Brendan Barry/Military Archives)

IRA training camp in Oldcastle, Meelick, County Mayo, 1921.
Back row, left to right: Brigadier Tom Carney; Jim McEvilly, Ballinamore; Captain John Carroll, Ballinamore; Bill Moran, Carracastle; J. B. Lavan; Captain Mick Brown, Aughaliska; Captain Campbell Kilkelly; Captain Murtagh, Pulronaghane; Harry McNicholas, Quartermaster.
Front row: Paddy Grennan, Kilkelly; Mick McDonagh, Kiledan; Matt Durkan, Shanaghy; Michael McNicholas; Pat Hyland, Captain.

(from *But They Are Forever Young: A History of the East Mayo Brigade, 1913–1921*)

The Sinn Féin group involved in the 1917 by-election in Kilkenny (pictured at the Victoria Hotel), in which Alderman William Cosgrave defeated Councillor Maginnis.
Back row, left to right: Dan McCarthy, Darrell Figgis, Reverend Dr Browne (Maynooth), Tom Kelly, Mr Flemming, Éamon de Valera and Sean Milroy.
Front row: Laurence Ginnell, Countess Constance Markievicz, William Cosgrave and Mrs Ginnell.

(BMH P 11 Mr Dan Lennon/Military Archives)

The North Longford Flying Column, photographed on Crott Mountain, 1 May 1921, following an ambush at Reilly's house at Fyhora, in which two Black and Tan soldiers were killed

(BMH P 14 Mr Michael McKeon/Military Archives)

memories of the Volunteer campaign in his area. Sullivan writes that 'from 1918 onwards we had in many unionist districts in County Monaghan a vigorous Ulster Volunteer organisation'. They were both well armed and vigilant. The nervousness of people who might be in sympathy with the Volunteers hampered whatever activity they might plan. Sometimes people were quite ready to pass on useful information to the IRA; later on, they might get cold feet. A case in point was the plan to raid a house at Ashfield on the Monaghan-Cavan border, on 15 July 1919, which had to be called off when it was learned that the British authorities knew all about it. Sullivan records: 'We heard afterwards that the young man who first reported about the rifles got scared about what he had disclosed and reported the matter.' In the general raid for arms, which was arranged to happen more or less simultaneously in many districts, 'we got very little arms in unionist houses, as the unionists had handed their firearms in before the raid took place'.

Sullivan, the OC of the Flying Column put together by Eoin O'Duffy some time before, was anxious to take on the unionists, but the 'Column men did not approve . . . the area being much too hostile and dangerous'. On one occasion, while engaged in an operation which was not going too well, Sullivan remembers one of his scouts advising him: 'If you are wise, you will go home also.' Sullivan recounts that it was on this same operation that

> a member of the Column left the Column billets for his home, and on his journey there he was arrested by British forces. This man gave all the information at his disposal to the British.

As a consequence, the British took the opportunity of attempting to throw a cordon around the billets where the Column was hiding. The members were able to escape – but only barely. The Column broke up, never to come together as a full-time Column.

There were other 'betrayals'; these were followed in 1921 in Monaghan by executions, which Sullivan never forgot. An intercepted letter led to the execution of one informer. Volunteers posing as British soldiers interviewed this man regarding the contents of the letter. Sullivan records:

> He took his visitors to the door and showed them the Volunteer Drill Hall . . . and said 'Many a night I was there peeping through the window

161

when drilling was taking place.' This man was shot as a spy on Good Friday night 1921.

On Easter Monday, two men, a father and his son, were executed for the shooting of an IRA man 'on the night of the general raid for arms' in Castleblayney. On the following Saturday, another man 'who fired on the Flying Column' was also shot. The execution which haunted Sullivan more than any of the others was that of a young man who had

> made a full confession of all he had told to the Tans, which I wrote down for him in the form of a statement which he signed. In this statement he emphasised that he told the Tans nothing but what they already knew.

But neither this statement nor Sullivan's efforts could save him: 'I protested against shooting him, and O'Duffy said it would be an example and a warning to others.' The young man was executed along with another man from the Monaghan area, at Aghabog.

The air of sadness which pervades many of the witness statements as the comrades recount the events of the last days before the Truce is heaviest of all in those dealing with the northern counties. P. H. Doherty from Carndonagh, County Donegal, who was a Commandant in the IRA in 1921, remembers the problems he and his Battalion had with informers while he was on the run. He explains: 'If I stayed in a particular house one night, the chances were that the house would be raided on the following night.'

Doherty tested out the situation by changing 'the particular locality where I was in the habit of staying' on several subsequent nights. It was an elaborate arrangement which should have put the informer off the track. Doherty continues:

> On checking up on all the circumstances a few days later, we came to the conclusion that the only person who was in a position to give so much information was a particular young man. Three months later the young man was arrested by members of the IRA, court-martialled and sentenced to death.

To his surprise, Doherty was not called on to give evidence. He considered the sentence too severe. He concludes:

The evidence was purely circumstantial and I suffered no ill effects. In addition, I considered that this boy was of slightly weak mentality. As it happened, I would say fortunately, he was handed over to me as a prisoner until such time as the sentence would be carried out. Immediately I got him alone I told him to run as far from the area as he possibly could and not return. He took my advice and never returned. . . . Whenever I remember the incident I feel happy that I allowed him to escape.

Doherty goes on to describe the strategy which the Active Service Unit he joined in May 1921 wished to pursue:

Our instructions were to avoid a large-scale operation and keep harassing the enemy so as to pin down a large number of British forces with headquarters in Buncrana so that these forces could not be utilised to assist in a large-scale round-up of our No. 1 ASU, already hard-pressed in the Dungloe-Burtonport area.

They attacked RIC patrols, demolished a bridge (by hand, having no explosives) and made a 'nuisance' attack on the RIC barracks. As in other mountainous areas, their practice then 'was to withdraw to the hills', where they hid in a sheep hut and kept warm by using about 'thirty blankets . . . which had been taken from a military store in Buncrana some time previously'.

Doherty writes a long and detailed account of the frenetic campaign to tempt the British forces into activity and 'consequently keep them on the move'. They travelled astonishing distances across mountains in order to raid the houses of unionists who would not know them. Doherty records what must have been a rare experience for him: encountering a sympathetic British army officer:

We next proceeded to the home of Colonel McNeece. On knocking on the door and announcing that we were members of the IRA, we were immediately admitted by the Colonel, who treated us very courteously, invited us to partake of some refreshments and discussed the political situation in Ireland. On being informed of the reason for our visit, he handed over a shotgun and cartridges and a very good telescope.

But this kind of encounter was rare indeed, not only in Donegal but in all the counties in the northern part of the island. Francis Connell from Tanderagee, Bailieboro, County Cavan, who was active with the local

Brigade at the time, reflects the experience of the other areas in 1920–21, where the intertwined nature of the population added its own complications:

> Enemy activity at this time increased considerably. The homes of officers and men of the Battalion were being raided day and night, with the result that few of us could sleep at home. We in turn raided the homes of both Protestant and Catholic parents whose sons had joined, or were about to join, the Ulster Specials. We told their parents that drastic action would be taken against them if their sons did not resign, or if they did not prevail on their boys not to join the enemy forces.

Many of the witness statements provide a table of contents like that of Nicholas Smyth, a member of the Irish Volunteers in County Tyrone, who was living in Dollymount Strand when he submitted his statement to the Bureau of Military History. But whether there is a table of contents or not, the sequence of events is the same, and generally ends with the Truce. Some, like Peadar de Barra from Corroga, Newry, have 'nothing much to report. The weather that summer was particularly warm, with long hours of bright sunshine.'

17

THE TRUCE IN THE NORTHERN CONTEXT

Not all the Northern statements end with the Truce for, if truth be told, the truce in the North was short-lived. James Short from County Armagh remembers the Truce period as one of training, drilling and other military exercises. He attended training camps at Killeavey, County Armagh. He remembers:

> None of our men was on the run during the period from July 1921 until May 1922. The 'B' and 'C' Special Constabulary were carrying on their usual procedure of patrols etc., with which we did not interfere, and they on their part did not annoy us in any way.

Nicholas Smyth also went to a training camp as soon as the Truce was declared. His camp was at Glenally in the Sperrin Mountains. The training was designed to filter down through the ranks as thoroughly as possible. Smyth writes:

> The first course given in the camp was for divisional Brigade officers. The next course which I attended was for Battalion officers. A later course was held at which all Company officers attended. . . . After our period of about two weeks in the training camps, we returned to our area and started training camps for the Company officers in the Battalion.

His namesake James J. Smyth, who had been Battalion Adjutant of the Lisnaskea Battalion, remembered with the other joint authors of the statement that the recruiting and training was stepped up with the coming of the Truce. The Fermanagh Brigade had their training camp at Carrigallen in Leitrim; the Tempo Battalion had theirs in Brochair Mountains outside Tempo. According to this statement, the Fermanagh

Brigade continued to drill and arm up to the signing of the Treaty. Towards the end of the statement, the authors record:

> Hostilities were resumed on the occasion of the cross-border raid early in February 1922. This raid developed into a series of fights, one at Carson's of Killyreagh, one at Cooper's and Elliot's of Enniskillen, and a final one at Belcoo. After this, Fermanagh was a hotbed. . . . In April 1922, the Volunteers in Blacklion Barracks captured Belcoo Barracks. After this came the round-up in May 1922.

John Connolly remembered that there was little activity 'during the first six months of the Truce period except training and drilling'. He goes on to describe an incident which reflected some of the tension in the area:

> About mid-January 1922 a number of 5th Northern Division officers [IRA] were travelling through Northern Ireland to take part in a Gaelic football match in Derry when they were held up and searched by Special Constabulary at Dromore, County Tyrone. Arms were found on some of the officers and they were detained as prisoners. When demands for their release were ignored, we received orders to kidnap a number of unionists from Six County territory and hold them as hostages.

Connolly duly went on to capture a policeman

> in a house outside Roslea village where he was visiting a girl. . . . the poor fellow was so scared that I purchased a half-pint of whiskey for him in Scotstown and I gave it to him.

Nicholas Smyth describes the football incident in considerably more detail:

> This capture of the Monaghan officers by the Special Constabulary caused a succession of events which was very much discussed at the time. A demand was made for the release of the Monaghan officers by General Eoin O'Duffy. This demand was ignored and the 5th Northern Division, under O'Duffy's orders, made an invasion of the County Tyrone and County Fermanagh areas and arrested a large number of prominent unionists who were held as hostages to be bartered for the release of the officers arrested at Dromore. After a great deal of negotiations the Monaghan officers were released and later the unionist prisoners were also released.

It was after this episode, Nicholas Smyth holds, that the Northern police became most aggressive.

The witnesses John Shields and James Short both refer to a plan the IRA had made to attack the British forces in the North of Ireland. Short refers to a Column

> organised to take part in the general attack on the British forces in the Six Counties area which was to have received the support of both sections of the IRA in Southern Ireland, who had split on the question of the acceptance or otherwise of the Treaty.

John Shields records some corroborative evidence. He writes:

> In the spring of 1922 we got a consignment of rifles from Dundalk military barracks. This consignment of rifles, other weapons and equipment, together with a large quantity of ammunition, was intended to equip the local Volunteers to take part in a general attack on British forces then occupying Northern Ireland – the six north-eastern counties. If we got any information about this planned attack, it is very vague in my mind at the moment. All our activities about the time that these arms were handed over to us pointed to an early intention to stage an all-out attack on British forces in the North on a large scale.

Connolly noticed that the Northern Government started to 'consolidate their position within the Six County area' in early 1922:

> Heavy lorry patrols of military and police were sent on all the country roads. B Specials commenced to carry out patrols in all local areas; a system of halting and questioning people going about their own business was introduced and government forces, both police and military, commenced to put up defences on all roads crossing the frontiers into Southern Ireland roads; bridges were being destroyed on the border line between County Fermanagh and County Monaghan. As it appeared to us that the British authorities in the North were preparing for a period of complete isolation which would prevent all access to and from Southern Ireland, we commenced a campaign of activities to prevent the cutting of road communication.

At this stage, Connolly and his Company was operating from a base in County Monaghan. He informs us that he and his comrades were supplied with ammunition from Clones barracks. He records:

167

We had to use the arms, rifles, etc. belonging to the pre-Truce IRA, as the authorities in Clones barracks would not give us rifles which were handed over by the British military when they were preparing to evacuate Southern Ireland. It was not considered good policy at this time to risk the capture of such arms by Northern Government forces.

There had been round-ups before the Truce in the Northern area. Peadar de Barra, a Brigade staff officer based in Newry, County Down, describes one of these:

A large force of police estimated at five hundred men moved into Corroga Company district and raided every house in the area. Several houses were raided on that day more than once. Every man, woman and child in the area was questioned.

But the round-up described by Shields, which happened on 22 May 1922, was widespread across the Northern Province in the six counties:

On the 22nd May 1922 [there was] a sudden large-scale swoop by the British forces from all their barracks and strong points in the Six County area in order to round up and capture all active members of the Irish Republican Army and their Sinn Féin supporters.

It was in this swoop that Shields himself was once again taken prisoner. Short's memory of the period is similar to that of Shields. He writes:

About May 1922, a Column was organised to take part in the general attack on the British forces in the Six Counties area which was to have received the support of both sections of the IRA in Southern Ireland, who had split on the question of the acceptance or otherwise of the Treaty. The plans made for this rising in the North were to operate as from the 19th May 1922. On the eve of this date the plans for the rising were cancelled by our Divisional OC, Frank Aiken. As the rising took place in a few isolated areas due to conflicting orders or the non-arrival of the cancellation orders, fighting started in County Antrim, North Down and County Derry. The Northern Government apparently got to know about the rising plans and they made a general round-up of all known IRA [members] all over the Six Counties area.

Short managed to escape into County Monaghan, with a number of others. He tells us:

We moved across into County Monaghan and took possession of Colonel Lucas's residence and out-offices at Castleshane, where we established a military post and engaged in an intensive programme of military training.

About a month after Short took over Castleshane, 'the Civil War broke out in Southern Ireland'. According to Short, the effects of the Civil War were disastrous for the republicans in the Northern counties:

> The Northern government were not slow to realise the weakening effect the Civil War had on the position of the IRA within the area, and they applied the pressure: raids and arrests were the order of the day. In areas where there were unionist majorities, the 'B' and 'C' Specials took complete control and instituted a reign of terror for republicans, to which we had no answer.

So ended Short's witness statement.

John McCoy, who had served as Adjutant under Frank Aiken, OC of the 4th Northern Division, remembered 'a number of wounded men [who] passed on through our area and sent for hospital treatment in Dublin'. He recollects:

> Many of the active IRA men from unionist areas were forced to evacuate their areas and come into the Free State . . . . At the end of May and early June, 1922, there must have been four hundred IRA men accommodated from Northern areas. About the same time there were so many nationalist civilian evacuees from Northern areas in Dundalk that several large vacant houses had to be used to try and accommodate them. . . . All the border towns in the twenty-six counties were packed with refugees. . . . It was estimated that about twenty-six to thirty thousand people had evacuated from Northern Ireland during the period March to June 1922.

Not all the Northern Volunteers continued the fight after the Truce. For example, Michael Sheerin, who had begun as a member of the Irish Volunteers in Tyrone, later joined the Irish Volunteers in Derry, and finished as a member of the Flying Column in County Donegal, went to Glenasmole Camp in the Dublin mountains. There he finished his course, but immediately afterwards secured a job as a wholetime paid official [in command] of the Civil Administration of the South Donegal District. . . . When the Treaty was signed I was just one of the many displaced persons of the period. The struggle was over. We were not the victors, and the struggle for an existence commenced. In December 1922, I joined the Free State army with the rank of Captain.

In contrast, Jack Shields's only regret at the end of his statement was the fact that he had been forced to spend so much of his time since 1916 'in prisons and internment camps. I feel that had I been at liberty during the time I was locked up, I could have done more to help in the fight for freedom'.

Shortly after his capture in the big round-up in May 1922, he and his fellow prisoners were taken to the *Argenta*, a steamship which was moored in Belfast Lough. In the *Argenta*, all the under-deck space had been converted into iron cages for the accommodation of prisoners. Shields writes: 'In my cage, which was known as "P2", forty-five men were accommodated. This was an average-sized cage.' The prisoners were guarded by the Special Constabulary. 'The vessel, in the position in which it was moored, was in constant danger night and day of being rammed by other shipping passing in and out to the Port of Belfast.' Shields goes on to describe conditions on the ship further:

> The under-deck conditions in the cages were so congested, and we were so crowded into such a small space, that there was not room for either chairs, tables or lockers. . . . We had to sleep in swing hammocks, one hammock suspended over another. Our food had to be taken sitting on the floor of the cage, which could not accommodate all the prisoners, or sitting in our hammocks. . . . The sanitary arrangements on the *Argenta* were most primitive. An open latrine was constructed . . . at the end of the cages.

The prisoners, including Shields, were outraged 'that no provision had been made for a chapel to celebrate Mass in'. In addition to the deprivations and insults inflicted by their captors, fights began to break out amongst the prisoners regarding the rights and wrongs of the Treaty.

Eventually, Shields was moved to Larne Workhouse. He describes the truly deplorable conditions of the workshouse – conditions that Shields and 'the staunchest republicans' endured. They set about making a tunnel. This was a long business, and all the remaining prisoners had been released before it was finished. Shields found it almost unbearable to witness the effect of imprisonment on republican prisoners and their families. He tells us the story of one such family. The man in question came from a small Tyrone town where his family had lived for generations. When he was arrested and imprisoned, he left his wife and family with no support. Worse still, a boycott of the family was initiated by the unionist section of the population, who represented about 55 percent of the people of the town:

> The attitude of the local unionists was bad enough. But later when the nationalist population became cowed and dispirited by the activities of the Special Constabulary in raiding their houses, threatening them, and halting them and questioning them when engaged in the ordinary everyday work . . . the nationalists, in order to curry favour with their Orange neighbours, started to copy the Orange section by boycotting this unfortunate wife and family as well.

The last straw was when the 'local Catholic clergyman' began to treat the woman and her family as outcasts. She came to see her husband. Shields saw this man as he returned from his wife's visit:

> I never saw such a change in any man in such a short period. . . . He gave me an outline of what his wife and family had gone through and then he exclaimed 'I have had to sign the form (promising good future behaviour) . . . I have renounced all I have fought and suffered for; I have eaten dirt.'

Nicholas Smyth had left the Tyrone area before the big round-up in May:

> [The IRA] were hard-pressed at the time and lost by capture a good lot of officers and men, including our brigadier, Mick Gallagher. . . . To make an estimate I should say that about 50 percent of our officers and men were captured.

Smyth and his comrades decided to 'make their way to Pettigo', he records:

> This was about the month of April 1922. The idea behind our evacuation of the North was to get properly organised, armed, trained and equipped with things which we needed badly, and return again to

171

Northern Ireland to carry on the fight as long as it was possible to do so. Pettigo lies on the border between Fermanagh and Donegal.

He and about forty other IRA men from the six-county area took over an old barracks in the town and settled down to wait. Smyth remembers that 'there was an air of expectancy about the place, and one felt that anything could happen'.

By the end of May, they were joined by other IRA men, bringing the number up to something short of a hundred. Against 'overwhelming numbers of British forces', they lasted a little more than a week. The story of this last stand is told in a witness statement prepared by John Travers (a member of the IRA in Fermanagh and Donegal in 1921) and four others, including Nicholas Smyth. Between them they remembered the details of the eight days from 27 May to 4 June 1922. The five men were anxious to give their account and record the following:

> [We were] active participants as members of the IRA Volunteer force in the events described. We have checked over the various versions which each of us remembered, and we have discussed and checked the statement with others who also took part. We are all satisfied that this document is as accurate as we can make it.

The statement is signed by all five men. It reads as follows:

> [It] began on Saturday, May 27, 1922. On that day, a hundred Specials crossed Lough Erne in a pleasure steamer called *The Lady of the Lake*, towing a number of small boats, and landed above Belleek. They marched to Magherameena Castle, the residence of the late Reverend L. O'Kierans, then PP of Pettigo, and ordered [him] to leave immediately, which he did. A party of thirty IRA Volunteers advanced down the railway line towards Magherameena Castle. On their way there they were intercepted by a patrol of Specials, who engaged them and then retreated to Magherameena Castle, pursued by the the IRA Volunteers. The Specials then abandoned the castle for good, retreated to their boats on the Lough Erne and withdrew to the Buck Island in Lough Erne, where they were reinforced by another hundred Specials with medical attendants who treated their wounded. The Volunteers had suffered but a few minor injuries.
>
> On Sunday 28 May, a number of [Specials in] Crossley tenders accompanied by an armoured car left Enniskillen to assist their comrades at Magherameena Castle, but they were intercepted as they

crossed into Donegal at Belleek by the IRA Volunteers. After a short but sharp engagement, in which the driver of the armoured car was killed, [the occupants of the car] retreated, leaving the Crossleys and armoured car, which were taken possession of by the Volunteers.

That evening, the IRA Volunteers in Pettigo got information that large contingents of A and B Specials were converging on Pettigo. The Volunteers blocked the bridges at Pettigo between Donegal and Fermanagh and took up defensive positions. That night, a substantial contingent of Specials advanced from their headquarters at Clonally, County Fermanagh, to Pettigo. They then opened fire on Pettigo with a view to obtaining a right-of- way through it to their beleaguered men on the Buck Island in Lough Erne. The Volunteers returned fire and, after a two-hour engagement, the Specials retreated to their convoy of Crossleys. Then on Sunday night, they attempted an outflanking movement with the aim of reaching their comrades on the Buck Island through Lowry. They would have to cross a narrow isthmus of Donegal territory, known as the Waterfoot, which juts out into Lough Erne between Letter and Lowry, both of which are situated in County Fermanagh. A section of the IRA Volunteers were sent to this isthmus on Monday morning, 29 May, where they entrenched themselves and prevented the Specials from crossing it. From then until Thursday 1 June, the Specials contented themselves with sporadic firing into the tower from the surrounding country-side.

On 1 June, a number of lorry-loads of British soldiers, followed by four Crossley-loads of Specials, advanced on the town of Pettigo. The Specials opened fire with rifles and machine guns on the IRA Volunteer outposts stationed on Drumharrif hill and at Pettigo railway station. The IRA returned fire, and then the British soldiers joined in with rifles and machine guns. This engagement lasted an hour and a half, during which a number of British soldiers were killed and others wounded. They then retreated. During Thursday and Friday nights, there was intensive sniping at Pettigo by Specials, who were now reinforced from Belfast. During Friday 2 June and Saturday 3 June, the British commandeered all the boats on Lough Erne and assembled them at Portonode. They used the boats to transport a Battalion of British soldiers across the Lough to Boa Island. The soldiers were marched through the island and from there were transported in the boats to [the village of] Letter, which is two miles below Pettigo.

In the meantime, another Battalion of British soldiers had advanced from Kesh to Lowry, with a view to joining the Battalion at Letter. This would entail them crossing the isthmus at the Waterfoot, but the IRA

Volunteer outpost, which had been in place since Monday, was determined to prevent this from happening. Throughout Saturday night, both Battalions of British soldiers made repeated attacks on the IRA Volunteers at the Waterfoot in the hope of dislodging them, but they failed to do so. During the intense fighting, a section of the IRA Volunteers crept from Pettigo, a distance of a mile, to assist their comrades at the Waterfoot.

During the week, a large party of Specials had gone into Donegal through Letteran, which is five miles from Pettigo, and had terrorised the people. Among other things, they shot and seriously wounded two girls. Now on the night of Saturday 3 June, the party of almost two hundred Specials tried to cross at Letteran from Fermanagh into Donegal, so as to attack Pettigo from the rear. A party of IRA Volunteers, foreseeing their intentions, intercepted them there and, after a fierce engagement, put them to flight, burdened with their dead and wounded.

The third engagement of this eventful night took place in Pettigo town. Two British Battalions tried in vain to take the town. Then on the morning of Sunday 4 June, a fleet of armoured cars and infantry again attacked the town, but the driver of the leading armoured was shot dead through the head, and the car overturned and blocked the road. Fire from the Volunteers prevented the British from clearing the way for some time. At this stage, a battery of howitzers artillery was brought into action by the British. Under this artillery fire, the unit of Volunteers covering the bridge was forced to withdraw to new positions, and the British then cleared the obstructing car and the barricade at the bridge and advanced into the town.

As this main thrust was being made, two other Columns of British troops, one which had been stationed at Letter and another from the right by Lough Derg road, attempted to join forces so as to encircle the town. Fire from the Volunteers on each flank kept them at bay and left the escape route open to the main body of the Volunteers, who withdrew to the hills and kept up a running fire until 5 PM, when they retreated to Donegal town. The machine-gun post of about eight Volunteers, which manned Drumhariff Hill covering the approach to the town, held their position until their ammunition was exhausted, and then the post was surrounded and captured. Three of the gallant defenders, Patrick Flood of Pettigo, and Bernard McCanny and William Kearney of Drumquin, were killed at their post.

While the fighting was taking place in Pettigo town, the post which manned the Waterfoot was heavily engaged by vastly superior numbers of British forces and was forced to surrender after two hours. Thus ended the Battle of Pettigo, a battle that is unique in the War of Independence in two respects: it is the only place where there was a stand-up fight with a defined battle line, and the only place in Ireland where artillery was used against the IRA.

So ends, too, the statement put together by the five IRA men and signed by them on 24 July 1952.

18

CONFLICTING LOYALTIES

Nowhere in Ireland were the complexities and inter-relationships engendered by the British historical presence on the island more evident than in the British army, particularly in 1920. The War of Independence stretched the British army, which at the time was also engaged in holding India.

John Flannery, of 2B Thomas Court, Thomas Street, Dublin, in the course of a detailed account of the Mutiny of the Connaught Rangers in India, indicates the complications of a mutiny for the imperial garrison. He records:

> Shortly after the men's leader had given the order to cease handing in the arms, a major of the Battalion came over to the RATA rooms, where a large body of men had assembled. He proceeded to address them . . . pointing out that there was a large supply of rifles and ammunition in the guardroom, and that it was necessary for the men's safety to have an armed guard placed over them. If the natives became aware that the guardroom and magazine were unprotected, he added, they would lose no time in attempting to secure their contents, and if such an attempt were successful, the natives would use the arms thus obtained to murder every European in the cantonment. When the officer had concluded, the men's leader assured him he had nothing to worry about as far as the arms and the safety of Europeans were concerned, as he had made the necessary plans to deal with any such attempt.

Joseph Hawes, who lived in Kilrush, County Clare, at the time he wrote his statement for the Bureau, remembered clearly how the men discussed events at home as they sat around a table in the canteen:

> I told them about a hurling match I had seen proclaimed by the British forces at the point of the bayonet, all assemblies being proclaimed

[banned] in Clare at the time. Some of the others spoke about what they saw in Irish papers and letters from home. During the discussion, I put up the point that we were doing in India what the British forces were doing in Ireland.

We are indebted to Flannery for a short history of the Connaught Rangers. They were, it seems, originally recruited in 1795, three years before another Irish Rebellion. Since their formation, they had fought against the Spanish in South America, and later against the Spanish and French armies on the Iberian Peninsula, after which they left for Canada, still in the service of the Empire. They fought in the Crimean War in the 1860s and, at the end of the century, against the Boers in South Africa. Naturally, they also took part in the Great War. Flannery writes:

> They formed part of the first British Expeditionary Force which land-ed in France. For their part in that war they were awarded thirty-seven place-names on their colours, which now lie in Windsor Castle.

On 24 November 1919, they were transferred to Wellington Barracks in Jullundur, Punjab. Jullunder was about three days' rail journey from the nearest seaport. Like many other events, the Mutiny of the Connaught Rangers began with the actions of one man. Farrelly records:

> On the 25 June 1920, about 2 PM, Private Dawson went to the Battalion guardroom and asked to be placed under arrest, giving as his reason to the guard commander that he was in sympathy with his country in its fight for freedom, and that he was taking this as a protest against the atrocious deeds committed on the people of Ireland by the Black and Tans. He concluded by stating that he was finished soldiering for England.

There was an immediate attempt made to cover up the incident, as though, even at this early stage, the authorities suspected that Dawson's stand might be contagious. His Sergeant-Major suggested 'that the man was suffering from the after-effects of slight sunstroke'.

But next morning, there were four more soldiers who 'made it very clear that they were finished soldiering for England, having just had twelve years' service with the colours'. Flannery remembers the scene:

> News of the action of the four men went round the barracks like wildfire. Small groups of excited men could be seen standing in every

177

direction, others were running here, there and everywhere, just like a swarm of bees that had been disturbed. The NCO thought the matter over very carefully.

The non-commissioned officer came to the conclusion that the four 'must be backed up by every Irishman in the Battalion who loved his country'. His preferred method of resistance was the passive method, but 'it was necessary that we should be prepared. . . . We would not lie down under blows while we were in a position to hit back.'

The NCO felt that it was vital to organise the campaign of passive resistance immediately

> if their four comrades in the guardroom were to be spared from the wrath of the authorities, who would deal very severely with them now that they were aware of the discontent in the Battalion.

It was a massive undertaking. In all, there were about eight hundred men; three hundred of these were up in the Simla Hills, 'as it was summer-time'. The remaining five hundred stayed at Jullundur. Flannery outlines the details of the campaign. The men who led the mutiny had no difficulty in persuading detachment after detachment to follow the pattern that had been established. Their officers did their best to persuade them to continue to carry out their duties. As Flannery records, when one of the Companies repaired to the guardroom and

> refused point-blank to come out, the Colonel then pointed out the seriousness of their behaviour and advised them to let the matter drop. Their action would not change the policy of the British government in Ireland; the only effect it would have would be punishment for themselves. But the men still refused to leave the guardroom.

Step by step, the leaders continued their campaign of passive resistance, keeping a careful check on any individuals 'who tried in any way to urge men of the Battalion to commit any act contrary to the policy of passive resistance'. Other meetings were held with the Colonel. Deputations were formed, and were invited to discuss the reasons for their actions. The culmination of this process was a meeting with the GOC of the Jullundur Brigade at the same time as five hundred men were on parade. The soldiers' spokesman put their concerns:

Turning around, he then addressed the general, and pointed out that the vast majority of the men on parade were men who had enlisted under the impression that they were going to fight for the liberty and rights of Small Nations, their own included. He put it to the general if it was a fitting reward for the sacrifices that thousands of Irishmen had made on many fronts throughout the Great War, and to these men on parade who came through that great ordeal, to return home and learn that their own fellow-countrymen and women were being shot down by orders of the British government. . . . He concluded his address by pointing out that the mothers and sisters of his comrades were being outraged by the Black and Tans, and asked him how could he expect the Rangers to remain loyal in the face of what was happening in Ireland.

The General remained silent in the face of this argument: 'He just heaved a sigh and asked their leader if he would give a promise that the Rangers would behave themselves.'

But of course the Rangers soldiers could not win, however magnificent their gestures of defiance. By 11 July, the authorities had by one means or another managed to place the ringleaders under close arrest: they were able to make one last effort to 'win the Rangers back to loyalty and they were successful'. Every man would be offered a free pardon

if he would become loyal once more to his Majesty, the King, and to the Colonel and officers of the regiment. . . . The officer gave the order that any man could do so by falling in on his own Company marker. There was a pause of a few seconds. . . . They commenced to fall in on their Company markers in sixes and sevens until the whole body did likewise. All became loyal.

The mutiny was over. The total number of men under arrest as ringleaders came to ninety. Forty-two of these came from their summer station in the Simla Hills. The authorities had found it much easier to deal with that section of the Rangers who were stationed in Solon. Two emissaries who had gone up to contact the Solon detachment had been arrested. At this point, Private J. J. Daly took command of about seventy men, marched them to the Officers' Mess, and 'there informed Captain Badham that they would not soldier further until the English dogs had been removed from Ireland'. The Solon mutineers attacked the magazine, and they were shot at point-blank range, with two of them being killed. 'Every man who could be identified as taking part in the mutiny was placed under arrest.'

When the mutiny was over, the prisoners were court-martialled and, although Daly was not the only one to be condemned to death, he was the only one to be executed. The others had their sentences commuted to imprisonment for life.

At daybreak on the morning of 2 November, Daly faced the firing squad. A detailed and heart-rending account of his execution was given to Lance Corporal Flannery by the Reverend T. B. Baker, who attended Daly in his last moments. Flannery duly included the account in his statement. The last of the Rangers prisoners were released on 9 January 1923.

Maurice Meade, who finished his busy military career as a member of the National Army, had begun by joining the British army in 1911. In his witness statement, he makes it clear that he had no interest in the national movement. He writes: 'Any private thoughts I had were given up to the hope of gaining my own independence.'

He had already begun to think of joining the British army when he went to Cork to visit his sister. He describes his first contact with the army:

> I saw a recruiting sergeant with red, white and blue ribbons flying from his cap. I was admiring this recruiting sergeant when this fine fellow came over to me and said, 'I say, young man, why don't you join the British army?' 'Begorrah, sir,' said I, 'I was just thinking of doing that!'

Meade was so impressed by the sergeant and his uniform that he was immediately hooked on the idea of joining up and, despite the best efforts of his sister, succeeded in formally joining the British army. Meade liked army life, particularly when he was transferred to the Channel Islands. He had a few shillings in his pocket and the opportunity to develop his talent for cross-country running.

When the First World War broke out in 1914, Meade was a member of the first Expeditionary Force to land in France. The Force made its way to Mons, where Meade, with many others, was taken prisoner. Meade suffered terribly as a prisoner, mainly from the hunger. He describes conditions:

> Our rations at the camp were very skimpy. Each man got a small loaf of bread which was supposed to last him for seven days. In addition to

that, we got a basin of black coffee morning and evening, and at mid-day a basin of soup which seemed to have been made from anything that came handy, because we used get pieces of rabbit skin and even horse hide mixed up in it from time to time.

Some of the punishments inflicted on the prisoners amounted to torture. According to Meade:

> For instance for anyone caught smoking, (the punishment) was to have our hands tied to a line above our heads so that we had to stand with arms stretched upwards for at least a couple of hours.

In mid-December 1915, all the Irish prisoners were transferred to a new camp at Limburg. There they were much better treated: 'We got extra underclothes and extra food and were generally made to feel comfortable.' They were gradually introduced to the idea of the formation of Casement's Irish Brigade. When they were shown the new uniform that had been specially designed for the Irish Brigade, Meade thought:

> It was a lovely uniform and looked very well. I wore such a uniform myself later and I also went to Berlin, where we were presented to the Kaiser, who came round and shook hands with each one of us.

As it turned out, Casement decided against taking the Brigade to Ireland, as it was too small. He advised the small band of Irishmen to join the German army instead, as a means of taking part in Ireland's fight for freedom. Only Meade took his advice: he joined the 203rd Regiment in Berlin and served six months against the British forces in Egypt.

Before the war ended in 1918, Meade was released from his regiment. He started to do very well in the business of buying and selling for a Berlin firm. He traded coffee with the local population and was generally having a very pleasant time, occasionally dressing up in his Casement Brigade uniform.

One evening, there was a tap on his shoulder: a British officer had found him. After three days, he and another Casement Brigade prisoner were lodged in the Tower of London to await court martial. They were tried for high treason, convicted, and sentenced to death.

Amazingly, Meade's luck held. He was given the King's pardon and returned home to Elton in County Limerick, where he was arrested again and handed over to military custody at Clonmel. He subsequently escaped from the detention barracks. The IRA had just then formed the East Limerick Flying Column, which might have been designed specially for Meade. The officer in command was Sean Forde – or Tomas Malone, to give him his real name. A man of courage and initiative, he was just the kind of officer to whom Meade could be completely loyal.

19

MEATH AND NORTH DUBLIN

The high point of IRA activity in County Meath up to 1920 must surely have been the capture of the RIC barracks at Trim. The occupation of the barracks, on the last Sunday of September of that year, was a spectacular achievement. Seamus Finn, Adjutant of the Meath Brigade, describes the edifice as follows:

> The barracks, a miniature fortress of stone walls and barred windows, stood in the centre of a plot of ground two acres in extent on the south side of the Fair Green which opened on two sides of it. Facing to the east it stood a hundred and fifty yards back from the Summerhill Road and was surrounded by a wall fifteen feet high. Strong iron gates barred the approach.

One member of the Trim police was heard to boast that the barracks was impregnable. This, more than anything, made the Meath Brigade determined to attack the stronghold. The operation required meticulous planning by the Brigade officers and the co-operation of the various Battalions. As Finn, the Adjutant, put it: 'Our plans worked like magic.' The IRA captured the barracks 'thanks entirely to the elaborate planning of the Brigade and local officers in conjunction with the information given by our contacts among the RIC'.

As we saw in Chapter Eleven, without the help of sympathetic members of the RIC the capture of the Trim stronghold could not have happened. Nevertheless, it was an important morale-booster for the IRA, particularly in Meath and the surrounding counties, and was an achievement not to be easily repeated.

The capture of the stronghold led indirectly to the resignation of Brigadier General Crozier, who had been placed in command of the Auxiliaries when they were established to help the RIC in Ireland. Seamus

Finn holds that Crozier 'resigned his command following the looting and burning of Chandler's public house in the hamlet of Robinstown' by the garrison of Auxiliaries and Black and Tans posted at Trim.

There is a hint of frustration in witness statements submitted by some of the Meath men. For example, Charles Conaty, who had been OC, 2nd Battalion, No. 3 Brigade, describes their long-drawn-out attempts at an attack on the RIC barracks at Oldcastle – the last one planned for 'the fair day in February 1921'. Conaty relates:

> Before the fair day Paddy McDonnell called us together and questioned each one in turn as to whether we had told anyone of our proposed attack. No one admitted having mentioned the matter to anybody. He told us that the RIC in Oldcastle knew of the time and date of our proposed attack. We had to call it off once again.

By the time the witness statements were being recorded, David Hall had a clearer view of Meath's role in the War of Independence. Hall, from Garristown, County Dublin, had noticed that

> any attempt that was made to do anything in the Dunboyne area was always cancelled by Brigade orders, and it took some time before it became apparent to us that the Brigade staff, who had their headquarters there, were determined to keep it a quiet area.

Hall points out that Dunboyne was the

> clearing house for all despatches to and from the north and north-west of Ireland. Likewise, arms and explosives and all types of small equipment were being passed through Dunboyne. . . . Our men were continually handling this sort of material and passing it along. This often entailed long journeys by cycle at night.

In the spring of 1921, the IRA in County Meath and the surrounding counties underwent a new and final reorganisation: the 1st Eastern Division was formed, with Sean Boylan as Divisional Commander. The men of Meath became close partners of the IRA in north County Dublin, particularly in the Fingal Brigade, and together they attempted one of the most audacious operations of the whole war. The plan was to attack the troop train carrying soldiers back to the Curragh from Belfast, where they had been drafted on the opening of the Northern Ireland Parliament by King George V.

The Fingal Battalion had some months of intensive training before the event. The training was given by Paddy Mooney, who had played an important part in the capture of Trim barracks. John Gaynor, Captain of the Balbriggan Volunteers, who lived at St Peter's Terrace in Balbriggan at the time he made his witness statement, describes the domestic arrangements of the Fingal Battalion:

> We were billeted in a hay barn at Smith's on the Oldtown–Dublin road near Oldtown. We got our food supplies from Taylors of Swords, which was delivered by their van to one of the local houses, where we picked it up. It was cooked for us in Smith's kitchen.

The food supply was augmented from time to time by the commandeering of an odd sheep. In his statement, Hall tells us that 'it was mostly from Mr Delaney of Portrane we took the sheep. . . . We always took the sheep at night, and the following morning gave a receipt for the animals.'

Gaynor marvelled at the people of Oldtown. He writes:

> It was a remarkable thing. . . . The British military or Tans in Swords were never aware of our whereabouts. The people of Oldtown area certainly knew how to keep their mouths shut.

This was indeed remarkable, considering that the unit was responsible for the burning of the coastguard stations along the east coast between Dublin and Drogheda. Gaynor relates that, in the course of the preparation for the burning:

> we gave the occupants the opportunity of saving any articles from the houses that they required. . . . they were not very interested in doing so. They informed us that they would be compensated adequately for what they lost. One man asked us to save his piano. . . . he would not be compensated for that.

Gaynor goes on to give a clear account of the attack on the troop train. But Commandant Matthew Barry, from Killsallaghan, County Meath, devotes his whole statement to an account of the attempt.

Matthew Barry, who was the Vice-Commandant of the 2nd Battalion of the 2nd Meath Brigade, arrived home 'shortly after dawn' on 30 June after a Battalion meeting:

I did not go to bed but immediately harnessed a pair of horses to a mowing machine and proceeded to mow three acres of meadow. I wanted to have this ready for making up when I returned, if ever I did so.

On 1 July, he assembled his men on their bicycles, and in the early afternoon they set out for Dunboyne. They were intercepted and guided along the byroads to a field near the Summerhill–Dunboyne road, where they remained for some hours. 'We seemed to be nobody's concern', he says, but, towards dusk, 'the Fingal Flying Column came into the field where we were. They walked through a thick thorn hedge just as if it did not exist.' He continued to be impressed by everything about the Fingal men, from their clothes to their bandoliers and Lee Enfield rifles. They were older than Barry and his group, 'who looked like mere boys'. They were brought across the road into a house, where they were provided with a meal. A priest heard their confession before they were paraded in two ranks, still 'with no idea of what they were heading for'.

They set off across country. Men slid into ditches or got caught in barbed wire as they tried to keep contact with each other. Eventually, they got on the road again 'and moved forward at a nice marching pace. . . . Everyone wanted to know where we were going. We had no sense of direction by now.' Someone thought that they were to go to Cork and were expected to jump a train travelling in that direction. At first, Barry thought of the meadow which he had left behind him, but after some hours had elapsed:

> the preservation of my skin seemed to be all that mattered. We tramped along the roads for what seemed endless miles. This was my third day and second night without sleep and, in addition, I must have cycled well over fifty miles.

On they tramped until, turning right off the main road, they found themselves 'in the yard of a not-too-big gentleman's residence'. At last they were told to get some rest. But instead, as Barry relates: 'As we entered the house, we could hear someone thumping a piano.' All thought of sleep abandoned, they joined a party instead.

It turned out that the house belonged to the Wardell family, who had been locked up in the harness room when the IRA commandeered their home some hours before. The house was situated alongside the main railway line to Cork. This proved to be the undoing of the whole operation.

As Barry writes towards the end of his statement:

> Although men were warned not to expose themselves, they were walk-
> ing around the yard with rifles slung on their shoulders. Some of the
> city-going trains were bound to have British officers, agents or sympa-
> thisers on them.

Obviously, the British authorities knew all about the operation early
on. The IRA, Barry amongst them, knew nothing of this, and the operation proceeded as planned. Barry writes:

> We swung out of the yard and along the carriage-way with Clinton in
> command, marching to the left rear of me about five or six paces
> behind. We had almost reached the outer yard or middle gate when I
> was amazed to see a British army lorry stop on the road at the outer gate
> and five or six soldiers jumped from it and ran through the gate in our
> direction.

Now the question for the IRA was how to escape. But first, they had
to make a stand against the British attack. Barry describes the gunfight in
extraordinary detail. Suffice it to say that he got away from the house
alive. He began crossing the fields again: he went through hay fields and
wheat fields, where he found some of his comrades. He describes a new
danger: 'Now an aeroplane, which had flown low down along the railway
line a few minutes previously, began to annoy us.'

John Gaynor too was annoyed by the plane. He writes:

> The aircraft apparently was not armed, as he made no attempt to fire on
> us and contented himself with diving down at us occasionally. He was
> probably indicating our whereabouts to his own side.

Gaynor and his colleagues succeeded in reaching the woods of the
Celbridge demesne, and the aircraft worried them no more. They continued to Dunboyne, spending the night in the castle. Next day, they reached
their camp at Mooretown. As Gaynor put it, 'We had accomplished an
enormous cross-country hike all for nothing.'

As for Matthew Barry, he too reached Dunboyne after many adventures. They found their bicycles as they had left them, and soon were
speeding for home. Barry remembers: 'strange to say, none of us felt hungry, although our last scant meal had been very early in the morning'.
After a day or so at home, Barry observes:

I was now feeling very refreshed again but unsettled, and I had a feeling that I would like to be behind the sights of a rifle again, and longed for the comradeship of my pals and the excitement of a fight.

Of all the stories from Fingal told to the Bureau of Military History, none is more astonishing than Gaynor's – one of the men who was sent to London to kill Lloyd George, the Prime Minister, and all his Cabinet. Early in 1918, the British government passed a Conscription Act for Ireland through the Parliament in London. It succeeded in uniting almost everybody in Ireland against the Act. Gaynor describes the reaction:

> There now developed a period of terrific activity. Anti-conscription meetings were held everywhere and were attended by huge crowds. The supporters of the Irish National Party and that of Sinn Féin united to oppose. . . . Even some of the Unionists joined in this opposition. Never before was there such unity of purpose in the country.

In April, Gaynor was approached by a Volunteer called Derham about a 'special job'. Derham and Gaynor had started a branch of the Volunteers in Balbriggan together a few years before. Gaynor writes: 'He (Derham) informed me that it would be a very dangerous mission and that the Volunteer Headquarters were finding it very hard to get volunteers for it.'

Gaynor agreed to undertake the mission. He was told to report to Dick Mulcahy, 'who was, I think, then Chief of Staff of the Volunteers'. Gaynor continues:

> Mulcahy informed me that a party of Volunteers under the command of the late Cathal Brugha were going across to London, where they would be joined by some Volunteers who were already resident there. The duty of his party of Volunteers would be to shoot the British Prime Minister and the members of his Cabinet when it was announced in the House of Commons that the King had signed the Conscription Act for Ireland.

It was not immediately clear where the Volunteers were to shoot Lloyd George and his ministers. Mulcahy left Gaynor in no doubt as to the nature of the risk he was taking. 'He gave me to understand that the chances of any of the party of Volunteers surviving subsequent to these executions would be one in a million.' Although he had the option of withdrawing, Gaynor, 'having volunteered . . . was not withdrawing now'. He was nineteen years of age.

A short time later, Gaynor was given his expenses, a date for travelling, and details of the route he would take. It was arranged where he would stay in London and who would be travelling with him. On no account were they to carry guns. The other members of the party were staying in different houses all over the London area.

They met Cathal Brugha at Hampstead Heath. It was important that they did not draw attention to themselves, Gaynor informs us:

> we used to loll around in small groups of two or three at different points and Cathal would come round each group and have a chat and give us the latest information or surmise of what was going to happen. Several times we were stopped by the police and interrogated, but our alibi was always the same – [we were] over in London looking for a job. There were so many Irishmen working in London at this time that this was nothing unusual, and the police were a soft lot and easily fooled. The police there were an extremely nice lot of fellows.

Gaynor found the waiting very stressful. They seldom went out during the day and found their days extremely monotonous. Gaynor remembers: 'you could see some of the lads beginning to look old and haggard under the strain, and I am sure many of them looked years older by the time they got back to Dublin.'

At last, they were each given an assignment by Brugha on Hampstead Heath: 'We were each required to draw a coloured bead from a hat, and each bead indicated the minister or person who was to be shot.' Although it was not finally settled, it looked very much as though Gaynor had drawn Lloyd George. He was told to travel to Wales and make himself 'thoroughly acquainted . . . with the Prime Minister's house there'. Although they were now fully familiar with the exterior of the House of Commons, as well the residence of their particular quarry, there was no definite idea as to how they would do the deed:

> The ideal way would be to shoot them all in the House of Commons. But whereas one or two of us might get into the public gallery in the house, it would not be possible, I think, for a party of fourteen Irishmen with Irish brogues to do so. . . . When we asked about escape plans, we were told it was every man for himself.

By the middle of August, the project was still on. The men were issued with their guns and ordered to hold themselves in readiness 'to strike any evening then'. But the call never came. Gaynor records:

> Lloyd George never made the announcement. The King had refused to sign the Conscription Act.

Gaynor could go home: the job was off for good. On his return to Balbriggan, Gaynor rejoined the local Company of Volunteers and took over the post of Captain.

20

WESTMEATH, LONGFORD, ROSCOMMON

AND THE OFFALY AREA

The testimonies of the many witnesses from all over the country corroborate each other's accounts of public events such as the conscription crisis, the 1918 election and the 'huge amount of work' put in by the Volunteers in ensuring the Sinn Féin victory in that election, as mentioned by Patrick Lennon of Summerhill, Athlone. All describe ambushes and attacks on police barracks, regardless of whether these actions succeeded or not. Most of them outline the organisation of the Volunteers and, in many cases, list the names of the officers. Many, like Patrick Lennon, are more interested in the embryonic development of the new independent State.

Lennon records: 'The Dáil met in January 1919 as the elected government of the Irish Republic, and the new Finance Department floated a loan.' He notes that the Volunteers 'were active in promoting this, by way of canvassing and collecting subscriptions. . . . it was surprising to see how well the people responded to the call.'

Lennon was pleased to record that the newly elected Dáil took over control of the Volunteers. There is a note of satisfaction in his depiction of the handing over of the reins of power:

> The Volunteers now began to act as policemen and to do police work. The RIC were no longer an effective force in this respect as the people had more or less ceased to cooperate with them. They had openly sided with the anti-Sinn Féin side during the election campaign.

Henry O'Brien from Athlone was at one with Lennon in his approval of Sinn Féin policing. He comments:

191

The Volunteers had now to take on the duty of policing the country and maintaining law and order. This they did right well, even in the towns where the RIC were still active.

There were problems for the Volunteers in dealing with prisoners, but both O'Brien and Lennon were happy to record the comparative success of Volunteer policing. Lennon notes:

Prisoners arrested by the Volunteers were kept in unknown destinations. . . . Such prisoners were made to work on the bogs and farms until their charges were disposed of either by the Sinn Féin courts or by Volunteer courts.

As for the Sinn Féin courts, they took the place of the British courts with remarkable ease. As O'Brien puts it: 'The British courts and the RIC, so to speak, were out of employment and were only supported by the few loyalists in the area.' According to Lennon:

Solicitors from Athlone practised in the Sinn Féin courts, including Mr Walker and Mr Hannon. . . . The people abided lawfully by the decisions of the Sinn Féin courts and only on rare occasions had the Volunteers to enforce the findings of the court.

As in other parts of the country, the pace of the war intensified with the coming of the Black and Tans and the Auxiliary forces. O'Brien records the formation of a Flying Column or Active Service Unit, listing their armaments and their billets. After initial training, they planned their first ambush, which was directed at a lorry-load of police on the main Dublin–Athlone road. Despite careful preparation, it was only partially successful. In the course of the fighting, 'two more lorries crowded with police drove up and halted'. O'Brien records: 'We realised quickly that we had hit up against something that we had not bargained for.' There was nothing for it but to retreat. Having commandeered a lorry belonging to Goodbody's of Clara, they drove to the Shannon, 'where they got boats and crossed over to the Roscommon side'. This first meeting with the Tans was a shock for them all, but on reflection they were not too impressed with the fighting qualities of this new force. Moreover, the Tans seemed easily confused. O'Brien notes:

When [the Tans] ran into a bit of trouble they jumped wildly from the lorries and seemed utterly confused and scattered around the place, firing their rifles wildly as they did so. On hearing the firing, a large number of cattle which were in the field stampeded towards the noise, and this, I am sure, added to the Tans' confusion, as they would be mostly town and city men from England.

Lennon had rather more respect for the Auxiliaries, the second force recruited by the British government. He describes them as

tough, stubborn fighters with a flair for acting the blackguard also. They were dressed to terrorise and usually went around with a rifle and bandolier of ammunition and a revolver or two strapped on their legs, and a few hand grenades hanging out of their belts.

At this point, the Volunteers were ordered to destroy communications in order to counteract the activity of the 'enemy forces'. They targeted the bridges, especially on the main roads. Lennon writes:

We destroyed the bridge on the main Athlone–Ballinasloe road at Summerhill. . . . Three or four days later the military and the Tans came out from Athlone, bringing with them a large number of men whom they had commandeered in the town. [They] consisted of bank clerks and businessmen from the town, who were not used to work of this nature.

They were forced to carry out temporary repairs on the bridge.

The people of Athlone were even more outraged by the behaviour of the Tans in the days following the Cornafulla ambush on the Athlone–Ballinasloe road on 2 February 1921. James Tormey, who had once served in the British army, was in charge of the Column. Henry O'Brien describes him as 'a man of fine physique and of a commanding disposition'. In the course of the fighting, Tormey was killed 'as he tried to cover the retreat of his comrades'. Lennon continues:

That night Tormey's body was recovered by the local Volunteers. . . . they took the body down the Shannon to Clonmacnoise cemetery and buried it there. The Tans discovered this somehow and they went to the cemetery and exhumed the remains and brought them to Athlone. Tommy's father identified the remains as those of his son.

Some of the witnesses from the midland counties like Offaly and Roscommon were concerned that their 'major engagements did not shine with the exploits elsewhere'. Patrick Boland, former TD from Ballycumber, Tullamore, County Offaly, and Brigade Police Officer, No. 2 Offaly Brigade, was anxious to remind whoever might read his witness statement that this situation was

> partly because the county was flat country and not suitable for ambushes, and rendezvous were not at all posts available; it was also partly due to the fact that control of arms and munitions were reserved for areas where more favourable circumstances for attacks prevailed. However, I would say that road-blocking day and night did its part to embarrass the enemy.

He went on to emphasise the extraordinary cooperation of 'the civil population who found shelter and food for the IRA' at a time when 'for such assistance the sentence was execution'.

For Thomas Brady, who was the Intelligence Officer in the 2nd Battalion, North Roscommon Brigade, the principal work of the intelligence sections was

> to watch, time and tabulate the operation of enemy patrols and their strength and armament and to watch out and detect civilians who might come under suspicion as enemy agents.

He recounts with some pleasure, one suspects, a particular achievement:

> The girl who is now my wife, Mary Ellen Brady, was then a student at the Grammar School in Elphin. Another girl in the school was doing a line – 'courting' – one of the Tans. The girl got information from her Tan friend that they were going to raid the Killina area. She told my wife about this and she immediately passed on this information to me. I called a meeting of the men of that area and told them not to sleep at home that night, that the place was going to be raided. Some of them, despite my warning, did stay at home and were arrested – I think about six.

Brady remembers that it was not easy to acquire any intelligence from the RIC men stationed in Elphin, but 'Constable Campbell, who was stationed in Strokestown, often gave us some useful tips, but he was not in a position to give us any big information'. He was a particularly useful friend on the day Brady was arrested by Captain Peak of the Lancers –

who were stationed at Strokestown. Brady writes: 'Campbell saved me by telling the Captain that I was not the Brady they were looking for, and I was released.' It is heartening to learn from Brady that 'there were no spies shot in the 2nd Battalion area'. This was not the case in other parts of the county.

Sergeant T. Crawley, who was Vice-Commandant of the 1st Battalion, South Roscommon, gives a somewhat chilling account of the conflict and his experiences in the last few months before the Truce. There were shootings on both sides, and feelings were so bitter that some in either group were loath to 'let go' when the Truce was announced. It was in this spirit that Sergeant King of the RIC was shot on the morning of the Truce. Crawley records his account of this assassination:

> We went into a shop to get a drink of lemonade, and when [we had been] only a few minutes there, Sergeant King came out of his own house on the opposite side of the street and proceeded to get on his cycle as if to go to the barracks. We left the shop. Ned Campion and I let him have it. He died immediately.

According to Crawley, Sergeant King 'was the principal man in the murder gang that was organised in the RIC in Castlereagh and was responsible for a number of killings around the area'.

Crawley signed his witness statement on 31 July 1952, almost thirty years after the 'National Activities' in South Roscommon. His anger regarding the whole question of spies and informers still burned within him:

> We were damned right from the start by having traitors and agents amongst us and in the area, and we were never really able to get control over this situation or eliminate that danger. Our Brigade Intelligence Officer was found out to be an intelligence agent for the British. He cleared out of the country and we never got him. Quite a number of men in the Castlereagh area were either shot in their beds by the RIC and Tans or taken out of their beds and shot, and all of these can be put down to the activities of that ruffian.

One of the most extraordinary executions was that of a Black and Tan who had admitted 'that he was on intelligence work' when he had the bad luck to be held up by Crawley's Battalion OC on a road near Ballangare. He records:

> Although this man, whom we now knew to be a Black and Tan, professed no religion, he agreed to see a Catholic priest. We got the priest for him and he was baptised. We bound him and drowned him by throwing him into the river Suck at Dunammon.

James Hynes, a member of the IRB throughout the War of Independence, worked as a lone intelligence agent. His job as a clerk in Mullingar Post Office gave him the opportunity of checking the mail for ciphers as it passed through. He enjoyed his solitary work. He remembers: 'on three occasions I was able to break down the cipher myself before the key had reached me'. He was so successful in keeping his role as an agent secret that, when he was finally arrested, the authorities 'had nothing definite', and he was merely interned.

There was at least one family of brothers in County Offaly who could rival similar families in Cork, Kerry or Mayo. There were five sons and one daughter in the Cordial family, and the five brothers were all members of the Volunteers. The family suffered for this devotion. Michael Cordial, quartermaster (Kinnitty) 3rd Battalion, Offaly Brigade, describes one raid on his home:

> Only my parents and my sister were there. On being informed that I was not at home, the raiders ordered my father, then a man of seventy-five years of age, to go on his knees and to say his prayers as his hour had come. A rifle was pointed at his forehead and my sister, fearing for her father's safety, seized the rifle and in the struggle that followed she disarmed the raider in full view of his companions, who stood looking on but did not interfere. Her action probably saved our father's life.

Cordial also records the tragic fate of the Pearson family – the details of which reflect the bitterness of this conflict. According to Cordial, the Pearson family were 'violently opposed to the national movement'. Some time before the Truce, they fired with shotguns on some Volunteers, one of whom was seriously wounded. The Brigade staff decided that the four male members of the family should be executed. On 30 June 1921, two of the sons were executed in the yard of their farm. The father and one of his sons were away from home. Cordial ends his testimony: 'The remaining members of the Pearson family left the district and did not return.'

In County Longford, the evidence submitted suggests a conventional guerrilla war. Leo Baxter is able to end his testimony with the happy words:

> There were no spies executed in this area. At least ninety percent of the people could be relied on and were on our side. The Protestant element amongst the people did not take any active part, except in a few instances where their numbers were greater.

Rather more information is available in the witness statement submitted by Frank Thornton, dealing with his activities on his release from Reading Jail in March 1919. Thornton, a 1916 man, was on 'the organising staff of GHQ which was controlled by Michael Collins'. Amongst other special projects, he was detailed to go to Longford. He records:

> I went to Longford along with Michael Staines. My job was to completely reorganise the Longford Brigade. We visited all the well-known men in Longford, and I remember Michael Staines and I visiting Sean McKeon at his forge in Ballinalee. He was then Company Captain of his own local Company. We went into the forge and after the usual introductions, we told McKeon what we were after, and his reply to us was 'You provide the rifles and we'll provide the men, and we'll guarantee that they fight.' So on that understanding we proceeded with our reorganisation.

Staines left for Dublin but Thornton stayed on to supervise the very thorough job of reorganising the IRA. More importantly, he was charged with the task of conveying the message which GHQ was sending out all over the country: 'The fight was now on; preparations had to be made immediately.'

Sean MacEoin 'took' Seamus Conway into the Volunteers in 1917. (Both men were living in Ballinalee in County Longford; each took an active part in the War of Independence and each joined the National Army in 1922.) Thus opened up a life of intense military activity for Conway, which really began in September 1920 with the capture of the RIC

197

barracks at Arva. From that time on, Conway records every engagement and every development in the War of Independence as he experienced it in Longford, right up to the Truce. By any measure, Sean McEoin dominates the account of those years. Conway records the end of the Arva fight:

> I next heard a lot of shouting out in the front. The first thing I could distinguish was Sean MacEoin shouting, 'Come out singly with your hands up.' . . . The police came out with hands up. There were about nine police altogether. The Sergeant asked MacEoin to do some damage to the barracks, as he said he could not stand over handing it up in such good condition, and he wanted to hang on to his pension.

On 1 November 1920, the North Longford Flying Column was officially formed, with Sean MacEoin in command. Conway records: 'we saw little of home again until the Truce. We usually billeted in an area being supplied with food and clothes and cigarettes by the local people.'

The shooting of the Lord Mayor in Cork, Tomas MacCurtain, had profound effects on the conflict in every part of Ireland where the Volunteers were active. Longford was no exception. Conway writes:

> On the eve of All Hallows day, District Inspector Kelleher was shot in Granard, and next day Constable Cooney was shot. This was done on receipt of an order from GHQ that all police were to be shot consequent on the death of [Lord Mayor MacCurtain of Cork].

MacEoin deployed his Column strategically in Granard and Ballinalee in order to deal with the expected reprisals. Conway remembered the ensuing fight at Ballinalee:

> As the night wore on we could see the glare of the fires in Granard. It was an awful wet and dark night. . . . in the morning we saw the lights of lorries approaching from the Granard direction. We were still inside the wall.

The ambush party allowed all the lorries through. Conway continues: 'Someone . . . ordered ten men to take possession of the square. . . . MacEoin called on them to halt.'

The fight began. Conway managed to throw a bomb into the lorry, putting their machine guns out of action. He continues the narrative:

We were lying down and kept up a continuous fire. One could not see any target to fire at and could only aim at the flashing from the enemy rifles. This went on for about two and a half hours.

The engagement ended suddenly when the lorries pulled away just as the IRA were running out of ammunition. They heard afterwards that some of the lorries did not get into Longford until the following evening, due to the fact that 'they went astray in the bad network of byroads in that area.'

Other ambushes followed, most of them yielding useful guns and ammunition. McEoin paid the penalty for his fame. He was recognised and arrested 'when returning from Dublin'. The Column soldiered on, determined 'to let them see that [McEoin's] arrest did not mean the end of everything'. They were active right up to the Truce. In May 1921, Conway and fourteen of his Column were billeted close to Arva. Conway relates:

Sometime about 8.30 I woke up and looked out. To my utter surprise I saw two Tans approaching. I shook up Seamus MacEoin and we shot the two and secured their rifles, revolvers and ammunition.

Two days before the Truce, which was arranged for 11 July, Conway was still looking out for good ambush positions near Castlepollard. Conway 'disbanded the Column – each man retaining his arms.' Conway ends his statement:

We were all glad to get back to our home to have a decent and regular supply of food, [and] your own bed to sleep on, and be able to relax and get away from the feeling of tension and always being on your guard.

21

KILDARE AND LAOIS

There is little doubt that the men from Kildare who took part in the 1916
Rising with him made a lifelong impression on Pat Colgan. At the
Convention held to select the candidate for the 1918 general election, he
put forward Eamon O'Kelly. He gives his reasons:

> He had been with us in 1916. He had been an organiser for the
> Volunteers in pre-Easter week days. O'Kelly sprung from the next door
> to 'Big House' Class. . . . Cardinal Cullen was his great-grand-uncle. . . .
> he had earned their intense dislike.

In the end, however, Domhnall Ua Buachalla was selected – the extraordinarily brave shopkeeper from Maynooth who was also a 1916 man.

Colgan made useful contacts at Frongoch Camp:

> I was sent to Hut 7, A lines. I had as hut companions, amongst others,
> Mick Collins, Frank Burke, William O'Brien, [head of the] ITGWU,
> Mark Wilson and Sean O'Duffy.

Colgan is proud to record 'being sworn into the IRB by Mick
[Collins] on the 16 December 1916'. In February 1917, Colgan was called
to Parliament Street, Dublin, to a meeting with Collins, Diarmuid Lynch
and Dick Mulcahy. Colgan writes: 'I was told it had been decided to
organise the Volunteers under similar conditions and control as existed
before the Rebellion.'

When the task had been completed, Colgan reported back to Collins.
They went on 'with the job of recruiting, which went very well'. The
Kildare Volunteers were kept busy with public parades throughout 1919;
drilling in public was banned by the British.

In 1919, immediately after the rescue of Sean Hogan at Knocklong,

Colgan was called to a meeting with Dick Mulcahy, the Chief of Staff. Colgan relates:

> [Mulcahy] was in bed with the flu. The interview took place in Cullenswood House. . . . he explained that it was decided to organise a unit to be known as the Special Reserve. It was to be recruited from known and trusted personnel. Its duties were to, if necessary, travel to various centres as directed by GHQ to carry out operations as directed. . . . I accepted. Mulcahy asked if there were any others of the Kildare men who had taken part in the Rebellion. . . . I nominated Tom Harris, Joe Ledwith and Timothy Tyrell of the Maynooth 1916 men.

North Kildare 'was in the direct line of communication between [the] west and south of Ireland to GHQ', as Colgan put it. Their geographical position kept the Kildare Volunteers very busy for the next few years. In fact, they were kept so busy delivering dispatches between GHQ on the one hand, and the west and south on the other, that Colgan was authorised to appoint a special courier: Michael Fay, a student at the time, who took on the job without pay.

By 1920, Colgan and some of his Kildare Volunteers were anxious to stage some event which might be more spectacular than carrying dispatches or raiding likely houses for guns. RIC barracks were being burned all over the country, but Colgan's preferred target was the old woollen mills at Celbridge, which the RIC had just begun to occupy. The mills were large and difficult to burn, but Colgan had reason to believe that there was an old underground tunnel connecting the mills to 'Breen's public house, Celbridge'. Colgan continues: 'I was very enthusiastic about the whole affair. It would give us a chance in a weak county of doing a big job.'

Not everyone agreed, however. Art O'Connor, who at the time was acting Minister for Agriculture, refused to mobilise for the burning, saying that destruction of buildings such as the mills was 'against the best interests of the national movement'.

It was a matter of great satisfaction to Colgan that he and Harris had been able to set up a most successful line of communication between Sergeant Jeremiah Maher RIC, clerk to the County Inspector RIC, who was stationed in Naas. Their chosen courier, Sean Kavanagh, had to be persuaded to become a member of the

IRA, as membership was a prerequisite for the job, but that was success-fully accomplished too. Colgan explains how: 'I instructed Harris to say to Kavanagh that unless he did as he was ordered he would be forced to leave Kildare.'

In September 1920, Kildare

> was divided, Tom Harris taking the section [including] Naas, Newbridge, Rathangan. I retained the extreme north of the county and [a] portion of South Dublin.

Colgan continued to keep in close touch with Collins in Dublin. In May 1920, 'the job in hand was the disarming of the RIC at Castledermott barracks, County Kildare, during an inspection by the County Inspector', of which Collins had previous knowledge. The oper-ation was to be carried out in conjunction with the Volunteers in Carlow, as Castledermott was in the Carlow Brigade area. The raiding party con-sisted of men from the Kill, Prosperous, Maynooth and Cloncurry Companies. The operation was a complete fiasco: it was dogged by acci-dents, misunderstandings and mishaps, and culminated in the taunts of an RIC man sitting on a wall: 'Ye can go home, there's nothing on today.' Colgan continues:

> Sergeant Maher reported later that at midday a message was received by the County Inspector, who immediately cancelled the inspection. How the County Inspector or the RIC at Castledermott learned of the attempted attack (if they did, and it would appear they did) was never discovered.

Colgan was arrested at the end of November and

> taken to the Curragh Camp, where I found also as prisoners, Tom Harris, Michael Fay, and my brother Pierce. . . . In mid-December we were removed to Ballykinlar Camp.

They remained there until the Truce in July 1921.

James Dunne, who was 1st Lieutenant in the Kill Company, and whose father, Patrick, was Captain of the same Company, reflects some-thing of the frustrating situation felt by the rank and file in other areas besides Kildare:

> In October 1920, Captain P. Dunne asked Commandant T. Harris to allow him to start a Flying Column in [the] Kill area, as he had ten or

twelve men on the run and could arm them. Commandant Harris replied that he had instructions from GHQ that a Column in the Kill area would cut the line of communication to the south of Ireland, which must be kept open for dispatches. After this order, the activities of the Company were reduced to blocking roads, raiding post offices, training, etc.

Frank Henderson (who had been Adjutant of the Dublin Brigade in 1921) had been transferred to the Department of Organisation sometime in mid-1920. Part of his job was to visit any area where there appeared to be a particular problem. He writes:

> During the hunger-strike of Terence MacSwiney, Lord Mayor of Cork and Commandant of [the] 1st Cork Brigade, an order was issued by GHQ to all Brigades that, in the event of MacSwiney being kept in prison and dying as a result of his protest, a number of members of the enemy police force in each Brigade area were to be shot immediately. . . . I was instructed to visit the South Kildare Brigade, which, I was told, had refused to obey the order.

Henderson describes what he found. It seems that the Volunteers were quite prepared to carry out other operations such as ambushes or attacks on enemy posts but they were unwilling to carry out this order, 'some giving it as their opinion that the proposed action would be murder'. Henderson continues:

> All but a few of the officers said that the police remaining in the area were very friendly, that they received information from them in regard to enemy movements and intentions.

Henderson had no choice but to 'inform them that I was authorised to dismiss them there and then from their commands for non-acceptance [of orders]'. Henderson remembers that

> this visit was a most unpleasant one for me, as I knew I was expelling from the IRA some men, including Eamon Moran of Ballysax, who had been for many years the standard-bearers of the republican movement in South Kildare. Appeals were subsequently made to GHQ.

W. A. Tynan, who lived in Monasterevin, County Kildare, at the time he gave testimony to the Military Bureau, had been quartermaster of the 5th

Battalion, Laois Brigade, in 1918 when the Battalion was formed in his father's house at Ballybrittas, County Laois. At the same time, Tynan was an active member of Sinn Féin and 'took a leading part in raising funds for the first National Loan, 1919–1920'. Tynan notes:

> The first interesting engagement I took part in as an IRA officer was the burning of the Heath RIC barracks on April 3 1920. . . . Unknown to us, the barracks had been vacated that evening, and so a fight was avoided. After surrounding the place and approaching with caution, armed only with shotguns, we called for surrender. On receiving no reply, [an] approach was made. Entrance forced, and the only occupant being the wife of the RIC Sergeant, we had her removed to safety, and burned the barracks.

This was a promising start, and GHQ felt justified in letting Tynan have some small arms – but not before enduring a lecture from Tom Cullen, a member of GHQ, when Tynan went to collect the guns. Tynan reports:

> We discussed the question of rifles with Tom Cullen, who accused us of not doing our bit in Laois. We pointed out that there were no rifles in the whole Brigade.

Cullen relented, and the rifles were to 'be sent on within a week, probably by canal'. By the time they arrived, Tynan was in custody. He tells the story:

> On the 26 August 1920, I saw a military lorry stopped on the Cross in Ballybrittas just across from my home. . . . I decided to hold them up and seize any equipment in the lorry. My father was away on business, my mother was away on holidays, and I was in charge of the shop at home. I sent for Volunteer Tim Kearney. . . . I gave him a loaded Webley, took one myself, and [we] partly disguised ourselves. I then closed up the shop, went out backways and came down on the lorry from behind, and called on the soldiers to surrender.

The soldiers duly surrendered. Tynan and Kearney searched the lorry for arms, found none, and set fire to the lorry. Tynan

> rushed home, opened the shop, and was standing at the shop door a few minutes later when one of the soldiers rushed up to me asking me where was the post office and telling me they were after being held up by two armed IRA men.

The phone call which followed called out British military and RIC support. Two thorough searches brought to light various incriminating documents, including a plan of the RIC barracks at Portalington and a document indicating why RIC man Lynch should be shot 'for having arrested and beaten Kevin O'Higgins, [and] having him strapped to a sidecar and publicly driven in this manner to Portarlington Station'.

Tynan was arrested. He telegraphed his father to come home. Father and son were both detained. Tynan senior was released, but his son was transferred to Mountjoy, to be court-martialled on Saturday 18 September 1920. Tynan refused to recognise the court and was sentenced to two years' hard labour.

Shortly after his conviction, Tynan was taken by ship to Belfast and transferred to Crumlin Road Prison. He found the food in Belfast 'the best received in any prison', but the work there – breaking stones – was very hard. His next prison was Walton Prison, Liverpool. He describes what happened there:

> We were all handcuffed in batches of six and on arrival at Liverpool were stripped by force and given convict clothing to wear. All prisoners refused to wear same and held out as long as possible, many remaining naked in their cells with nothing but a sheet for several days.

A month later, Tynan was transferred once more, this time to Usk Prison in Monmouthshire. He completed his sentence, and was released on 23 December 1921, almost six months after the Truce.

Another County Laois man, Edward Brennan, who joined the IRA in 1920, was immediately appointed Adjutant of the Company. When the 6th Battalion, Laois Brigade, was formed, he was appointed OC. He had two encounters with the Black and Tans, from both of which he escaped unscathed. Brennan attributes the second escape to a prescient dream:

> On the night previous to the hold-up, I dreamt I was raided and the document found, with the usual terrible consequences. Owing to my dream I hid the document before starting that morning, and so escaped punishment.

The hold-up was unusual in other respects. Brennan was cycling towards Rathdowney 'in the spring of 1921' when he met a friend. While he was talking to his friend for a few minutes, two lorries approached. One of them was in the charge of a District Inspector called Mooney. Brennan relates:

> Immediately he saw us he called a halt and ordered us to put up our hands and be searched closely. When the searchers found nothing in our pockets, the District Inspector, who all this time was moving around us with a revolver in his hand, ordered our clothes to be taken off and searched. We were standing naked on the road. Again they found nothing.

22

Carlow and Kilkenny

Daniel Byrne, who lived at Grangeford, Tullow, County Carlow, when he made his statement regarding the activities of his local Company, refers to the failed attack on the RIC barracks in Castledermot in June 1920. He was one of those Carlow men who was ordered to join the Volunteers from Kildare at Castledermot. He writes:

> The intention was to hold up the RIC in the barracks there during an inspection parade by the [District Inspector]. There were contingents there from all the surrounding Battalions, and everything was in readiness for the attack, but the CO of the Brigade, who was to have led the attack, failed to turn up, so the whole thing was called off.

Byrne had a much happier memory of another (successful) engagement. He records:

> On Easter Sunday night, 1920, six members of our Company carried out a raid on the income-tax office in Carlow. The Volunteers were William Mara, Michael Quinn, Har Twamley, Michael Walsh, Paddy Murphy and myself. We entered the office and filled up the documents in corn sacks and carried them away to a motor car. We then brought them out the country and burned the lot.

Patrick Burke, of 3 Mall Lane, Waterford, started his long service with the national movement in the Fianna, when he was serving his time as a coachbuilder in Waterford city. By the time he transferred to Bagenalstown in 1915, he was already a member of the Irish Volunteers. There was no Company in Bagenalstown, so he and a few others started one at Royal Oak, about a mile and a half away. There was no Brigade Headquarters in Carlow, so they affiliated with the Kilkenny Brigade. Burke records:

We had about forty men in the Bagenalstown Company, comprising men from Paulstown, Royal Oak and Wells. Our drill instructor was an ex-RIC man named Murphy.

Burke did not take part in the 1916 Rising, although he tried his best to carry out the orders he received on Holy Saturday, 1916, 'to capture the RIC barracks in Borris, County Carlow'. He notes:

On Easter Sunday, 1916, the men, to the number of thirty or so, turned up as instructed. . . . we were to proceed to Borris, about seven miles distant, in small groups. This was done mainly by towpath on the Grand Canal, to avoid notice. A chap named Finn, in charge of a donkey and cart, took the arms by road.

The party of Volunteers had covered about two-thirds of the journey when word came that the exercise was cancelled. The informant 'was after being told by some Dublin men who had come down by car from Dublin with the countermanding order from Eoin MacNeill'.

It was the summer of 1917 when Burke and his comrades began reorganising the Bagenalstown Volunteers. They had very few arms and, apart from the few raids on some farmhouses, Burke saw little chance of procuring more. But the Bagenalstown men were remarkably resourceful. Burke reports:

I remember about that time that a man named Jim O'Rourke, a painter by trade who worked with my firm, discovered, in a book he was reading, a formula for making explosives. With the idea of putting this formula into practical use, I consulted Brother Francis of the De La Salle Christian Brothers in Bagenalstown. I knew perfectly well that he was very sympathetic towards the cause and that, if he could be of any assistance, he would gladly help us.

Burke was right in his assessment. Brother Francis was able to enlist the help of his science teacher and

with the aid of a mixing drum which I [Burke] made, the ingredients for making the powder were put together. . . . This made a highly explosive powder. We made about a stone of the stuff.

Soon afterwards, Burke liaised with the Volunteers in Athy, who were engaged in a similar enterprise.

In 1918, Burke returned to County Waterford, where he continued his intensely active service, organising the Volunteers, raiding for arms, and engaging in ambushes. He describes:

> On various occasions during the winter of 1920 and early 1921, we lay in ambush at night in the hopes of engaging the enemy, but we were unsuccessful. I recollect one winter's night in 1920 when the Stradbally Company lay in ambush . . . with about thirty boys armed with shotguns and rifles.

In February 1921, Burke was arrested and imprisoned in Dungarvan barracks. He was passed on from military barracks to military barracks, ending up in Beare Island via Spike Island. He was released on 1 December 1921.

The witness statement submitted by John Hynes, Vice OC of the 4th Battalion, Carlow Brigade, is an unhappy one. It deals mainly with the problems caused by a particularly eccentric townsman from Borris called Kennedy. Kennedy owned a public house and a chemist shop, and had completed his education at Trinity College. He was no longer a Catholic and, according to Hynes, 'was continually passing insulting remarks about the Catholic religion'. He was not a popular man: a condition he appeared to enjoy. He entered in to a long, hostile relationship with the Volunteers. 'He was always sneering at them', according to Hynes. Kennedy went from one outrage to another. Hynes describes:

> Kennedy became more aggressive. One day after that he fired at a Volunteer going through the town. He went out at night-time with a revolver in one hand and a flash lamp in the other and fired at anyone he thought was a Volunteer. He very often went to Gowran and accompanied the RIC and Black and Tans to raid IRA men's houses. . . . Kennedy drove his car through the town with the wheels on the footpath and fired into Dr Dundon's house when passing it.

Hynes details what amounted to a long-drawn-out gun battle between the IRA and Kennedy. By March 1921, the IRA Company, tired of his taunting, was determined to kill Kennedy. They prepared an unusually elaborate ambush plan for the assassination. Hynes reports:

I went to the Battalion OC, Pierce Murphy, and told him the information I had received and that I was going to shoot them. I mobilised twelve men at Harry Doyle's, at Ballingrane, about one mile south of Borris. I divided them into three sections with four men in each. I took charge of No. 1 Section and I put P. J. Byrne in charge of No. 2 Section and I instructed Gerald Murphy, brother of the Battalion OC, to take charge of No. 3 Section. The Battalion OC did not come with us. Nearly all the men were armed with shotguns. I was armed with a double-barrel shotgun.

He explained his plan of attack to the party and deployed his men accordingly:

As arranged, I let them [Kennedy and his group] proceed until they reached the position occupied by the centre section and then blew the whistle. . . . Kennedy drew his gun.

Kennedy was duly shot, but not before firing 'six shots at us'. He then fell down, dead.

Edward J. Aylward, who came from Callan and reached the rank of OC of the 7th Battalion of the Kilkenny Brigade, looks back with a critical eye on many aspects of the war in Kilkenny. Callan came late to the Volunteers. He was a student in St Kieran's up to 1918, when all the 'boys of military age returned to their homes'. As a Volunteer, he 'had more contact with the 7th Battalion, Tipperary, than with Kilkenny city'.

The Active Service Unit of which Aylward was a member involved more men from Tipperary than from Kilkenny. When some arrests by the British authorities thinned out their command structure, the unit 'carried on without any specific orders from Brigade or other sources and made no records or reports of our day-to-day activities', according to Aylward. He goes on to make a startling statement:

I learned afterwards, long afterwards, that the Chief of Staff, General Mulcahy, had sent a message of congratulation to the OC of the Kilkenny Brigade regarding the fight at Garrycricken House, but at the time it took place we did not even know that we had a Brigade Commander. In fact, a man named George O'Dwyer had been appointed as Brigade Commander of the Kilkenny Brigade, but we did not know about this until approaching the Truce.

According to Aylward, the Kilkenny Brigade had been in a 'disorganised state' ever since some vital lists written by Ernie O'Malley fell into British hands on his arrest at Inistioge in October 1920. The other commanders were arrested around the same time also. For whatever reason, Aylward did not find the Brigade staff or the other Kilkenny Battalions cooperative.

The rift between Aylward and Kilkenny is evident in the wholly contradictory nature of the accounts of the same event in two different witness statements, one made by Aylward, the other by Martin Cassidy, who had joined the Volunteers in 1914 and was OC of the 1st Battalion, Kilkenny Brigade.

It appears that Aylward and the other members of his Active Service Unit were invited into Kilkenny to shoot 'the County or District Inspector, who had made himself particularly obnoxious'. Aylward continues:

> Why the Kilkenny men could not have done this themselves, I do not know, but Sean Hayes, Paddy Ryan and myself went in and, arriving at the outskirts of the city, we found ourselves high and dry. We did not know the local set-up and there was nobody to act as our guide or to orientate us on the situation. Actually we had a local guide up to a point, but when we reached St Kieran's Church, the local guide left us.

Aylward maintained that the County Inspector never turned up as they waited behind the wall of St Kieran's College. They had to abandon the project.

Cassidy tells a different story. According to him, it was a well-planned operation, and he gave the details of the operation to Aylward in plenty of time. Mr White, the District Inspector, was well protected, but Cassidy had identified a weakness in his defence. The District Inspector walked to work and back each day. He had only two routes to choose from, one via the High Street, the other via Abbey Street. Cassidy writes:

> I gave all these particulars to Aylward and explained to him that a scout placed at the corner of Abbey Street and Parliament Street would not only be able to see White leaving the barracks, but would be able to indicate the route which White was taking. No matter which route White took, he would have to pass . . . alongside the wall or quite close to it. . . . as Aylward was for some years a student in St Kieran's College, he was familiar with the locality.

211

Worst of all, Cassidy holds that White did exactly as he had predict- ed and that he reported White's movements to Aylward, who 'with six or seven of his Column were waiting on the Circular Road'.

For some reason that is not explained, instead of moving in White's direction, 'they were actually moving away from the direction in which White and his party were coming'. Needless to say, they did not engage with White and his escort. Cassidy ends: 'To say the least of it, Oakes and I were bitterly disappointed.'

Cassidy would be the first to agree that, after the successful attack on Hugginstown RIC barracks in March 1920, there was little activity in Kilkenny city, particularly when compared to the activities of Aylward's unit. Cassidy attributes this to 'the fact that both Tom Treacy, the Brigade OC, and James Lalor, the Brigade Vice OC, were taken into custody.' On 8 December, Ernie O'Malley was arrested at the house of James O'Hanrahan. Cassidy reports:

> Amongst documents captured by the Auxiliaries was a list of the Battalion officers whom [O'Malley] had met. . . . The British forces immediately started a round-up, and amongst others arrested were Peter de Loughrey . . . acting OC for Tom Treacy.

After this setback, George O'Dwyer was appointed Brigade Commandant. This appointment did not work out, according to Cassidy. O'Dwyer continued to give most of his attention to 'the 3rd, 4th and 5th areas . . . with the result that . . . I rarely saw him', Cassidy reports.

Garrett Brennan, who was Deputy Commissioner of the Garda Síochána when he signed his name to a detailed statement on 30 March 1959, remembers too many failed operations about which the British forces must have had previous knowledge, whether by design or accident. Describing a series of such failures, Brennan writes:

> It looked as if the enemy were getting information about our plans, and an old Fenian said that the family of one of the prominent men in the IRA had been traitorous in the Fenian days. This old man said the IRA man could be no good. Strange how tradition dies hard. After that we never took this man into our confidence. He was gradually edged out of the organisation.

Shortly before the Truce, the ambush at Coolbaun took place, in which two IRA men were killed and one wounded. From its very beginning, this operation was dogged by disagreements on the choice of site, late delivery of dispatches, or dispatches not being delivered at all. Brennan writes:

> 'A' Company did not turn up. They never got their dispatch. It was held by the Battalion Commander. With the 'E' Company they were to be posted along the River Deen to cover the footbridge at Boran's, Loon, but they were not so informed in the dispatch.
>
> 'E' Company did not turn up either. Their explanation was that they had been to Attanagh railway station with Ballyouskill Company on the previous Monday night and thought one night in the week was sufficient when they all had to work next day after a night out on Volunteer work.

And so it went on. The last straw for Brennan was when he was shown a copy of the dispatch that had been sent to the Brigadier. It read:

> To Brigade Commandant,
>> Sorry. I don't believe in your action.
>> Wishing you luck.
>> Commandant
>> 3rd Battalion.

The upshot was that 'there were not sufficient men at Coolbaun to cover all points of the approaches, in the absence of the Companies who failed to turn up'.

Miss Dreaper, a well-known unionist who farmed about four hundred acres nearby, found no obstacle in her way when she set out to alert the authorities about the planned ambush. Brennan explains:

> The military at Castlecomer got their information that a party was mine-laying at Coolbaun in this way. The farm labourer told his mistress – Dreaper – of being held up at Rock Lane. She set off on foot by the fields and by the foot bridge over the Deen river at Borann's cross and by the Loon road to Castlecomer Barracks, where she was seen to arrive about 9 AM. The whole bungled operation made things very easy for the authorities.

23

WEXFORD AND WICKLOW

Wexford was proud of its rebel past, and even more proud of the fact that the county was one of the few areas outside Dublin where the Volunteers had taken a stand during Easter Week in 1916. It is scarcely surprising, therefore, that the witness statement submitted by Andrew Bailey, from Fethard-on-Sea, was, in a sense, a commissioned task. He had been asked to write a history of the South Wexford Brigade despite the fact that he himself had not been a member of the Volunteers during the 1916 period. Bailey writes:

> There were only two Companies of the Irish Volunteers in South Wexford during the 1916 Rising. . . . Both Companies . . . mobilised for the Rising, and stood to for a portion of the week.

Bailey names Sean Sinnott as the senior officer in the Wexford area as a whole but singles out Robert Brennan as one of the leaders. Brennan and four others from Enniscorthy were sentenced to death, afterwards commuted to penal servitude for life.

Patrick Carton's memory of his association with the Volunteers went back to 1914, when he and his comrades were drilled by a succession of former members of the British army. Carton, who was a member of the North Wexford Flying Column, records that 'W. J. Brennan-Whitmore, another ex-British soldier, also helped to train us. He taught us Morse code.' His Company was not mobilised on Easter Sunday or on any of the days following.

Patrick Doyle, his two brothers, and a group of friends joined the Enniscorthy Battalion of the Irish Volunteers, but as they lived so far from the town, they were unable to attend parades or take part in the normal activities of the Battalion. They were forced to become Auxiliaries. In spite of this reduced status, Doyle reports:

Late on Wednesday of Easter Week 1916 we got word to report without delay to the Battalion in Enniscorthy. I cycled to Enniscorthy and went to Sinnotts' [on] Slaney Street.

They were set to work at once 'on outpost duty and on police duty in the town itself'. On Saturday night, they were given wire-cutters and told to

go to Ballindaggin and to cut all the telephone wires, to close all the public houses . . . and to call on the young men of the district to join the Volunteers and to take part in the Rising.

About a hundred recruits joined on the spot, Doyle reports: 'The Parish Priest, Canon Meehan, advised the young men to join.' But when his brother Tom returned to Ballindaggin, 'he told us the Rising was over – that the Volunteers in Dublin had surrendered.'

Later, when the Rising was well over, Doyle was a useful contact for the Volunteers in GHQ Dublin. When District Inspector Lee Wilson was shot in Gorey, Doyle tells us that the five men who shot him 'drove to my place, a distance of about twenty miles'. Doyle, who had been sworn in to the IRB in early 1916, is able to tell us the names of all five men:

The five men were Frank Thornton, Liam Tobin, both from Dublin, Jack Whelan, Enniscorthy, Joe McMahon, a native of Clare, who was working in Enniscorthy, and Mick Sinnott, Enniscorthy, who drove the car.

Doyle was eventually able to get rid of the car, despite intense police activity in the area. He includes in his testimony what amounts to directions for building an underground dug-out, 'which we used as a dump in a corner of a field on our lands'. He relates:

It was seven feet wide, ten feet long and seven feet high. The side and walls were built of stone, with an opening in one corner. From side-wall to side-wall we placed wooden beams at intervals of a foot or so, and over the beams were spread sheets of corrugated iron. We then covered it with about three feet of soil, and on top we replaced the sod, which had been carefully skimmed when we started the job. The entrance to the dug-out was concealed. In fact it was so well done that it was never discovered, although our house and lands were constantly searched by the RIC and military.

John Carroll was a full member of the Enniscorthy Battalion. For the two years before 1916, he underwent the orthodox training which every full member of the Volunteers was expected to undergo. 'It included foot drill, arms drill, musketry and scouting', he reports. On Sundays, they sometimes went on route marches, field exercises and manoeuvres; they collected any arms they could. Carroll was able to say: 'When the Rising took place, every man in the Company was armed with either a rifle, a shotgun, or [a] pike'. The Volunteers made the pikes themselves.

When the Volunteers in County Wexford reorganised and reformed from 1917 onwards, the manufacture of munitions and the procurement of arms became an overriding preoccupation for many. According to Carroll, some of the bombs used in the attack on Clonroche RIC barracks were made at Breen's coach factory in Enniscorthy.

At the end of August 1918, Seamus Rafter, Vice Commandant of the Brigade, was fatally wounded while he was engaged in the manufacture of munitions at his premises in Enniscorthy. 'His death was a severe blow to the Volunteer movement', wrote Carroll, but the event did not deter Carroll from the dangerous practice of 'bomb throwing'. Carroll continues:

> These practices were held at an old ruined house near Kilcannon. It was known locally as the 'Haunted House'. The bombs were home-made and were called 'Tailer Bombs'. They had a tail like a kite, so that the nose of the bomb, in which the exploding mechanism was placed, would first strike the object at which it was thrown. We soon became very accurate at bomb throwing.

In his witness statement, Michael Conway from Carraghmore, Ballycullane, County Wexford, gives testimony of what must have been a rare experience in the War of Independence. He is described as 'Survivor of Explosions at St Kearns Saltmills'. Conway sets the scene:

> an old unoccupied house at St Kearns, Salt Mills. Members of the Company assembled there at night to make bombs [to use against] Foulksmills and New Ross Barracks. On the night of 12 October 1920, fourteen members of the Company were in this old house. . . . Candles and cart lamps were used to light the house, and sacks had been placed at the windows to prevent the light from being seen from outside. There was a large quantity of explosive material in the house.

Part of the Volunteers' tasks involved cutting the wire off the detonators. One of the men was using a penknife for this job and cut the wire too short. Conway continues:

> It struck fire in his hand and he dropped it on to the floor. I was standing up at this time. I heard a report like a revolver shot. Then I saw a blue flame sweeping across the house. The next thing I heard was Captain John Timmins shouting, 'Run men, we will all be killed!' Almost immediately a terrific explosion occurred. I thought I was split from the top of my head down. The roof was blown up and landed some fields away. I was blown up too and I thought I was up to the stars, and when I came down again I fell on a tree which was growing at one end of the house. The bough broke with me and broke my fall into the house again, and stones from the wall fell on me. I was at this time almost unconscious. When I came to a little, I heard great moaning. I was smothering from gas and was gasping for breath. I was naked, as my clothes had been burned off me, and I was red with blood. All that was left on me were my two boots, and they were badly tattered. With the help of other men I dragged myself from under the stones and I was laid on the green sod.

Conway and nine others survived the explosion.

Christopher Byrne, who lived at Ballykillivane, Glenealy, County Wicklow when he signed his witness statement on 27 September 1954, felt it necessary to explain the special circumstances in County Wicklow in the lead-up to, and during, the War of Independence. It might appear that, compared to County Wexford, for example, the part played by the men and women of Wicklow in the movement was negligible. Byrne was disturbed by this misjudgement and set about putting the actions of the Volunteers in Wicklow in context. He writes:

> It must be remembered too that Wicklow was the last county in Ireland that was added to the Pale. They hadn't got our people till after 1700 and they weren't safe in the hilly districts till after 1800.

He reminds us that the way in which the Volunteers were spread into Brigades outside the county gave a false impression of inactivity:

> And further let it be noted that Wicklow was divided into several outside Brigades. Tinahely, Shillelagh, and in fact south from Aughrim was

217

in Wexford Brigade. Baltinglass was in Carlow Brigade and all the rest of west Wicklow was in either Kildare or Dublin Brigades. Bray also was in South Dublin Brigade, so that our entire territory was from Delgany to Arklow, taking in Roundwood, Laragh, Rathdrum, Avoca, Ashford and Glenealy; and in that area we had two villages which sent the most recruits to the British army from any village in the British Empire during World War 1, viz. Rathnew and Newtown-Mount-Kennedy.

Byrne's own activity dated back to 1913, when he had attempted to 'organise Wicklow'. Like many in the republican movement, he was a member of the GAA and attended the Congress held in Dublin on Easter Sunday 1916. The people he met on that weekend were well aware of the big question that was exercising the minds of republicans: should there be a Rising or should it be abandoned? Byrne went home to Wicklow. He records: 'On Tuesday I heard Dublin "was out". Wednesday and Thursday I spent trying to get some information but failed. On Friday I heard that Wexford was out.'

In 1917, Byrne 'started off again organising both Sinn Féin and the Volunteers. . . . We soon had sufficient Companies to form two Battalions.' Byrne was proud of the quality of the officers in charge of the organisation he had put together, particularly Tom Cullen, who was Vice Commandant of the East Wicklow Brigade. But Wicklow lost Cullen when he 'was recalled to Dublin, where he was kept for the remainder of the struggle'. GHQ, in the persons of Michael Collins, Michael Staines and Austin Stack, had made the decision, much to Byrne's disappointment. He writes:

> I suggested bringing Tom Cullen back to Wicklow. There were a number of Wicklow men in Dublin who had fought in 1916, and I wanted a couple of them sent with him. They would have roused the whole county, and Wicklow would have been as good as in Fiach MacHugh's or Michael Dwyer's times.

Matthew J. Kavanagh, who had joined the Irish Volunteers in 1914, provides us with an eye-witness account of the meeting held at Woodenbridge in September of that year, and John Redmond's address. He records:

> We had a route march to Woodenbridge, where Volunteers from all the county were assembled in a big field, near the railway station. John

Redmond rode into the field on a white horse, and addressed the assembly. He was accompanied by Con McSweeney, national teacher, Aughrim, and later a Major in the British army. Pointing out the fact that we were a fine body of men, Redmond said that he felt proud to be able to address us, and that he thought we would serve the cause of Ireland by fighting on the fields of Flanders. As a result of his speech, practically all the men dropped their rifles in the field and walked away. I dropped my rifle there on the ground.

Kavanagh, who lived at Bridge Street, Arklow, County Wicklow, at the time he made his witness statement, had the distinction of being the recipient of a spirited reprimand from Michael Collins in person. Like so many other Volunteers at the time, Kavanagh was worried about the arms situation. The Arklow Company had been trying to get some stocks of weapons together. Kavanagh relates:

> We collected the ingredients for making gunpowder from local chemist shops, and we collected lead for the purpose of making buckshot. We were actually making pikes as well.

When a friend told him that he could supply him with some revolvers and ammunition if he could collect them himself in Liverpool and pay cash for them, Kavanagh readily agreed to purchase about £50 worth. When he got to Liverpool and met Neil Kerr, who was supposed to give the arms and ammunition to him, they had already been collected by GHQ. He returned to Wicklow. A few days later, he was collected and brought to Cullenswood House on Oakley Road, and met Michael Collins for the first time. He recounts:

> Collins started off with a terrible harangue and abused me at a frightful rate, for daring to interfere by tapping a Headquarters source of supply for arms. Michael Staines, who was present during this interview, said something on my behalf, whereupon Collins appeared to change his view towards me. He shook hands with me and congratulated me for trying to secure arms. He said there were so many people trying to avoid getting them. He agreed to give me six revolvers for cash and three hundred rounds of ammunition. They were not the type of revolver which I was actually looking for, but a .38 revolver made by Harrington and Richardson of America.

No man loved Wicklow more than Robert Barton; despite the fact that he did not personally engage in the use of physical force in the War of Independence, he spent a disproportionate amount of time in prison during these years. Barton appears to have enjoyed his efforts at outwitting the prison authorities, especially if he succeeded in escaping. His plan to escape from Mountjoy was successful, thanks to the help of his comrades and 'Joe Berry, a plumber warder'. He remembers the details:

> With the saw [brought in by Dick Mulcahy], I cut out the bar, the ladder came over the wall, I scaled it and dropped into a blanket. My rescuers were led by Rory O'Connor. Mick Collins was in a street nearby waiting to congratulate me.

Barton was anxious to repeat the success while he was in prison in England. He writes:

> When I was a prisoner in Mountjoy, I could always get in touch with Michael Collins through Joe Berry or some other sympathetic warder, but in Portland I was altogether out of touch.

But it seems that he was not completely out of touch. He tells us:

> I wrote a letter while I was in the silence cell with a piece of lead out of a pencil which I had retained – a tiny piece of lead which I had concealed in a seam of my coat. I used a piece of paper torn out of the back of a Bible and pushed it under the door to a warder who was related to the gardener of an aunt of mine living in Hampshire. That letter got through to Michael Collins.

Barton is certain that he would have escaped if he had not been released first.

24

WATERFORD

At the time of the War of Independence, Waterford was a special place with a special history, and most of the local witnesses who submitted statements were at great pains to explain how this situation came about. Michael F. Ryan, who was Brigade Engineer with the East Waterford Brigade during the relevant years, goes back to the founding of the city for an explanation. He writes:

> First the city was a Danish settlement, and a little while afterwards it became an English city, and thus it remained except on isolated occasions. . . . There was no '98 or Fenian tradition in the city.

Thomas Brennan, who, like Ryan, served with the East Waterford Brigade, is more concerned with the difficulties of electioneering in Waterford on behalf of Sinn Féin. He acted as personation agent in Ballytruckle for the Sinn Féin candidate, Dr White. He remembers:

> Our men were continually beaten up whilst engaged on such jobs as conveying voters to the poll, and everything possible was done by opposition mobs to prevent republican sympathisers from going to the polling booths.

Brennan analyses the opposition:

> There were three anti-national elements in those days, viz. the unionists comprising the ascendancy classes; the element known popularly as the 'Ballybricken pig-buyers', which was entirely pro-Redmond and pro-British; and those who had connections with the British army, i.e. soldiers' wives and families, and ex-British army men who were pensioned off. These three elements formed a most formidable opposition to anything appertaining to republicanism.

There were two elections in Waterford in 1918: the first was the by-election in March following the death of John Redmond, the leader of the Irish Parliamentary Party. The members of the Fianna, of which Moses Roche was a member in his early days, 'did all the bill-posting and the painting of slogans on walls and footpaths in support of Dr White.' Brennan records:

> It was necessary for the conduct of this important by-election of March 1918 that organisers be brought to Waterford from Sinn Féin HQ Dublin and from almost every strong republican centre in the country. I remember the following . . . Eamon de Valera, Sean McEntee, Harry Boland, Darrel Figgis, Laurence Ginnel, Joseph McGrath, Joe McGuinness, Longford, and Arthur Griffith.

William Keane, who came from outside Waterford city, remembers being

> ordered into Waterford city to help in the election campaign of Doctor White. . . . The Redmondite mobs, mainly composed of ex-British soldiers and their wives – and the pig-buyers from the Ballybricken district . . . carried on in a most blackguardly fashion. Anybody connected with Sinn Féin [was] brutally assaulted with sticks, bottles, etc.

The RIC were no help, Keane notes:

> The police in Waterford did nothing to help keep any sort of order; in fact they openly encouraged attacks on republicans and stood by and laughed when republicans were being brutally beaten up by gangs of Redmondite followers.

Sinn Féin lost the by-election in March and the general election at the end of the year, which was conducted in a similar manner. Keane notes: 'As a man from the Flying Column said to me years afterwards, he had tougher fighting in Waterford during these elections than ever he had with the "Column".' Brennan, however, records a viewpoint which certainly merits attention:

> It was in my opinion at the time, and it still is my opinion, that the bringing in of Volunteers from outside was bad policy from the local republican standpoint. I am convinced that this course of action was against the interests of Dr White, the Sinn Féin candidate and a local man. It simply irritated the Redmondite mobs further.

Brennan continues:

> It is also a rather significant fact that, just a year afterwards, i.e. in 1919, a municipal election was held in Waterford city which resulted in a resounding success for the Sinn Féin candidates. On this occasion no Volunteers from outside were brought in to the city.

At the same time as the citizens of Waterford were becoming exercised by the political events taking place in their city, other activities were taking place at dead of night not far from them. James Mansfield was from Dungarvan and had joined the Volunteers as early as 1913. He took no part in the Volunteer movement after Redmond's speech at Woodenbridge. He was back in action, organising and drilling, from 1917 onwards. There was a grave shortage of arms. He records:

> Early in the year 1918, I received orders from the Brigade OC to try and contact German submarines which were operating off the south coast of Ireland against British merchant shipping in the course of the First World War. The idea was to secure some guns from the Germans. We put to sea at night in boats off Stradbally, a village on the Waterford coast, situated about five miles east of Dungarvan. There was a password (which I cannot remember) to be given to the German submarine commander. . . . We spent many nights on this task, but we never did succeed in contacting any of the German 'U' boats.

The shortage of arms continued to be a problem. In order 'to increase our meagre store of arms', Mansfield records, 'the raiding of farmhouses and houses of the landed gentry was begun' [in 1919]. 'All the time, we were constantly on the lookout for arms', Keane tells us. He was able to locate likely sources mainly through information supplied by 'friendly servants'. Generally, the task of removing guns from their owners went without a hitch, but a man 'named Shanahan, at Coolfin', who resisted, was tied up 'with a rope I had brought with me' and warned 'not to leave his position for twenty minutes'. Keane's most interesting encounter was that with Major Congreve at Kilmeadon, County Waterford. Keane recounts:

> The OC and other Volunteers held up Major Congreve while I and four others went upstairs to search for arms which a friendly servant had previously told us were up there. In a wardrobe we discovered two shotguns (silver-mounted) and some cartridges. Meanwhile, Jimmy Power

was explaining to the Major that our object in raiding his house for arms was to make certain that we would get them before they fell into the hands of the British. . . . Major Congreve said that as far as he was concerned he would not report the raid or the taking of the guns if the Volunteers would give him a promise to return the shotguns when all the trouble was over. . . . Jimmy Power gave him the promise to return the guns and as a matter of fact did return them in perfect condition to their owner after the Civil War in 1923.

According to Keane, 'upwards of fifteen members of the staff [of the Mental Hospital in Waterford] were members of D Company, and all of them were active members' – a circumstance which he found invaluable when choosing a safe place for the arms which were collected in the raids.

The refuge provided by the psychiatric hospital was particularly welcome on occasions such as the aftermath of what became known as the Tramore Ambush. Keane makes special mention of the hospital when he expresses his desire to pay tribute

> to friendly members of the RIC and to put on record the fact that a man named Neligan of the Waterford city RIC was very helpful in passing on information to us. Were it not for him, both Nicholas Whittle and Mick Wylie, who were brought wounded to the Mental Hospital, Waterford, after the Tramore ambush in January 1921, would have been captured.

In 1954, the year in which Keane signed his statement, the Tramore ambush was still a touchy subject. Several of the Waterford witnesses give accounts of the engagement, in varying detail. Andrew Kirwan, who was with the Bonmahon Volunteers from 1918, is admirably concise in his account:

> Briefly, the planned attack on the British was that a few shots were to be fired at the RIC in Tramore, to scare the garrison, who would summon assistance from Waterford, eight miles to the east. The British relief party was to be ambushed when they reached a barricade erected on the west (Tramore) side of the Metal Bridge. No shots were to be fired by the east Waterford men until the military lorries ran up to the barricade and then came under fire from the west Waterford men. Actually, what happened was that the British were fired on by some east Waterford men before they (the British) ran into ambush position. The fighting

then developed entirely on the eastern side of the Metal Bridge, where the military got out of their lorries and engaged the men from east Waterford, who lost two killed, and two wounded.

Brennan reports:

> During the day of 8 January 1921, news of the ambush was all over the city of Waterford. Various stories were told of the numbers killed and wounded on both sides.

Thomas Brennan did more than most to save the wounded men, taking them first to the mental hospital, and then, after they 'had been seen by someone who was considered untrustworthy', removing them. He records:

> It was eventually decided to shift the wounded men across the river Suir to the home of a family named Walsh of Portnascully Mills, Mooncoin, County Kilkenny. . . . They received medical attention from Miss Walsh of Portnascully, who was a nurse and who is now my wife.

Jack O'Mara, who lived at Knockboy, Ballinamult, County Waterford, on 6 December 1955, when he signed his witness statement, had good reason to remember the date of the signing of the Truce. He was in jail at the time while the military authorities awaited the arrival of a soldier witness who would identify him 'as being present when Sergeant Hickey was captured and brought away for execution. Before the witness turned up, the Truce of July 1921 was signed.' Sergeant Hickey 'had apparently been acting as a "spotter" for the British raiding the previous night', according to Michael Mansfield (a brother of James Mansfield) and Vice Commandant, 1st Battalion, West Waterford Brigade.

Sergeant Hickey's execution took place during the Burgery ambush, a long and hard-fought engagement which took place on the main road from Waterford to Dungarvan and is described in some detail by O'Mara. Shortly before this ambush, George Plunkett, brother of Joseph Plunkett and an officer with GHQ, had come from Dublin to join the West Waterford Flying Column. Michael Mansfield sets the scene:

> The Column invariably travelled at night-time, on foot, across country, sending scouts ahead. These scouts, in addition to keeping a lookout for enemy forces, would contact the Company Captain in the area in which we were to billet. About half a dozen men from the local Company

would mount guard at night with a few of the men from the Column. The Column was paraded twice a day by the OC, and field exercises carried out. Each man carried about fifty rounds of rifle ammunition, most of which was captured at Piltown [a successful ambush mounted at Piltown on 1 November 1920].

The Burgery ambush was a costly operation for the Column. According to Michael Mansfield, none of the officers agreed with Plunkett when he insisted on going back to the scene of the initial successful attack 'to look around for guns which [had been] discarded by the British'. He continues:

> Plunkett was determined to go ahead with the idea so . . . he set off with five or six men towards the Burgery, Dungarvan. Crossing a field near the road where most of the fighting had taken place the previous night, Plunkett's party ran into heavy fire from a party of military and Black and Tans. Sean Fitzgerald was killed outright and Pat Keating mortally wounded.

O'Mara finishes the story:

> We pulled out then, but Plunkett and another man, whose name I cannot recall, remained behind to see what could be done for Keating. They did succeed in getting him away from the place and into a house in the district, to where a doctor was brought. The poor fellow died of his wounds the same night.

25

THE TESTIMONY OF THE WOMEN

Nowhere is the value of the work done by the Bureau of Military History more evident than in their collection of witness statements made by the women involved in the national movement in the period 1913–21. Not only do they provide eye-witness accounts of the main events of these years, but they also offer crucial evidence of the importance of the women's activities in the War of Independence. Most, but not all, of the women who gave statements were members of Cumann na mBan.

The key to the importance of the Cumann na mBan was its structure, which provided a national network that was both efficient and reliable. Brighid O'Mullane was instrumental in developing the structure of the organisation, and her approach was followed by others. She remembers that, starting 'on a push-bike':

> it was my custom to contact the Volunteer OC, who gave me the names of reliable girls. Having got the names, I convened a meeting, generally at the private house of one of the girls; occasionally it might be at a local hall or even a barn. I first lectured the girls on the aims and objects of the organisation, and the work they would be asked to do. I had a good deal of prejudice to overcome on the part of parents, who did not mind their boys taking part in a military movement, but who had never heard of, and were reluctant to accept, the idea of a body of gun-women. It was, of course, a rather startling innovation, and in that way Cumann na mBan can claim to have been the pioneers in establishing what was undoubtedly a women's auxiliary of an army. I fully understood this attitude and eventually, in most cases, succeeded in overcoming this prejudice.

As soon as each branch was established, she would get them to elect a President, a Captain, an Honorary Secretary, a Treasurer, and committee members. Each officer had clearly defined duties. O'Mullane advised them to meet, if possible, weekly. Before I left them, I always tried to get the local doctor or nurse to give the branch a course of first-aid lectures, and an IRA officer to instruct them in drill, signalling, despatch-carrying, cleaning and unloading arms. Each branch paid an affiliation fee of ten shillings to Headquarters.

Their training indicates the services that were provided by Cumann na mBan. O'Mullane lists these:

The carrying of arms and ammunition, despatch carrying, intelligence work, getting safe houses for wanted men, looking after the wounded, when necessary, seeing to the wants of prisoners, and collecting funds for the Volunteers. For the latter purpose, they organised concerts, ceilidhthe, aeridheachta.

Margaret Broderick-Nicholson, who had joined Cumann na mBan in Galway in 1917, carried out all her duties for the organisation diligently. She was particularly good at interrupting British recruiting meetings:

moving through the people and singing national songs until the meeting collapsed or we were ejected. . . . I was asked by some Volunteer offi-cers to take up intelligence work, which I did, and this partly consisted in keeping an eye out for RIC patrols and the carrying of dispatches. I did a lot of work at the latter from the Brigade to the Battalions. . . . I was very well known to the different officers in each area.

She also began to become well known to the police.

Margaret Broderick was not averse to engaging in physical force directly, if the occasion demanded it. She describes one such occasion:

I remember getting up on one policeman's back and getting my two hands round his throat. He wriggled to knock me off. . . . Another RIC man intervened and pulled me off. I grabbed the second fellow's cap and beat him on the head with the hard peak, and the other fellow swung round and struck me with his revolver on the side of the head above the ear. I was half stunned and staggered against the wall, when someone shouted 'This is no time for fainting!' I shook myself back to life, but by this time they had Shiels [the Volunteer being arrested] inside the barracks.

Broderick and her comrades from Cumann na mBan collected all the stones they could find and broke every window in the barracks. 'We then reformed and commenced our march back very "*bronach*" indeed'.

Broderick was a 'marked woman'. She describes what appeared to be a special raid on the Broderick home with herself as the target. She remembers:

> I thought at first they were going to shoot me, but they took me out and closed the door, then grabbed my hair, saying 'What wonderful curls you've got', then proceeded to cut off all my hair to the scalp with very blunt scissors. I might say they did not handle me too roughly, which is strange to say. There was no further comment until they finished, when they pushed me towards the door and said 'Goodnight'. All spoke with English accents. I had to have my head shaved by a barber next day in order to have the hair grow properly.

Afterwards, Broderick was reliably informed that 'at least one RIC man was seen to point me out to the Black and Tans'.

The testimony provided by the remarkable Cooney sisters is given under the name of Annie O'Brien. By the time their stories were recorded, Annie was married to Denis O'Brien, a prominent republican. She shared her witness statement with her sister Lily. Both girls had been part of the garrison which fought the British forces in Marrowbone Lane Distillery in 1916. After the surrender, they stayed with the men, marching behind them 'in ranks of four, keeping step' as far as Richmond Barracks. O'Brien remembers:

> separated from the men . . . we were all – twenty-two of us – brought into a large building up the stairs . . . where we were divided for the night, eleven of in each of two rooms. A British military sergeant had charge of us and brought us tea in a bucket and some hard biscuits. . . . We ate and drank what we got, as we were hungry.

Next morning, they were lined up in the square and marched off to Kilmainham. This was a filthy place, and the food was bad. It also had extremely bad associations for the sisters. It was while they were there that their dear friend Con Colbert had been executed, together with Michael Mallin, Eamon Ceannt and Sean Heuston. They were released soon afterwards, and eventually got home, riven with grief.

When we got in, the first thing we said to our mother was: 'Mother, Con is gone.' We thought she did not know it but she had seen it in the paper that morning.

With these memories fresh in their minds, the women set about reorganising their branch of Cumann na mBan. O'Brien relates:

The part of Cumann na mBan, our branch included, was to collect money at the church gates, holding flag days on the streets, organising different functions such as ceilidhithe and concerts. We did the collecting and others were organised as distributors, who brought the money to the houses who were in need of it.

In addition, they continued to attend lectures in first aid at No. 6 Harcourt Street, 'which were given by Dr Kathleen Lynn, Paddy McCarvill, who was not yet qualified, and Dr Geraghty, who lived in Westland Row.'

They resumed their military training 'and took part in all public funerals such as [those of Thomas] Ashe, Coleman and Pierce McCann', O'Brien notes. They then took a significant step, as recorded by O'Brien:

Sometime during 1918, during the autumn as far as I can remember, it was decided to re-form each branch of Cumann na mBan into a semi-military organisation governed by a Captain, First and Second Lieutenants, an Adjutant, a Quartermaster, Section Leaders and Squad Leaders.

In September 1918, Cumann na mBan held a meeting

to protest against the continued detention of the women who were in English prisons . . . Mrs McBride, Countess Markievicz and Mrs Clarke. The speakers were all women, and they spoke from a jaunting car.

Despite the fact that they were involved in serious subversive activities throughout the period, the sisters escaped arrest until early February 1921. In 1920, they helped their father carry armaments, consisting mainly of bomb cases, to a secret dump; 'paraded round Mountjoy during the hunger strike singing national songs and praying'; and took turns manning the first-aid station set up by the IRA in South Frederick Street. Their riskiest venture was taking part in the disposal of the guns on the morning of Bloody Sunday, after the earlier synchronised assassination of

British agents. On the night before, the sisters were asked to be ready and waiting at 6 o'clock, at University Church, 'as there was a big job on'. O'Brien continues:

> We were at the church at the appointed time and, to avoid attracting attention, we went into the church in turns, two at a time, and attended Mass while the third remained in the porch and watched. We heard the shooting quite near, as the operations were in progress in that area, and after waiting during what seemed to us an eternity, the three fellows came along walking pretty smartly and handed over their guns to us, one each, in a laneway between the church and Harcourt Street corner. We put the guns in our pockets and proceeded home via Cuffe Street and other lanes, avoiding main roads.

When O'Brien was eventually picked up by the British after a raid on her home, they had very little to charge her with. She was taken to the Bridewell, where she met many more women prisoners, including four women 'who were all teachers in [the] Dominican Convent, Eccles Street'.

A few days later, O'Brien was moved to Mountjoy, where she was able to meet other women political prisoners. They included Eileen McGrane, Peg McGuinness from Roscommon, and Miss Keogh from Gorey. 'Some time after that, Frances Brady and Molly Hyland came, and Linda Kearns also.'

Eileen McGrane was the OC of the prisoners. By the time she submitted her witness statement, she was married to Dr Paddy McCarville, who had helped to instruct the members of Cumann na mBan; her witness statement is signed with her married name. The Rising in 1916 came as a great surprise to her, and she was disappointed in her efforts to join it. She had been a student of Tom McDonagh's, one of the executed leaders, and was clearly greatly moved by the events of Easter Week. On returning to UCD after the Rising, she immediately threw herself into the nationalist movement. She joined Cumann na mBan, undertook rigorous training, and bought a uniform. She records: 'I bought mine from Harry Boland.'

When McGrane graduated in 1918, she was a respected member of Cumann na mBan. After a brief spell of teaching in a Protestant school in Armagh, she was asked by Cumann na mBan to take up 'some active organising' in Counties Armagh, Down and Louth. Later on, she was sent to west Clare 'to visit all the Cumann' na mBan members there.

McGrane put forward the proposal referred to by Annie O'Brien, which sought to define the position of Cumann na mBan in the nationalist movement. McGrane states:

> We had a Cumann na mBan Convention. . . . I put forward the proposal that we should reorganise Cumann na mBan on military lines in view of the fact that we were co-operating with the Volunteers. Up to then each branch had a president, vice-president and secretary. The proposal was to abolish that system and substitute a captain, lieutenant and adjutant. The proposal was well received by the younger delegates. . . . it was carried by a large majority.

McGrane's witness statement is a litany of names of active dedicated women in every part of Ireland. Like so many of the other women involved in the movement, her work as an organiser enabled her to develop a profound knowledge of the whole country. She was in close contact with 'the Republican Government headquarters' and was able to let Michael Collins have the use of a small room in the flat which she shared with two other women. She writes:

> No official personnel were located there. Mick Collins, Tom Cullen, Arthur Griffith and others came from time to time for conferences or to collect or deposit papers. The principals had a key to the door of the flat and access to the key to the office, which was in my custody. The only servant we employed was a cleaner, Mrs McCluskey, whose husband was caretaker to the National Bank.

Maureen McGavock, who later married Sean Beaumont, was able to continue her job of teaching at Scoil Bhride, 70 Stephen's Green. She was a member of the Executive of Cumann na mBan in 1918. She notes:

> We used to meet Ernest Blythe, Desmond Fitzgerald, Liam Mellows, Piaras Beaslai and others there in connection with Volunteer and Cumann na mBan business.

McGavock describes a vital development for which Cumann na mBan must take most of the credit. Of Scoil Bhride, McGavock writes:

> despatches used to be left there for us to be forwarded through town and country by lines of communication organised by Cumann na mBan.

The establishment of these lines was the result of a request from GHQ of the IRA, which found the post utterly unsafe. Leslie Price organised a reliable system of communication which consisted of Cumann na mBan girls walking from branch to branch in the towns and villages. The best line of communication was the one to Cork through Celbridge. To test its efficiency she cycled every yard of it herself as far as Cork.

The two Cunningham sisters, Mollie and Nora, both members of the Macroom branch of Cumann na mBan, were engaged in the usual activities of the organisation. Mollie writes:

> several new types of duties fell to be performed by members . . . It was nothing unusual for me to take two or three revolvers at a time from one Company area to another.

As their home was a 'receiving station' for dispatches, the sisters were 'regularly engaged in the delivery of these messages to the appropriate officers or units'. According to Nora, as time went on 'these operations became more dangerous when the enemy decided to install a lady searcher' at a point where the messengers had to pass within a few yards of the sentries at Macroom Castle.

Alice Cashel was a very early member of Sinn Féin. She was a member of the Cork branch of that organisation for some years before 1916, when the membership never rose above ten. The Volunteers had not yet been founded, but Tomas MacCurtain and Terence McSwiney were both members. Cashel was a sister-in-law of James O'Mara; O'Mara had been an MP and had run in the 1918 general election – very successfully, according to his wife, who also submitted a witness statement. O'Mara had been asked by de Valera to organise the Republican Loan.

It so happened that Alice Cashel was able to take up residence in the house called Cashel in Connemara. In 1918, she was appointed an organiser of Cumann na mBan. While organising in Newry, she was instructed to go to Derry and join de Valera and Sean McEntee, who invited her to speak at organising meeting. She writes: 'My instructions were to follow in their traces and organise branches of Cumann na mBan.'

In August, she was ordered to go to Clifden, where she proceeded to hold a meeting despite a warning from the RIC that she would be arrested if she did so. She describes events:

> We held the meeting near the square. It was broken up by the police, the platform, planks on barrels, being pulled from under our feet. We stayed on until the last plank was taken. Then I re-organised the women in the street and marched them out of the town and held my meeting on the monument base which stands on a hill outside Clifden.

From that point, she was a marked woman. She felt that she should leave the district, and decided to cycle to Galway. Just then, she heard from her friend Countess Markievicz. Cashel tells us:

> On the morning of the Clifden meeting I had a letter from her from Holloway Jail in London telling me that she was sending me her bicycle as she knew mine was decrepit – she had used it in the Armagh election. It arrived that morning, just in time for me to go 'on the run'.

The RIC continued to pay special attention to Alice Cashel, especially after she went to live at Cashel House. She was arrested and kept prisoner for a week. On her release, bonfires were lit on Cashel Hill, and there was general rejoicing. The following summer she was co-opted onto Clifden District Council, and later selected as representative on the county council, where she was elected vice-chairman. Before this, she had taken the unusual step of founding a branch of the Volunteers in Cashel, after obtaining the authority of the Volunteers HQ in Galway. She explains:

> [The Volunteers] patrolled the fairs, seized the poteen which they brought up to Cashel House, and on order poured away on the lawn. These IRA patrols got the poteen traffic well under control.

She entered enthusiastically into the administration of the fledgling State. She was elected a county justice and presided openly in court; she settled a stubborn land question with the aid of Robert Barton's newly founded Land Bank. Towards the end of her statement, Cashel writes with some satisfaction: 'In that summer of 1920, the writ of the Republic ran.'

But further trials awaited her. Firstly, she was attacked by the Black and Tans in her own house. She escaped capture by getting out at the back of the house, over the wall on to Cashel Hill and [then I] lay for some time in the bed of a dried-up stream. . . . After that I went to Dublin. While there I found that family business necessitated my going to Paris.

But in the event Cashel had little time for family business. While in London, on her way to Paris, she read in the *Daily Mail* an account of what her county council had been getting up to in her absence. She hurried back to find that the council had been suing for peace, without authority. Her arrangement for the collection of rates, whereby the council retained them out of reach of the British administration, had been rescinded. Cashel, in her capacity as acting chairman, called an extraordinary meeting of the county councillors and rate collectors with the intention of restoring the rates arrangement, but she was arrested and no meeting was held. She was removed to Galway Jail, where, after six weeks, she was summoned before a field general courtmartial and sentenced to six months' imprisonment. From prison, she continued her work with the county council. She explains:

> the secretary of the council used to come to see me, and I gave him instructions and he reported to me on the meetings of the council.

The work undertaken by the Cumann na mBan members was onerous and often dangerous. Brighid O'Mullane writes:

> Having regard to the extent of the area for which I was responsible, I might say I was always on the road, re-visiting and re-organising the branches which I had formed. Long journeys – say from Dublin to Enniskillen – I would do by train, but the journeys within the counties were all done on a push-bike. These journeys were by no means all hardship, although I sometimes had to do sixty miles a day, as I made many friends who were always glad to see me on my return visits. The life was strenuous, as I generally worked in three meetings a day to cover the various activities of each branch. My meals were, of course, very irregular, and the result of this sort of life, which I led for about three years, i.e. to the Truce, was that my weight was reduced to six and a half stone. I got many severe wettings and consequent colds, which I was unable to attend to. The reaction to this came during the Truce, when I broke down and had to get medical attention.

One of the most intrepid women of the War of Independence, Linda Kearns (or Mrs McWhinney, her married name), was never a member of Cumann na mBan but was an early member of Sinn Féin. She was first drawn to the movement 'in 1911 or 1912, as a trained nurse', after visiting a typhus hospital in Belmullet. She writes:

> It was not a hospital at all: it was only an old barn that was converted to this purpose. You could see the sky through the ceiling and walls and the patients were lying in filth on the floor . . . . It occurred to me that it was time that the government that was responsible for this state of affairs should be expelled from the country.

Although she was never a member of Cumann na mBan, Kearns lectured some members in first aid. On the first night of the Rising, she set up a clinic for wounded Volunteers: 'I walked around the streets then during the week looking to see if I could give assistance to any wounded Volunteers.'

Kearns was first asked by Michael Collins and Diarmuid O'Hegarty to carry messages to Alec McCabe in County Sligo in 1917. McCabe was a member of the IRB and of course, although she did not know it, both Collins and O'Hegarty were important members of the same organisation. She delivered messages for the IRB for 'several years'. Sometimes she carried more lethal freight on the train – her usual mode of transport before she bought a car. The car made her even more useful to the nationalist movement. She writes:

> I was told to go to Frank Carty at the Harp and Shamrock in Sligo. . . . from then on I was taking orders from Frank's Brigade. . . . I was used now chiefly for carrying guns before and after an engagement. It seemed as if a couple of Flying Columns were using the same material. I would bring them to Chaffpool one day and perhaps the next day back to Grange.

She provided the transport for the guns captured by the IRA at the Cliffoney ambush (in which four policemen died and two were fatally wounded) and carried the tins of petrol that were intended to be used in the destruction of the barracks at Dromore. She remembered a particular rendezvous that took place 'on the Saturday after Bloody Sunday' involving:

Jim Devins, who was in command, Eugene Gilbride and Andy Conway. They were looking for a car. . . . They had a lot of equipment with them, including some revolvers. I was to take all the arms and equipment. Jim Devins then took me a little way along the shore of Lough Gill and he said to me 'Have you taken the oath?' I said 'No.' 'You had better take it now. . . . those are my orders.' I repeated the oath after him. It was a thrilling and unforgettable moment in the dark of the night by the side of the road.

They drove back through the town of Sligo; on the road out again, the car was halted by the Auxiliaries and Kearns was made to drive back to Sligo Barracks. Kearns records: 'The police recognised the rifles that we had captured. It was then they saw red; they beat us up, calling us murderers.' The long night began. Kearns continues:

The Auxiliaries adopted a devilish plan, probably to wear down my nerves. They took the boys out one by one, and we heard a shot each time and we thought it was the end.

The Auxiliaries then changed tactics and promised that, if only she told where she was going and who she was going to meet, 'I would be allowed to go home and nobody would hear of the episode.' When the Auxiliaries left:

the RIC took me on again. . . . a notorious fellow . . . gave me a bad time. He beat me about the head and chest and broke one of my front teeth. A real Cockney Black and Tan who was among them protested. After this, they put me in the mortuary . . . and locked me up.

Next morning, Kearns found, to her great relief, that 'the boys' were still alive. After a few days in jail in Sligo, they were all put on a destroyer and were eventually put ashore at Buncrana and marched from Buncrana to Derry Jail. She was the only woman prisoner in the jail. She was put into the hospital there, which she found quite comfortable. She continues:

A nurse, who was a friend of mine living in the town, sent me in my meals from a restaurant. The warden who was looking after me was an old man, and he brought me an iron, so I washed and ironed all my clothes.

Kearns was moved from jail to jail. She found Armagh quite comfortable too, especially when she 'ordered her dinner every day from the hotel'. But her good fortune didn't last. On 11 March 1921, she was sentenced to ten years' penal servitude. A couple of weeks later, she was put on board a boat for Liverpool, where she was imprisoned in Waltham Prison. This prison was not comfortable, to say the least. There she met Eileen McGrane for the first time.

Kearns was not a compliant prisoner. Eventually, after she had gone on hunger strike and been in the prison hospital, she was sent back to Ireland, to Mountjoy. She remembers that, on 14 September 1921:

I arrived in Mountjoy, where I was given a great welcome. I was given a lovely tea, the first decent one I was given for a long time. I was very sick and was put into the hospital. Eileen McGrane and K. Brady were there in the hospital too.

Kearns crowned her rebel career by escaping from Mountjoy as soon as she had recovered her health. Neither of her friends, McGrane and Brady, would join her in the escape attempt. The escape included all the familiar methods: the key, the rope, the wall. She arranged a noisy football match to coincide with the escape attempt:

While playing football on the appointed evening, we pushed our ball down towards the door and Eileen McGrane promised to keep up the noise. I opened the door quietly and the four of us slipped out and raced towards the appointed spot on the wall.

A short time later, she was in Dr St John Gogarty's car being transported to his aunt's house in Earlsfort Terrace. Dr Gogarty was a friend of hers. She was passed from safe haven to safe haven, ending her work for the IRA by imposing some order on the Volunteer camp at Ducketts Grove in Carlow. She came back to Dublin the night the Treaty was signed. She never got her car back.

Mairin Cregan, later Mrs James Ryan, was closely associated with the national movement from well before the Rising (see *Witnesses: Inside the Easter Rising*). In July 1919, she married Dr Jim Ryan, who was also deeply implicated in the movement, and went to live in Wexford town, where he had his practice. In her own words:

I joined the local branch of Cumann na mBan. . . . we took part in every political activity there, and took our share of the consequences – raiding was one of them.

She describes one raid in some detail:

Between 1 and 3 AM in December 1920, [the military] broke in through the dining window downstairs; they were fully armed and were wearing light rubber slippers.

They had crept upstairs so quietly that they were already in her bedroom 'when she turned round to dress'. They were looking for her husband. Cregan went downstairs to the drawing room, where she found the officers searching through her papers. When she tried to stop them doing this, they ordered her to leave the room. She refused. Two soldiers dragged her forcibly from the room. She remembers:

I stood against the wall outside the door and refused to go further. At that point Captain Parke came out of the room. I had already noticed that he was under the influence of drink. He had lost his left hand in the war and usually wore a hook attached to the stump. During raids this hook was replaced by a dagger. He stood quite close to me now, waving his revolver and dagger in my face while we argued. I did not think he intended to kill me, but I certainly feared that the revolver would go off by mistake, and I made a most fervent mental Act of Contrition. Eventually they went away.

Cregan's ordeal was far from over, however. Her first child was eight months old, and apart from her young sister from Killorglin, who was visiting her, she was left all alone when her husband was captured and retained in custody on Christmas Eve. Worse was to come. As part of a reprisal exercise, and because she refused to hang a poster that had been given to her by the military, Cregan too was taken prisoner. She records: 'I asked to be allowed to see my baby before leaving, and they sent a soldier with me while I was doing so.'

Eventually, Cregan was handed over to the civil authorities at Waterford Jail. 'I was signed for and delivered', she writes:

Certain members of the House of Commons, Commander Kensworthy, Wedgewood Benn and Jack Jones, asked Sir Hamar Greenwood awkward questions about my arrest since I had an eight-month-old baby at home.

On 20 February, Cregan was tried for her offence (refusing to post the Proclamation) and sentenced to three months for not paying a fine of £50. She was quietly released and returned to Wexford, where she was reunited with her baby. Indefatigable as ever, she continued to work for the movement until the Truce.

Some of the witness statements are valuable for the light they cast on the family, friends and acquaintenances of the women witnesses. In particular, Dulcibella Barton gives a unique insight into her brother Robert and her cousin Erskine Childers. Living in County Wicklow, she provided the indispensable service of offering hospitality to Volunteers who were 'on the run'. She writes:

> I had many Volunteers on the 'run' staying in Annamoe. Many of them came from Cork via Rockwell College. Kevin Barry's brother used to drive them over in a pony and trap. They stayed as long as they liked. In many cases they were on their way to Dublin and I was able to get them there by old roads which were only known to Wicklow people.

According to Barton, Dan Breen was 'very nice and quiet' and Liam Lynch was 'a very good-looking man and so quiet and gentle'. Dulcibella was never arrested herself, she was glad to say: 'I could not have endured being in jail, used as I was to open-air life.'

Mrs A. K. Wordsworth was yet another woman whose hospitality was invaluable to the IRA. She lived at Leinster Road, Rathmines, with her eight-year-old daughter and her sister Dorothy Stopford, who was studying medicine at Trinity College. Her aunt was Mrs Stopford Green, who was a friend of Roger Casement and was well known in nationalist circles in the North. Mrs Wordsworth writes: 'I was always willing to take in wanted men but steadily refused to house arms or ammunition, as I was asked to do more than once.'

President de Valera stayed with her for a week when he had to leave his former abode at short notice. She writes:

> The next morning at breakfast there was an account of an ambush on the military at Kilbrittain. My daughter said, 'I think Kilbrittain is a very

good name for a place in Ireland.' The President was much amused, saying, 'Do you think we want to kill all the Britains [*sic*], Mary?' He had to stay mainly upstairs as I had to negotiate the child's daily governess, with all his papers round him. . . . I came in one day to find a small Fianna boy in the hall raising the seat of his bicycle to accommodate the President, on which he rode away.

Two other 'wanted men' who were looked after by Mrs Wordsworth were Liam Mellows and Sean Etchingham. She remembers:

The same two spent Christmas 1920 in my house, and I shall never forget how much they frightened me by not getting in until after curfew on Christmas Eve because they had been buying presents for my daughter's Christmas stocking.

Maeve McGarry signed her witness statement on 31 March 1953 as a member of Cumann na mBan, but the contribution of herself, her mother and her family went far beyond the duties of an ordinary member of the organisation. Her mother was one of the few who knew of the Rising planned for Easter Monday 1916; she was sent as a courier to Limerick with the message that the Rising was to take place. While her mother was away from home during that fateful week, Maeve held the fort. Her biggest problem was getting some food for herself, as well as dealing with the numerous visitors: 'There were so many coming in and out that all the food was consumed.'

The visitors continued to come long after the Rising. There was little going on that Maeve's mother did not have a hand in. There were constant meetings in No. 5 Fitzwilliam Square. Maeve's mother was 'in the Corporation and a councillor for the Fitzwilliam Ward since 1919'. In addition to all this, the family was asked to accommodate important delegates, as well as arranging receptions for them. Maeve writes: 'We had a great big crowd in the house that night for the dinner, which was supplied by Mitchell's [restaurant].

Mrs McGarry's great service to the national movement, however, was the acquisition of a house where de Valera could be accommodated on his return from America. Maeve remembers: 'It was about the middle of May we took up residence in Glenvar. We could not have a maid, so I did all the work.'

The witness statements of the women include two made by undercover agents: one in Dublin, the other in Cork. The story of Lily Mernin is fairly well known. Michael Collins's 'little gentleman' went about her business as a shorthand typist in the lower Castle Yard so quietly that she was still a typist, in the Department of Defence, at the time she made her statement. Her carefully made copies of vital information all ended up with Collins, the Director of Intelligence. In her statement, she gives us a glimpse of her work:

> Each week I prepared a carbon or a typed copy, whichever I was able to get. Sometimes I would bring these to the office placed at my disposal at Captain Moynihan's house, [in] Clonliffe Road. He had a typewriter there and I typed several copies of the strength returns [of the British armed forces] and any other correspondence which I may have brought with me that I thought would be of use. I left them on the machine and they were collected by some person whom I did not know. I had a latchkey for the house and nobody knew when I came or went.

The other undercover agent was Miss Annie Barrett of Killvullen, County Cork. Annie Barrett's father was a Fenian. She was a graduate of the Munster Civil Service College. She entered the Post Office Service as a telephonist in 1906. In 1919, she was appointed supervising telephonist at Mallow, and continued to serve in that capacity until she retired in 1945. She writes: 'My first contact with the Irish Volunteer Organisation was made through my brother, who was a wireless operator. This was early in 1918.'

Barrett's statement is not as long as some, but almost every page of it deals with information that was passed on, or not passed on, which made a difference to the conflict:

> I arranged . . . to relay all military and police messages passing through Mallow during my spells of duty to the Mallow Intelligence Section of the Irish Volunteers.

She was thus able to alert the Volunteers to the intentions of the military in arranging for the collection of arms in the area. Naturally, the Volunteers decided to collect the arms themselves.

Mallow was a key centre for the whole of Munster, and Barrett learned of intended raids before they happened, so that appropriate action could be taken by the Volunteers. She passed on 'several messages regarding enemy plans and intentions'. She continues: 'Information regarding the enemy's intention to carry out arrests was more or less a general feature throughout late 1919 and 1920.'

Barrett was connected with the capture of Mallow military barracks:

> When the raid was over the military came to the post office and, with post office engineers, had the line repaired. When the lines were again in order, the British were sending urgent messages to Fermoy . . . but I delayed the messages, giving the excuse, 'The lines must still be faulty.'

The IRA members avoided capture, partly due to Barrett delaying the arrival of the British forces. Her information helped the IRA plan several ambushes, which she lists, and in 1921 she was able to warn the Cork Column that a round-up was about to be made in their area. On that occasion, she overheard one of the officers say: '[Sean] Moylan must have tapped the lines.'

She was never at any time under suspicion by the British forces. She ends her statement: 'I always managed to maintain friendly relations with them'.

26

THE CAPITAL CITY

While we should not downplay the importance of any of the statements submitted by participants in the War of Independence, whose activities were mainly in places outside the capital, there is no denying that the place to be was Dublin. Beneath the highly visible structures of British government, there were the first faint traces of a new State, proclaimed at the meeting of the First Dáil in 1919. The conflict that had been begun in 1916 continued, some of it openly in the streets of the city, but most of it in more subtle ways: in prisons, through the interception of post, in the undermining of the judicial system, in the establishment of the Dáil, in the establishment of government departments, and by means of statements and representations to foreign countries. The post-1916 separatists were in effect aiming to break the claim of the British government and Parliament to rule and legislate for Ireland. The best vantage point for an overall view of these changes was Dublin, which was a good place to meet people.

To judge from John Shouldice's witness statement, prison was an even better place to meet people. Shouldice was living in Inverness Road, Fairview, when he made his statement. During the War of Independence, he had been Captain and Acting Adjutant in 'F' Company, 1st Battalion, Dublin Brigade, IRA. He describes the arrival at Dartmoor Jail, after the Rising, of nationalist prisoners who were considered important. 'There were prisoners there from Wexford, Galway, Clare, Louth and mostly Dublin', Shouldice writes. He continues:

> The last prisoner to come in was Eoin MacNeill, President of the Volunteer Organisation up to Easter Week. Although he was responsible for calling off the big parade on Easter Sunday, no hard feelings against him appeared to be evident amongst the other sixty-odd

prisoners. It was typical of de Valera in regard to the leadership which he had shown then and later, as on the morning after MacNeill's arrival at the prison, when he came down from his cell to join us in the morning prison parade, Dev, to the consternation of the Chief Warder and his assistants, stepped out from the ranks and gave the order 'Irish Volunteers – Attention – Eyes Left' and he and we saluted MacNeill. It was a thrilling moment for us.

Dartmoor was not an easy prison to be in. Shouldice loathed the food and, like many a convict before him, hated the winters. He writes: 'About late autumn the fogs or moor mists came over. These were very unpleasant as the prison walls ran with moisture.'

Shortly before Christmas 1916, Shouldice and his fellow Irish prisoners were transferred to Lewes Prison. He writes:

The winter of 1916–17 was very severe. The frost was practically continuous up to March or April of 1917. Sometime before our transfer to Lewes, during exercise periods, we were allowed to trot round the circle to keep warm. . . . When we were removed from Dartmoor we were chained together in batches of six by means of a steel chain through handcuffs. That journey was very enjoyable. We sang rebel songs on the way and even danced. When changing from the Dartmoor railway line to the main line we had a delay. . . . On the platform our squad, who were chained together, consisted of Bob Brennan, Harry Boland, Dick King, Con Donovan, myself and another whom I cannot recollect. Bob asked Dick, another Wexford man, to give an exhibition of Irish dancing, Bob lilting in great style. We held up the chain, and King, who was a Leinster Champion dancer, gave a selection of jigs and hornpipes which delighted us, and even the English travellers and railway officials who were on the platform, and they warmly applauded the performance.

Life in Lewes was much more pleasant, and Shouldice found the work for which he applied – gardening – congenial. Included in his working party were Tom Ashe, Sean McGarry, Seamus Melinn and de Valera. Shouldice continues: 'While we were working, Tom Ashe used to sing us traditional songs and tell us amusing yarns, mostly true, of his young days in Kerry.'

The news from Ireland was good. Count Plunkett won the Roscommon by-election for Sinn Féin. Some unknown genius got the idea of putting up a well-known Longford republican for election when the

North Longford parliamentary constituency became vacant. His name was Joe McGuinness, and he was a prisoner in Lewes. McGuinness is for-ever associated with the slogan: 'Put him in to get him out.' He was duly elected and, according to Shouldice, 'There was nearly a riot in the prison when they got the news. . . . The prison rang with the cheers of 130 Irish convicts.' Towards the end of May, de Valera, Ashe, Hunter, Harry Boland, Bob Brennan and others worked out a campaign to force the hand of the authorities. Shouldice explains: 'If our demands were not acceded to, we would proceed to break every prison regulation that lay in our power.' He joined in the ensuing campaign wholeheartedly, and took the consequences.

The campaign for the release of the Irish prisoners in English jails was at the same time taken up in Ireland, and was successful. Shouldice, who had by that time been moved to Maidstone Prison, remembers:

> The Governor, referring to the graceful action of the government, made a little speech and said that they now hoped that on our return to Ireland we would be good boys and cease our extreme methods of political agitation.

The 'boys' returned to Dublin. They were some of the last prisoners to be released.

Not all the men who fought in 1916 in Dublin were sent to jail. Apart from those who were executed, some escaped arrest. Nicholas Laffan, Captain G Company, 1st Battalion, Dublin Brigade in 1916, attests:

> Some of these men who had been out in the Rising were told on Sunday morning prior to the surrender that, if they wished, they could try and get away during the armistice, which lasted until 10 AM that day. They did so, and hid in the North Dublin Union grounds until after dark, when they made their way along the railway line to Cabra.

Frank Henderson, whose position as an officer and an organiser gave him a special expertise with regard to the structure of the IRA, writes a clear account of

> the work of rebuilding the Irish Volunteers, which began immediately after the return of the men who had been interned at Frongoch. It was

arranged in Dublin that the Companies would come together as soon as the men had spent Christmas with their families.

Henderson was Captain of F Company of the 2nd Battalion, Dublin Brigade. The Battalion Headquarters was located in Clonliffe Hall, situated at the end of a tree-lined avenue, close to Clonliffe Diocesan College. Henderson thought it ideal for the Volunteers' purposes. At Clonliffe Hall, they began, in Henderson's words:

> a period of unremitting intensive organising, training and planning which did not cease until the Truce (and for those of us who took part in the Civil War, until the Cease Fire Order in April 1923).

The aim of this programme, which was begun in each of the Dublin Battalion areas, was to knit together the members of the Battalion into a disciplined and trained force which, 'when the time came for action, played an efficient part in breaking down foreign domination in the country'.

The first step in the reorganisation was the appointment of officers for all the Companies: captain, lieutenant and second lieutenant. Henderson provides us with the names of all of the officers. 'The sections were re-formed, NCOs appointed, and a Company Council formed.' He could not remember the names of the NCOs.

The Battalion Staff officers ranked in order downwards from commandant through vice-commandant, adjutant, quartermaster and intelligence officer to other staff officers with special duties, such as transport. What might surprise us at this distance in time is the number of councils that were established by the Volunteers, each one requiring its attendant paperwork, however minimal, according to Henderson – not to mention the meetings. Each Company had its own council, as did each Battalion and Brigade. Henderson gives us the details, from which we can deduce the implications for the councils' members, who were mostly still part-time soldiers. He writes:

> The Battalion Council was presided over by the Battalion Commandant, and the other members were the Vice-Commandant (who was responsible for the Special Services i.e. First Aid, Intelligence, etc.), Adjutant, Quartermaster and Company Captains.

In the Brigade Council:

> The Brigade Commandant presided over the Brigade Council, which was formed, in addition to himself, of the Vice Brigade Commandant, Adjutant, Quartermaster, Intelligence Officer, the Commandants of each Battalion of the Brigade, and any other Staff Officers (First Aid, Transport, etc.), whom the Brigade Commandant ordered to attend. These councils were conducted under conditions of strict military discipline. Matters of organisation, discipline, arming, training, etc., were discussed and orders from the higher councils passed on.

The meetings may well have been short. Henderson emphasises: 'It was, of course, understood and accepted by all that the presiding officer had to be obeyed when he issued orders . . . at these councils or elsewhere.'

Oscar Traynor, who in the course of time became Brigade Commandant, remembered the council meetings too:

> The council met at least once a week, when each Battalion Commandant gave a detailed report of the activities of his unit. Intelligence reports were also discussed at these meetings. Battalion officers who had special schemes or plans in regard to attacks on the enemy would discuss these matters at the Brigade Council meetings. On occasion these plans would be improved as a result of the general discussion.

Once the Volunteers were on the way to being organised into an army, people like Henderson and Traynor were anxious that the men get some practice in military matters besides the endless drilling and the odd weekend manoeuvre.

The overriding concern of the Volunteers, officers and men, at that time was the procurement of arms. It goes without saying that the surrender by the insurgents at the end of the Easter Rising had stripped the Dublin Volunteers and the Citizen Army of all their arms. Henderson was in charge of his Company at all the parades that were held in connection with the death and funeral of Thomas Ashe. He remembers that he was only able to arm a few of the Volunteers. Even when some of the men were able to acquire some rifles, revolvers and ammunition from contacts in the British army, or when they had made successful raids on enemy posts, Traynor remembers:

The general equipment of the Battalion, however, was poor and on many occasions, when a large-scale attack was being launched on a particular object, it was found necessary to transfer equipment from one unit to another. In this way, the fight was vigorously carried on.

One of the first tasks allotted to Frank Thornton on his arrival in Ireland from Reading Jail had to do with the urgent necessity of procuring arms. Thornton records:

> I immediately reported for duty to Mick Collins and was instructed to report to Dundalk in connection with a job that was to be carried out there – a raid for Ulster Volunteer arms at Ballyedmond Castle.

In the late summer of 1918, a member of Henderson's Battalion in C Company named Tom Bourke, who worked as a checker in the Great Northern Railway at Sheriff Street, suspected that 'a large consignment of gelignite (and probably detonators)' was to arrive at Sheriff Street soon. Henderson continues:

> I told McDonnell to pick his men. . . . After a long delay . . . Burke brought word one evening that a railway wagon had arrived full of wooden boxes of the explosive. The boxes had been unloaded into one of the goods sheds and was to lie overnight there with one solitary DMP constable, who was unarmed, protecting it. McDonnell's plan was to enter the railway yard after dark with a party of Volunteers by scaling the walls in Oriel Street, which would then be practically devoid of traffic or pedestrians, come silently on the policeman, and quietly remove the boxes to waiting Volunteers over the wall in Oriel Street. . . . The coup was a complete success.

The British military scoured the north-east of the city in the days which followed, but none of the gelignite was ever recovered by them.

Shortly after this, Henderson had another stroke of luck. He came to hear of a military store at the North Wall which contained rifles belonging to a military post. These too were captured and 'dumped safely', and added to the stock of armaments.

It was sometimes easier to make contact with sympathetic members of the British army than it was to take possession of the goods after a deal had been made. Christopher Farrell was a member of A Company, 3rd Battalion, Dublin Brigade from 1917 to 1921. He was living in Upper George's Street, Dun Laoghaire, when he signed his statement on 2

December 1951. He had been authorised to conduct negotiations with two soldiers from Wellington Barracks for the delivery of a quantity of rifles. Farrell remembers:

> The Grand Canal forms the rear boundary of the barracks which is situated between the bridges – Harold's Cross and Sally's bridge. Inside the barrack railings . . . is a small red-bricked house known as the schoolmaster's house. This house offered cover. . . . It was decided that I would swim across the canal at this point.

Farrell made about fourteen crossings with the rifles strapped to his back, obtaining about fifty rifles in this way. 'It was winter and on several occasions I swam through a thin coating of ice', he notes.

On 20 March 1919, a most fruitful raid took place in north County Dublin. Seventy-five rifles, bayonets and sets of equipment, six thousand rounds of ammunition, and a portion of an aeroplane were captured 'without the firing of a single shot', Henderson records. The target was the military post at Collinstown, which was 'unknown to practically everyone'. Henderson writes:

> In 1918 and 1919 the British were carrying out extensions to the buildings and the airfield, and hundreds of Dublin city and county artisans and labourers were employed there by the civil contractor who had been appointed. A large number of these . . . were Irish Volunteers, belonging to the First Battalion, and to the unit recruited in the Finglas area.

Word reached Tom Byrne, OC 1st Battalion, who passed it on to Dick McKee, the Brigadier; McKee recognised how important the operation might be. Henderson notes: 'There followed several months of planning and postponing.' When all difficulties had apparently been resolved, the matter of the specially trained dogs posted at the entrance to the military post arose:

> These dogs were reported to be 'man-eaters' which would devour any strangers approaching the post. They were also supposed to start loud baying at night-time.

The difficulty was overcome when

> the men who were selected to deal with them had cultivated their friendship beforehand and were able to approach them without causing any noise that might arouse suspicion in the minds of the garrison.

There was another solution to the problem of supplying armaments for all the engagements which the leaders of the Volunteers were surely planning in 1917. Dublin Volunteers tried manufacturing the armaments themselves, with varying success, as did Volunteers in many of the country areas. James Foran, who had fought in the South Dublin Union in 1916, was back in action again by 1917. He and a Volunteer named McGlynn formed No. 4 Company, Engineers, with about fifty or sixty men. In 1919, Foran became ill and was in hospital for some months, but when he recovered, he tells us:

> I built two furnaces. I had to excavate the ground and go down six feet and put in two squares and build up the furnace with bricks. This place was beside the Telephone Exchange in Crown Alley. The British were in occupation of the Telephone Exchange . . . and we were never caught. . . . I never noticed how many grenades we turned out. They used to come twice a week and take three or four sacks of them in the car – not full bags. . . . It was marvellous the way we got away with it, we were very lucky. We were never raided. All the other fellows working there in the usual way at the usual foundry work never gave us away.

Meanwhile, James L. O'Donovan was working away at an earlier stage of production at University College Dublin. It was not generally known that he was Director of Chemicals, General Headquarters Staff, of the IRA. In fact, it was not generally known that he was a member of the Volunteers. Mulcahy, whom he knew through his friendship with the Ryans, had asked him not to join any unit of the Volunteers, although his brother was openly active in the movement. O'Donovan escaped attention from the police and got on with his research work in explosives, using the facilities provided by the college. He reveals an extraordinary list of co-workers in the research field: '[As well as Michael Lynch, Mulcahy and the Ryan family,] Tom Dillon was another contact and with him at Larkfield, Rory O'Connor and the Plunketts.' Dillon worked away in an attempt to get a native supply of explosives, apparently unnoticed by other academics in the college. Yet on one occasion, O'Donovan reports:

> the liquid blew up during my preparation of the poison gases . . . and the laboratory superintendent . . . found me wandering about in instinctive search of water after being blinded.

251

There were no repercussions. The superintendent was a man called Perry, whom O'Donovan thought unlikely to be in sympathy with the aims of the Volunteers, but he did not give him away. As the war went on and its scope expanded, the nature of O'Donovan's work changed. He started 'getting stuff' from England. Unexpected contacts were most useful at this point. When O'Donovan went to Liverpool, his contact was a Dr Daly, whose sister did secretarial work for Liam Mellows. But his best source never came under suspicion:

> In the latter stages, pre-Truce, I got a lot of chemical raw materials through Francis Fitzgerald, who owned a chemical factory in Greenwich. He was a brother of Desmond FitzGerald. He was an extremely useful introduction. It took time to develop this source of supply because the quantities involved were very much bigger.

The obsession with the procurement of arms followed the members of the Volunteer mission to the USA. A short witness statement submitted by the Very Reverend T. J. Shanley and others from 216 West 68th Street, New York, has as its subject: 'Purchase of arms in America and arrangements for transport to Ireland'. The combined statement describes a series of attempted deals which all fell through, including one which aspired to the purchase of an Austrian ship 'to put her into the Irish trade'. Harry Boland, one of the leaders of the American mission, evidently felt the pressure from Headquarters back home. Shanley writes:

> When the 'East Side' was chartered, Harry Boland, McGee and Gleeson were at lunch in a place in either Fulton or Nassau Street, and McGee said to Boland that the shipment of such a large number of pieces of machinery would be very hard to handle. Harry said: 'I am forced to do this. The "Big Fellow" is riding . . . out of me.'

The 'Big Fellow' was presumably Collins. At this time, Collins was simultaneously a member of Dáil Éireann, Minister for Finance, President of the Supreme Council of the IRB, Director of Organisation, and Director of Intelligence, the last being arguably the post in which he was most effective. His links with Thornton went back to their time in England. Both had returned to Ireland with the Kimmage Garrison in 1916, as had Seamus Robinson.

Thornton is at pains to express his respect for other high-ranking officers as well as Collins – officers such as Mulcahy, Brugha and Gearoid

O'Sullivan. He describes the initial steps taken by the intelligence section at GHQ, the section of which Collins became director almost from the beginning:

> The first office opened by GHQ intelligence in the city was over Fowler's in Crow Street, off Dame Street, which was right bang up against Dublin Castle. Here Liam Tobin, Tom Cullen [and] myself, together with Frank Saurin, Charlie Dalton, Charlie Byrne [and] Joe Guilfoyle, started off our operations.

Thornton explains the hierarchy of the intelligence system. It shadowed the ranks that were already in place in the IRA. He writes:

> Each Company appointed an intelligence officer for its own area. This intelligence officer was responsible for setting up a system for the collection of information of all sorts through the medium of agents acting within, and outside, the ranks of the enemy forces. He employed people in all walks of life, special attention being paid to movements of troops and location of enemy spies, and the securing of positions in enemy centres for our own agents where possible.

The Company reported to the Battalion intelligence officer: 'He [the Company intelligence officer] passed on what was useful to his Brigade IO.' It was a useful system. 'The Brigade Intelligence Officer was always in touch with both his own intelligence staff and the GHQ Intelligence Branch.'

Oscar Traynor reminds us how the intelligence system fitted into the whole structure of the IRA. Traynor, because he was officer commanding the Dublin Brigade, was a member of the Army Council. He writes:

> This council seldom met in the same building twice in succession. Notices for attendance at these meetings were typed on tiny pieces of tissue paper, which could be quickly destroyed or swallowed if the necessity arose.

The Minister for Defence, Cathal Brugha, presided over these meetings. The officers attending were: Richard Mulcahy, Chief of Staff; J. J. O'Connell, Assistant Chief of Staff; Gearoid O'Sullivan, Adjutant General; Sean McMahon, Quartermaster General; Michael Collins, Director of Intelligence; Diarmuid O'Hegarty, Director of Organisation; Liam Mellows, Director of Purchases; Piaras Beaslai, Director of

Publicity; Rory O'Connor, Director of Engineering; Sean Russell, Director of Munitions; and Oscar Traynor, Officer Commanding the Dublin Brigade.

The general discussion at these meetings usually centred around the reports of the various directors. Naturally, the most interesting of these discussions centred around the Director of Intelligence, and to a lesser degree the Director of Organisation.

Traynor goes on to deal with a subject which came up occasionally at these Army Council meetings. He attests:

> Occasionally authority would be sought for the execution of spies, and these, I understand, were usually submitted to a Committee of the Cabinet and later returned for action to the Army Council. These things could not be discussed by the government because, first of all, they were army reports which had to be discussed by the council, and if there was anything in them, the Minister for Defence, who was Chairman, would say 'We will have this matter dealt with and report later.' . . . I was told then that in every case the authority of the government was required for the execution of spies. . . . Unauthorised executions were not permissible.

Thornton, who was given the special task of compiling the information on every known member of the new British Secret Service Organisation, corroborates Traynor's report. He writes:

> I had the honour to be in charge of that particular job of compiling all that information and got the very unenvious job of presenting my full report to a joint meeting of the Dáil Cabinet and Army Council, at which meeting I had to prove that each and every man on my list was an accredited Secret Service man of the British government. This, as everybody can realise, was not an easy task, but proves one thing, that is that our government and our army were not going to allow any man to be shot without the fullest possible proof being produced of his guilt.

To a large extent, the War of Independence in Dublin was a contest between two intelligence organisations: that of the British government and that of the IRA. In addition to the intelligence structures in the ranks of the IRA Companies, Battalions and Brigades, there was another, as Traynor describes:

The Special Intelligence Squad was a special Headquarters Squad of fighting men, who were reserved for use by Michael Collins in the event of their services being specially required by reason of urgent intelligence which he might receive. They were completely separate.

Thornton reveals:

Mick McDonnell was the first OC of the Dublin Squad and remained OC until some time after Bloody Sunday, when his health collapsed and he was sent to California. About this period, Paddy Daly took over.

The single most memorable operation against the British Secret Service in Dublin was the shooting on Bloody Sunday, 21 November 1920, of nineteen operatives in the British Secret Service. Vincent Byrne, 2nd Battalion, Dublin Brigade, and a member of the Squad, records:

This operation which took place on the 21 November 1920 was a Brigade one, members of the 1st, 2nd, 3rd, and 4th Battalions, the [Active Service] Unit, Intelligence staff, and Squad taking part.

Byrne remembers the details of the Bloody Sunday operation in vivid detail, and devotes several pages of his statement to that fateful morning.

The operation was a daring counterblow to the activities of the Black and Tans throughout the country. According to Thornton:

The activities of the Intelligence Department were not confined to this country. They were entrusted with the carrying out of a very big and important job in the city of London.

Their job was to compile all the information necessary for the kidnapping of twelve members of Parliament, including some Cabinet ministers. Thornton himself spent some time in London on this work.

Life was more mundane for the Volunteers who were left at home, even if, like James Corrigan, a member of the 1st Battalion, you made it into the Active Service Unit. Members of the Active Service Unit were paid soldiers. Corrigan recollects Oscar Traynor's talk on their formation:

[We were told that] we were now joining a unit that was formed for the purpose of engaging the enemy in the streets of Dublin and that we were to be the paid soldiers of the Irish Republican Army – our main tactics would be guerrilla warfare – hit and run – and that was to continue night and day and that we were to regard ourselves as full-time soldiers.

They were free to stand down at this point if they did not feel up to standard. Corrigan did not stand down. He continues:

> My arms consisted of a short Webley revolver and twelve rounds of ammunition. The Active Service Unit Headquarters was situated in a small shop in Temple Bar.

The burning of the Custom House was probably the largest operation undertaken by the ASU, the Squad, and units of the Dublin Brigade. It took place on 25 May 1921 and was expensive in terms of IRA prisoners taken. We have Oscar Traynor's account of a meeting, held early in the new year of 1921, when the destruction of the Custom House was proposed and decided on. De Valera, who was not long returned from the United States, spoke at this meeting. Traynor reports:

> (de Valera) made it clear that something in the nature of a big action in Dublin was necessary in order to bring public opinion abroad to bear on the question of Ireland's case.

The burning of the Custom House fitted the bill and duly took place, with rather more casualties on the British side than on the nationalist side. Traynor reports:

> Altogether we lost five killed and about eighty captured. . . . Everything within the four walls of the Custom House building was reduced to ashes. The fire was still burning ten days after the attack. The fire brigades were unable to go into action for a considerable time.

Patrick Daly, the Officer Commanding the Squad, gives his verdict on the Custom House operation:

> The attack on the Custom House put a great spirit into the whole Brigade, for I think there was not a single Company in Dublin but went out that night to hit up enemy forces, which they did to very good effect.

Daly goes on to describe the amalgamation of the Squad and the Active Service Unit under his own command:

> After the burning of the Custom House, the Squad and the Active Service Unit were amalgamated into one. We had approximately eighty men between the two units; the remainder were either prisoners, wounded or killed.

Daly reorganised this group and made several changes. He records:

> When I took over I told the men that we were having no staff officers.
> Every officer and NCO would be a leader in attack. The Lieutenants
> would not alone take orders from me, but they would look for jobs and
> keep the men employed. Every Tan and military lorry was fair game, but
> no individual shootings of civilians must take place; no man had the
> right to say who was a spy. Headquarters were the only people who
> would give an order for an execution. I kept in touch with [the] Brigade
> OC as well as Intelligence, and the two half-Companies worked very
> well, as a day never passed without some lorry being hit up, sometimes
> with very good effect. British dispatch riders were constantly being
> relieved of their motor-bicycles and dispatches. Laundries were invaded
> and military clothing destroyed. Provisions going to military barracks
> were seized. The enemy was harried in every way possible.

As 1921 progressed, things began to slacken off. The announcement of
the Truce came as a great relief for people like Stephen Keys, who was a
member of the 3rd Battalion, Dublin Brigade, in that year. He writes:

> I do know that things were getting on my nerves. It was no joke going
> out two or three nights each week for months, and the strain was begin-
> ning to tell on me. Still I continued to go out and I would not bring a
> grenade back. It was not so bad when our grenades exploded, but too
> often they were duds. When this occurred we were left in a very unen-
> viable position, as the grenade was our main weapon of attack.

27

In Retrospect

The Truce, when it came, was hugely popular all over the country, particularly amongst those people who had taken no active part in the War of Independence. Some of the combatants were not so sanguine. Eamon Broy, the famous spy in the Castle, had misgivings. In an account of a conversation he had with Michael Collins, on the evening of Broy's release from prison, he remembers:

> Mick was worried about too much rejoicing going on all over the country following the Truce and too much relaxation.

Broy himself was

> disagreeably surprised to see many fine and highly strung young Irish Volunteers, who had been teetotallers when I had last met them, drinking whiskey neat. It was bound to have a bad effect on them, especially after the long struggle they had endured.

Some people did not believe that the Truce would last. According to Michael Brennan from Clare, this group included Michael Collins. Brennan remembers:

> I went to Dublin on July 12th or 13th and reported at GHQ. Collins, Mulcahy, Gearoid O'Sullivan and others all emphasised that they didn't expect the Truce to last very long and that it must be used to improve our organisation and training. I left them quite convinced that we had only got a breathing space and that a resumption of the fighting was an absolute certainty.

Oscar Traynor, Brigadier of the Dublin Brigade, records that on the declaration of the Truce our general instructions from the Chief of Staff was that we were to intensify our training, and with this instruction in view, training camps were operated all over the country.

In the decade when the Bureau of Military History was assembling the archives of witness statements, Michael Collins was the subject of intense interest – as he has been ever since his tragic death at the age of thirty-one. Some of the witness statements express the thoughts of his contemporaries, many of them close comrades, about Collins. As one might expect, they vary considerably.

Patrick Colgan, from Maynooth, was a prisoner with Collins at Frongoch. They shared a hut with four others. Colgan gives his memories of that time:

> Mick Collins – gay good humour all through our time in Frongoch; his kindness in sharing his issue of two cigarettes with me, who received the same issue as he did. I being sworn into the IRB by Mick on 16 December, 1916.

In 1917, on one of his re-organising trips, Ernest Blythe remembers:

> I should say that when I was going from Cork to Bantry on my first trip, I travelled west in the train with Michael Collins and Diarmuid Hegarty, who were going to speak at an Aeridheacht in Bantry. I had met Collins for a few minutes in the National Aid office when [I had been] released from Reading or released from Arbour Hill, after giving my undertaking to go North, but could not say that I knew him well until the day we travelled west from Cork. The first time I ever heard Collins deliver a public speech was at the Aeridheacht. He spoke very vigorously, but the time had not yet come when he could grip the crowd. Although his reputation was growing, it was by no means made, and he did not reckon as any more important than an ordinary local speaker.

Charles Dalton, a member of IRA intelligence, remembered his first meeting with Collins:

> When I walked into the room I saw several staff officers assembled. Among them was the Director of Intelligence, Michael Collins. I knew Michael by sight but this was the first occasion on which I saw him face to face. He was sitting at a table, and he gave me a friendly nod when I

reported to him. I felt very important to be in such company, but at the same time the presence of Michael completely overawed me.

Frank Thornton, who was the Volunteers' Deputy Director of Intelligence from 1919, had known Collins since 1915. In his own words:

I liked Michael Collins. I was a great admirer of him. I recognised at an early stage, even as far back as my first contact with him in Liverpool, that he was a dynamic type of individual and, although at that period he was not in any directive position, still he was an outstanding individual on that famous day in Liverpool in 1915. Later on, working with him on organisation, I had a very quiet admiration for him which developed as the years went on.

Laurence Nugent, a Lieutenant in 'K' Company, 3rd Battalion, does not display quite the same enthusiasm for Collins. After the release of the prisoners and their return from Frongoch, Collins first came to prominence as Secretary of the National Aid Association. According to Nugent, Collins owed his election to 'the Plunkett influence'. Nugent continues:

With those who did not know him well, he was not at all popular. He was inclined to be aggressive and impatient in his manner, and he had no time for anyone who wanted to delay over the reorganising of the Volunteers.

Nugent hints at intemperance:

He enjoyed a good drop of whiskey, and while he was acting as Secretary of the National Aid in Exchequer Street his favourite bar was The Stag's Head, where there was a whiskey barrel known as 'Mick's Barrel'. If you met him there you would meet the genial, good-natured man gushing with friendship. I met him frequently on matters dealing with arms during this time, and under these circumstances certainly he never drank to excess.

Almost as if he had heard Nugent, Thornton also deals with the issue of drink. He writes:

In some of the criticisms that have appeared from time to time about Mick Collins it has been suggested that he drunk [sic] to excess. These statements are lies. As one who was very closely associated with him during those stremuous days, I can say that Collins rarely took anything, and when he did it was a small sherry.

Mrs Sean O'Donovan, who was Harry Boland's only sister, knew Collins well. She remembers an intriguing episode:

It must have been some time before the Truce that Mick Collins asked me to go to Mountjoy Jail with flowers for Mrs Llewelyn Davis, who was imprisoned there, though I don't know for what. I took a bouquet three times for him. He brought them himself to me on a bicycle. It struck me as funny for Mick Collins to be bringing flowers, and I used to joke him about it. Flowers and Mick Collins did not seem to go together. I fancy there must have been some good reason behind it and that it was not merely gallantry. I must say that, although Mick made no personal appeal to me as a man, he was a Trojan worker and kept everyone up to the mark. He had that quality that everything he would do, he would do well. He was very disappointed that Harry and Gerry did not go with him at the Treaty.

In his witness statement, Eamon Broy gives considerable attention to Collins, to whom he was devoted. Possibly the most striking passage dealing with Collins is the following:

I remember one morning about a quarter past nine I went to keep an appointment with Tommy Gay in the vicinity of Tara Street. I was casually watching the traffic coming from the direction of Butt Bridge and going along Tara Street when who should I see but Michael Collins cycling in the stream of traffic. As I had no direct business in talking to him at that precise moment, I did nothing to attract his attention. Such a proceeding, in any case, would have been risky in drawing attention to him and to myself. He did not notice me and passed on. He wore a high-quality soft hat, dark grey suit, as usual, neatly shaved and with immaculate collar and tie, as always, seeming ready for the photographer. His bicycle was of first-class quality and fitted with a lamp and many other accessories. He looked like a bank clerk or stockbroker or 'something in the city' and cycled on as if he owned the street.

Maeve McGarry, in whose house in Blackrock Éamon de Valera had lived in the months just before the Truce, is able to throw a little light on the relationship between de Valera and Collins. She remembers:

The night before he travelled to London, Collins came, and the two of them spent hours walking up and down in the garden discussing things.

261

De Valera and Collins were devoted to each other. Collins worshipped the ground that de Valera trod on, and while de Valera was in America Collins went down to Greystones to Mrs de Valera every week to see that all was well there and to bring her her husband's salary. De Valera was equally fond of Collins. Some years later, when he came to 31 Fitzwilliam Street to look for consulting rooms for his son, he asked to see the room which Collins used to use.

One suspects that the Bureau of Military History was particularly interested in recording Robert Barton's opinion of Collins. Not only were they close associates whenever Barton was not in prison, but they took opposing sides on the Treaty.

Barton was one of the signatories of the Treaty, and he includes in his witness statement a convincing explanation of the position he took on that fateful document. He explains why in the first place he signed the Treaty, and secondly how he opposed it. On Collins, he writes: 'I had a very high estimate of Mick Collins. He was an indefatigable worker and a most efficient administrator. We were on very friendly terms.' Sadly, the friendship was broken:

> Our relations were completely severed after the Dáil debates. I never spoke to him again and never saw him. We spoke after we returned from London and we spoke occasionally during the debates but, once the vote was taken, as far as I remember, I went home and took no further part.

Seamus Robinson, who had placed such value on acquiring Collins's endorsement of the Soloheadbeg ambush, had become disillusioned with GHQ in the course of the War of Independence, according to his statement. He expresses himself freely, with all the hindsight of thirty years and a bitter Civil War behind him. There was something of the age-old quarrel of 'the generals behind the lines and the misunderstood fighting men at the front' about Robinson's testimony. He calls Collins an 'artful dodger' and accuses him of arranging a phoney attack on Lord French. He writes:

> However, Mick was able to give the impression to the Volunteer officers from all over the country that he not only organised the attacks that had begun in Dublin but that he also led them, taking part in them!

But Robinson, who must have known Collins from the Kimmage Camp days in Larkfield before the 1916 Rising, in which they both took part, was deeply angry at the influence which Collins was able to exert at the time of the Treaty. He suspects the complicity of the British press, ably assisted by the 'anti-national press' in Ireland. He writes:

> Towards the end of 1920 and the beginning of 1921, the British press had been changing its description of Collins from a 'thug' and a 'murderer' to a 'daredevil'; romanticising him with damnation that praised him in the sight of the Irish people. He was 'seen' all over the country leading the Column from Dublin to west Cork, where he had been 'seen' riding on a white charger like King William at the Boyne. But it was Tom Barry who rode the horse because of a strained foot and King William rode a brown horse. This sort of journalism is not history but it is blatant propaganda. In the case of Mick Collins it put him on a pedestal where he did not properly belong. It enhanced his undoubted influence beyond all bounds. 'What's good enough for Mick Collins is good enough for me' – as Deputy after IRB Deputy declared before announcing his decision to vote for the Treaty.

Very few other witness statements extend as far as the Treaty debates. Most end at the Truce, and quite a few cover only that extraordinary week around Easter of 1916. There are a few which express hints of earlier dissension, which might later develop into huge fissures. Barton, for example, when he returned from prison in England, noticed that there was

> internal dissension which had not existed when I was arrested. . . . dissension in the Cabinet developed while I was in jail. Previously we had been a very happy family. When I returned, I found personal animosity between members of the Cabinet; this very much disturbed me. There were differences of opinion between Cathal Brugha, Austin Stack and de Valera on one side, and Michael Collins and Dick Mulcahy on the other. Ministers were not co-operating in the way they had before. I think Cathal Brugha felt that Michael Collins was getting too much control of the army.

Blythe records something of the same discord, but in far more detail. From the beginning of the War of Independence, these relationships were greatly complicated by the varying attitudes towards the IRB within the independence movement. People like Cathal Brugha made it clear that, from the very first meeting of Dáil Éireann, and particularly once an independent government had been established, there was no role for the IRB. But at Frongoch, the IRB greatly increased its membership – much to the disgust of Robinson, who had no time for the IRB either.

Frank Henderson was well placed to observe the situation when he worked with the Department of Organisation. Henderson noted: 'There was a close liaison between [the Department of Organisation] and the IRB', but he saw nothing strange in that. Henderson was a member of the IRB himself. He continues: 'Many of the most reliable officers in Brigade areas were also the local IRB Centres. The Director of Organisation [Diarmuid O'Hegarty] was an important IRB official.'

Things were beginning to change, however, and Henderson noticed a tendency 'for some of the more active Volunteer officers not to regard the IRB as seriously' as they used to do. Henderson relates in some detail an incident which he regards as significant. Shortly after the Truce had been announced, Henderson was asked by the IRB to go to the north Wexford area during the August bank holiday weekend

> to visit the IRB Circles there and to bring them a message from the Supreme Council. . . . I received my instructions from Gearoid O'Sullivan . . . who was the Centre for Leinster. He was also the Adjutant General of the IRA.

Henderson visited every IRB Circle in the area over the weekend. The message which the Supreme Council wanted Henderson to pass on was to

> warn them that negotiations which were proceeding between represen-tatives of our country and those of England might possibly conclude with an offer by the British government of a compromise which could not be accepted by the republicans, but which would be so tempting that there would be a great danger of its acceptance being advocated by many influential people.

Henderson could not have been surprised by the message. What did surprise him, however, was the last-minute information that was given to him almost as he boarded the train for Wexford. He records:

> Before I departed for Wexford on Saturday afternoon, I was told that Cathal Brugha, the Minister for Defence, would be travelling to County

264

Wexford on the same train as I would, and that I was to avoid him. This latter instruction seemed to me to be an intimation of a serious estrangement between the chiefs, whom I had regarded up to that moment as peerless in their unity and their leadership of the resurgent nation, and I was deeply troubled.

Austin Stack's posthumous testimony, submitted by his widow Mrs Una Stack (who was herself the widow of an RIC officer), leads us through the peace talks in the months before the Treaty. The talks began immediately after the Truce had been drawn up and signed by both sides. Stack was one of the party who accompanied the President, Éamon de Valera, to London to meet the British Prime Minister, Mr Lloyd George. Stack remembers:

> We remained in London for about eleven days. During that time the President and Lloyd George met on three occasions, I think. . . . After the second interview, we had reason to believe they were not going beyond Dominion Home Rule.

This was found to be the case when the British put their proposals in writing, to be considered 'at a meeting of Cabinet ministers and others at the President's house at Blackrock.' Significantly, Stack recollects:

> I got the impression strongly forced upon me that Griffith and Collins and Mulcahy (who had also been invited) were inclined to view the proposals favourably – that is that they were in the main acceptable [to them]

It was decided to submit the terms to the Dáil, which was summoned for 15 August. Stack continues:

> They (the British proposals) were rejected unanimously and enthusiastically, though everyone knew of England's threat to renew the war.

Correspondence between de Valera and Lloyd George was resumed. Following some disagreement between the two leaders on the status of the representatives as emissaries of 'a free and independent nation', the correspondence stalled, but, Stack continues:

> Lloyd George writes de Valera another letter suggesting that the previous correspondence be all wiped out and issuing a new invitation to our

representatives to meet Britain's representatives in London.

The talks were on again. Stack describes the Cabinet meeting:

> It was suggested early that the President should go himself, but he had his objections. He pointed out that he was in the position of head of state as well as head of the government, and that, in his absence, it would be always said they had to consult the President and their other colleagues in Dublin.

The meeting went on to select five plenipotentiaries. A further Cabinet meeting or two, a couple of discussions on what was meant by 'external association', the settling of the instructions for the plenipotentiaries, and all was ready for their departure to London. They left early in the second week of October. Stack continued to be uneasy, particularly when Griffith appeared to ignore his advice. Stack writes:

> I mentioned the absolute necessity of procuring the services of some constitutional lawyer from America or Europe, if necessary, to look after our interests. Mr Griffith promised to look after this; I had a private conversation with him afterwards – it may have been some days later – and he repeated his promise . . . but as it turned out the plenipotentiaries got no constitutional lawyer to act with them in London.

There were other issues which disturbed Stack and made him wonder what the plenipotentiaries were up to in London:

> For some time – perhaps a fortnight – we used to receive detailed accounts of the discussions and we followed them closely. There was nothing alarming to us in any of the reports up to about October 25th.

The question of allegiance to the Crown had also come up:

> The President then and there . . . dictated a letter to Mr Griffith, informing him that our views 'were giving in too much to the English in important matters' such as the Republican Courts.

It seems that the courts might continue to function but that no decrees were to be enforced.

On the question of defence, Stack records:

> Our people in London, without consulting the Minister for Defence, agreed that there were to be no more arms imported into Ireland.

Towards the end of October, the detailed reports from London ceased as the negotiations began to be narrowed to about four participants. Stack reports that it was decided that 'Collins and Griffith should meet himself and another British minister to discuss matters from that time forth.'

Robert Barton, who was a plenipotentiary and a signatory of the Treaty, comments on this development:

> Possibly Lloyd George also felt that he could make more progress with Griffith and Collins than he had made with a full delegation.

Barton and Gavan Duffy acquiesced to Lloyd-George's request to reduce the number of negotiators. Barton continues:

> It was not until later that Gavan Duffy, Childers and I realised that Griffith and Collins were prepared to settle for less than we thought it possible to obtain. We had trusted them fully. We had complete confidence in them up to that time. Griffith fought magnificient actions during the full conference. We had no reason to suppose at the time that he would agree in private to anything which he had not been agreeing to with five of us present . . . It was decided that one of us must go to Dublin to acquaint the Cabinet and de Valera that we were not at all sure that the reports given us of what transpired at private conferences were comprehensive.

De Valera and the Cabinet thought that Barton, Duffy and others were exaggerating. In Barton's opinion, de Valera retained his confidence in the plenipotentiaries, particularly Griffith, right up to the moment when 'Duggan handed a copy of the Articles of Agreement to President de Valera at the Mansion House'.

But on 30 November, before that point had been reached, the plenipotentiaries sent a dispatch, signed by Griffith, to Dublin. The dispatch included what amounted to a draft treaty, and a letter asking for a Cabinet meeting to be called for Saturday 3 December 1921. Stack was glad to arrange a full attendance of the Cabinet members to meet all the plenipotentiaries. The meeting began at 10 o'clock in the morning and lasted all day, ending at 6 PM, 'just in time to enable the delegates to catch the night mail [boat] back to London', Stack notes. He continues:

> The discussion throughout was on the main questions – allegiance to the British Crown and Partition. . . . Griffith argued all day in favour of acceptance.

But when at last 'Cathal Brugha turned to him to him, saying "Don't you realise that if you sign this thing, you will split Ireland from top to bottom?" the truth seemed to strike Griffith very forcibly, and he said: "I suppose that's so. I'll tell you what I'll do. I'll go back to London. I'll not sign the document but I'll bring it back and submit it to the Dáil and if necessary to the people."' Everyone was happy with this.

On 6 December, Stack was surprised to read 'on the back page of the *Independent*, under "Latest News", was a paragraph saying that a settlement had been reached and an agreement signed between the British and Irish representatives at 2.30 o'clock that morning. I did not know what to think.'

That evening, President de Valera was to preside at a National University event celebrating Dante in the Mansion House. Stack remembers:

> he (the President) was about to lead the way into the round room, when who should arrive but Mr E.J. Duggan and Mr Desmond Fitzgerald".

They presented a copy of the signed Articles of Agreement to de Valera. Duggan informed the President that it had been arranged 'that the thing be published in London and Dublin simultaneously'. It was a fait accompli: Griffith had broken his pledge not to sign the fateful document.

Both Barton and Stack continue the narrative of the succession of Dáil assemblies and endless meetings. Barton writes:

> There were several meetings, covering several days. I remember the *Independent* screaming that the talking should stop and the vote must be taken.

At the Department of Local Government, where Kevin O'Higgins was Assistant Minister, there was no doubt amongst the staff as to how the vote should go. Seamus Ua Caomhanaigh remembers the day of the Cabinet meeting which would consider the Treaty. He writes:

> when leaving the office to attend that meeting of the Cabinet, the girl members of the staff followed [O'Higgins] halfway down the street urging him to vote against the Treaty, and it was not until he had got away from them and was some distance ahead that he turned round and shouted: 'I'm going to vote for it.'

APPENDIX

THE WITNESSES

Aghas, Nora, sister of Thomas Ashe

Ahern, Robert C., Intelligence Officer IV and IRA, Cork 1917–21

Aherne, Maurice, Constable in DMP 1921, IRA Intelligence

Aughney, Eilis, Member Cumann na mBan Dublin, 1921

Aylward, Edward J., Commandant IRA Kilkenny, 1921

Barrett, Annie, Intelligence Agent IRA Cork, 1921

Barrett, James, Member IRB 1913, Officer IRA Galway 1920–1921

Barrett, Joseph, Member IRB 1908, Officer IRA Clare 1917–1921

Barry, Matthew, Captain, Meath IRA, 1921

Barry, Tom, OC Cork No. 3 Brigade Flying Column 1920–21; Commandant General IRA 1921

Barton, Dulcibella, Sister of Robert Barton

Barton, Robert, Signatory of Anglo-Irish Treaty, 1921

Baxter, Leo, Commandant IRA, Longford, 1918–1921

Beaumont, M., née Maureen McGavock, Member Executive Committee Cumann na mBan, 1918

Berry, Patrick Joseph, Prison Warder Mountjoy, 1921; Intelligence Officer

Bloxham, Elizabeth, Member Executive Cumann na mBan

Blythe, Ernest, Minister Dáil Éireann, 1921

Boland, Patrick, Officer IRA Offaly, 1921

Bolger, John C., Attached to GHQ Intelligence IRA

Booth, Frank, Member IRB Belfast

Bradley, J. J., Registrar, Dail Court County Cork, 1920

Brady, Bernard, Commandant IRA Cavan, 1921

Brady, Hugh, Officer IRA Leitrim, 1921

Brady, Margaret, née Sweeney Member Cumann na mBan Leitrim

Brady, Thomas, Officer IRA Roscommon, 1921

Bratton, Eugene, Constable RIC Meath, 1916–21

Breen, Dan, Quartermaster 3 Tipperary Brigade IRA; Author *My Fight for Irish Freedom*

Breen, Sean, Officer IRA Wexford

Brennan, Edward, Commandant IRA Laois, 1921

Brennan, John, Constable RIC Offaly, 1921

Brennan, Joseph, British Official Dublin Castle 1920, Governor Central Bank

Brennan, Michael, OC East Clare Brigade IRA, 1921

Brennan, Patrick, Officer IRA Wexford, 1921

Brennan, Robert, Publicity Department , Dáil Éireann, 1921

Brennan, Timothy, Constable RIC Offaly, 1921

Browne, Monsignor, Friend of Sean McDermott, Brother of Mrs Sean McEntee

Broy, Eamon, IRA Intelligence Agent in British Police Dublin Castle

Bryan, Dan, Officer IRA Dublin 1918–21, Director of Intelligence 1948

Bulfin, Eamon, Lieutenant IV, Dublin, 1916

Burke, Patrick, Officer IRA, Waterford, 1921

Byrne, Christopher, Member IRA Carlow, 1918–1921

Byrne, Daniel, Officer IRA Wicklow 1921, TD and Senator, Dáil Éireann

Byrne, Thomas P., Member Irish Brigade, South Africa, 1900–1902, Captain IV
    Dublin, Commandant IRA Dublin 1921

Byrne, Vincent, Officer IRA Dublin, Member 'The Squad' and ASU, 1919–1921

Cahill, James, Member IRB and IV Cavan, 1914–1917; Member of ASU, Dublin,
    1921

Cannon, Patrick, Commandant IRA, Mayo, 1921

Carroll, John, Captain IRA Wexford

Carroll, Nicholas, Vice Commandant IRA Kilkenny, 1921

Carton, Patrick, Member IRA Flying Column Wexford

Casey, Patrick J, Commandant IRA Down, 1916–1921

Cashel, Alice, Member Cumann na mBan Galway, Vice Chairman Galway
    County Council, 1920–1921

Cassidy, Martin, Captain IV and IRA Kilkenny, 1917–1921

Cassidy, Patrick, Commandant IRA Mayo, 1921

Ceannt, Aine Bean, Ceannt, Widow of Eamon Ceannt, executed 1916

Clarke, James, Intelligence Officer IV Kerry, 1918, Officer IRA Kerry, 1921

Cogan, Denis, Office of Land Bank, 1919

Colgan, Patrick, Commandant IRA, Kildare, 1921

Colley, Harry, Officer IV 1915–1919, Adjutant IRA Dublin Brigade 192–1921

Collins, Maurice, Member IV and IRB, 1916

Conaty, Charles, Officer IRA Meath, 1921

Conneely, Martin, Officer West Connemara Brigade IRA, 1920–1921

Connell, Francis, Commandant IRA Cavan, 1921

Connolly, John T., Captain IRA Fermanagh, 1921

Connolly, Joseph , Commandant IRA Offaly

Conroy, David Joseph, Battalion Officer, IRA West Clare, 1921

Conway, Michael, Commandant IRA Limerick, 1921

Conway, Michael, Member IRA Wexford, 1921; Survivor of explosion at
    Saltmills, Wexford 1921

Conway, Seamus, Commandant Flying Column IRA Longford

Cope, Sir Alfred, Assistant Under Secretary for Ireland, 1921

Cordial, Michael, Battalion Quartermaster, Offaly, 1921

Corrigan, James, Member of Fianna Éireann 1913–1916, GPO and Hibernian Bank 1916, ASU Dublin 1919–1921

Corrigan, William, Member of South Dublin Union Garrison 1916, Brother of Michael Corrigan, Chief State Solicitor

Cosgrave, William T., Member of Marrowbone Lane Garrison 1916, Minister Dáil Éireann 1919–1921, President Dáil Éireann 1922

Crawley, Thomas, Vice Commandant IRA Roscommon, 1921

Cremin, Michael, Member IV Dublin 1916, Captain IRA Dublin 1921

Cronin, Michael, Clerk, Dáil Court, Cork, 1921

Crothers, Christopher, Member ICA, 1916, IRA Dublin 1920–1921

Crowe, Patrick, Member IRA Kerry 1921, Communications & Intelligence Glanmire Railway Station

Cunningham, Mollie, President Cumann na mBan Macroom, 1916–1921

Cunningham, Nora, Member Cumann na mBan Macroom, 1917–1923

Curran, Monsignor M. J., Rector Irish College Rome

Czira, Sydney, who wrote under the pen name 'John Brennan', sister of Grace Gifford, widow of J. Plunkett, executed

Dalton, Charles, Member The Squad, 1921

Dalton, Emmet, Officer IRA Dublin, 1921

Daly, James, Captain IRA Kerry, 1921

Daly, Patrick, Lieutenant IV, Dublin, 1913–1916, Member of ASU, 1920–1921

Daly, Una, Secretary to Liam Mellows, executed 1922

Davern, Michael, Commandant IRA Tipperary, 1921

Davitt, Cahir, Judge, Dáil Courts, 1921

de Barra, Peadar, Member of Corroga (Co. Down) Company Irish Volunteers 1918–, Brigade Staff Officer, 1921–1922

de Burca, Doctor F., Member IRB

Deasy, Jeremiah, Officer IRA Bandon, Cork

Deasy, Liam, Brigade and Divisional Officer IRA Cork, 1921

Dillon, Geraldine, Sister of Joseph M. Plunkett, executed 1916

Dobbyn, Seamus, Member Supreme Council IRB, 1917–1921

Doherty, Michael, Commandant IRA Donegal, 1921

Doherty, PH, Commandant IRA Donegal, 1921

Donegan, Maurice, Battalion Officer IRA Cork, 1921

Donnelly, Simon, Captain IV and IRA Dublin, 1916–1921, Chief of Republican Police

Donnelly, Stephen, Captain IRA, Mayo, 1921

Doyle, James, Manager Gresham Hotel, 1920; Witness of Execution of British Agents, 21/11/1920

Doyle, Patrick , Rev. Father, Parish Priest Naas

Dryer, Albert T., Doctor; Secretary Irish National Association, Australia

Duffy, John, Member RIC working for IRA Roscommon

Duggan, George C., Assistant to Under Secretary for Ireland, Dublin Castle, 1919–1921

Dunne, James, Commandant IRA Kildare, 1921

Egan, Patrick, Lieutenant IV, Dublin, 1916; OC Battalion Communications, Dublin, 1917–1921

Farrell, Christopher, Officer IRA Dublin, 1921

Farrington, Annie, Owner Barry's Hotel, meeting of GHQ IRA officers

Feehan, John, Quartermaster 4 Western Division, 1921

Finn, Seamus, Officer IRA Meath, 1921

Finucane, Matthew, Member IV and IRA Kerry, 1921

Flannery, John, Participant in mutiny of Connaught Rangers, India, 1920

Foran, James, Member IV Dublin, 1916

Furlong, Joseph, Member IRB, Wexford, 1908, IV London, 1913; GHQ Staff IRA, 1920–1921

Gavan-Duffy, Louise, Sister of George Gavan-Duffy, Secretary Cumann na mBan, 1916

Gaynor, John, Captain IV and IRA Dublin, 1921

Gerrard, Captain E., British Army Officer in Dublin, 1916–1921

Gibbons, Sean, Member IRB, 1917; Commandant IRA Mayo, 1921

Goulden, J. R. W., Son of RIC man who was engaged in Tourmakeady Ambush, Mayo, 1921

Gribben, Hugh, Commandant IRA, Down, 1921

Hales, Donal, Trade Representative, 1919–1922, Brother of Sean Hales

Hales, William, Member IV and IRA, Cork, 1918–1921; Brother of Sean Hales

Hall, David, OC 1 Brigade IRA, Meath, 1921

Harling, Sean, Officer Fianna Éireann 1921, Courier Dáil Éireann 1920–1921

Harris, Thomas, Member IV, 1916

Haugh, Liam, Senior Officer IRA Clare, 1921

Hawes, Joseph, Participant in mutiny of Connaught Rangers, India, 1920

Healy, Sean (Blackrock, Co. Dublin), Captain IRA Cork, 1921

Hearne, Patrick, Fianna Éireann, Waterford, 1921

Hegarty, Patrick, Officer IRA Sligo Mayo, 1921

Henderson, Frank, Captain IV Dublin, 1916, Commandant IRA, 1917–1921

Hennessy, Sean, Lieutenant IRA Cork, 1921

Henry, Michael, Officer IRA Mayo, 1921

Heron, Aine, Captai, Cumann na mBan, Dublin, 1916

Hevey, Thomas, Adjutant IRA Mayo, 1919–1921

Hewson, George, Member IRA Mayo, 1921

Higgins, Patrick, Captain IRA Cork, 1921

Hilliard, Michael, Captain IV and IRA, Meath 1917–1921

Hobson, Bulmer, Member Supreme Council IRB 1915, General Secretary IV 1916

Hobson, Mrs Bulmer (Clare), née Gregan, Courier to Kilkenny, 1916

Hogan, John Joseph, Officer IRA Cork, 1921

Holland, Robert, Member IRB; Fianna Éireann & IV, 1909–1916; Member IRA Dublin, 1917–1921

Holohan, James, Commandant IRA Kilkenny, 1921

Houlihan, James, Captain IRA Kerry, 1921

Houlihan, Timothy, Captain IRA , Kerry, 1921

Howlett, Thomas, Officer IV and IRA Wexford, 1917–1921; OC South Wexford Brigade, 1922

Hunt, Jim, Commandant IRA Sligo, 1921

Hurley, James, Officwer IRA Cork, 1921

Hynes, Frank, Captain IV Galway, 1914–1916; Captain IRA Cork, 1918–1921

Hynes, James, Member IV Mullingar 1915–1916; Intelligence work for IRB 1919

Hynes, John, Commandant IRA Carlow, 1921

Ibberson, Geoffrey, Lieutenant British Army, Mayo, 1921

Ingoldsby, Augustine, Secretary Cumann na nGael, 1898

Irvine, George , Member IRB and IV, 1907–1916

Kavanagh, Andrew, Officer IV and IRA Wicklow, 1918–1921

Kavanagh, James, Official Department of Local Government Dáil Éireann 1921, Accountant Sinn Féin Executive, 1918–1919

Kavanagh, Matthew, OC East Wicklow Brigade IRA, 1920

Keady, Margaret, Courier IRA Dublin, 1920

Keane, William, Commandant IRA Waterford, 1920–1921

Kearney, Patrick, Member IV and IRA, Dublin, 1913–1921

Kennedy, Jeremiah, Officer IV and IRA, Kerry, 1916–1921

Kennedy, Tadhg, Officer IV and IRA, Kerry, 1916–1921

Kenny, Joseph, Captain IV Bray-Wicklow 1916; Member IRA South Dublin 1917–1922; Civil Servant Land Commission

Kettrick, Thomas, Officer IRA Mayo, 1921

Keys, Stephen, Member IRA Dublin, 1918–1924

Kidd, Davis W., Witness of raid by British Military at Kilmashogue, 1920

Kieran, Peter, Member Sinn Féin, 1906–1921; Member IV Louth, 1914–1921

Kirwan, Andrew, Officer IRA Waterford 1921, Member West Waterford ASU

Laffan, Nicholas, Captain IV Dublin, Captain IRA Dublin 1917–1921

Lawless, Sr.Eithne, Secretary to Michael Collins

Leahy, Michael, Captain IV Cobh, Cork Brigade Vice Commandant IRA Cork, 1921

Leahy, Thomas, Member Irish Citizen Army, 1916

Leddy, Con, Commandant IRA Cork, 1921

Lennon, Patrick, Member IV and IRA , Westmeath, 1917–1921

Luddy, Patrick J., Commandant IRA Cork, 1921

Lynch, Diarmuid, Member Supreme Council IRB, 1917–1921

Lynn, Kathleen Dr, Member Irish Citizen Army, 1916

MacEntee, Sean, Senior OfficerIV and IRA 1916–1921, Member Dail Cabinet 1932–1948

MacGarry, Maeve, Member Cumann na mBan, 1913–1921

MacGuill, Feidhlim, Brigade Intelligence Officer IRA Antrim, 1920–1922

Madden, Denis, Officer IRA Waterford, 1921

Maguire, Conor, Judge Dáil Éireann Courts 1920–1922, Attorney General 1932–1936, President High Court 1936–1946

Malone, Thomas, Sean Forde, Commandant IRA Limerick, 1921

Manahan, Liam, Captain IV, Limerick, 1916; OC Galtee Brigade IRA, 1921

Mannix, Patrick, Constable DMP 192; Associated with IRA Intelligence

Mansfield, James, Commandant IRA Waterford, 1921

Mansfield, Michael J., Officer IV and IRA Waterford, 1914–1924

Matthews, Sean, Member IRB Waterford 1910; Commandant IRA Waterford 1921

McArdle, T J., Secretary Department of Local Government, Dáil Éireann, 1919

McBrien Harold, Commandant IRA Sligo, 1921

McCarville, Eileen, née McGrane, Captain University Branch, Cumann na mBan Dublin

McCabe, Alec, Member Sinn Féin and IV 1913; Supreme Council IRB 1916

McConville, Sean, Commandant IRA, Armagh, 1921

McCoy, John, Commandant IRA Armagh, 1921

McDonagh, Sister F., Sister of Thomas McDonough

McDonnell, Peter, Officer IRA Connemara, 1920

McElligot, Patrick J., Member IRB 1911 and IV 1914–1919; Commandant IRA Kerry 1921

McEllistrim, Thomas, Officer IV and IRA Kerry 1916–1921; OC ASU

McGarry, Sean, Member Supreme Council IRB

McGleenan, Charles, Commandant IRA, Armagh, 1921

McGowan, Martin B., Commandant IRA Sligo, 1921

McGowan, Tady, Commandant IRA Sligo, 1921

McGuill, James, Commandant IV Dundalk 1916; Centre IRB Louth 1919–1920

McMahon, Peadar, IV Limerick 1917–1918; Organiser IV 1918–1921; Secretary Department of Defence 1925–1958

McNeill, Josephine, Officer Cumann na mBan, 1917–1921; Widow of James McNeill, Governor General Irish Free State 1928–1934

McSwiney, Eithne, Sister of Terence McSwiney

McSwiney, Muriel, Widow of Terence McSwiney

McWhinney, Linda, née Kearns, Officer Cumann na mBan, 1914–1921

Meade, Maurice, Member Irish Brigade, Germany 1916; Member IRA Limerick 1921

Mee, Jeremiah, Constable RIC Kerry 1919–1920; Led Mutiny Listowel 1920

Meehan, Bernard, Lieutenant IRA Sligo, 1921

Meehan, Patrick, Constable RIC Meath 1921; Co-operated with IRA 1918–1920

Meldon, Thomas J., Member IV Dublin 1915–1920; Officer IRA Dublin 1921

Melinn, Joseph, Member IRB and Fianna Dublin, 1905–1912; Lieutenant IV Tralee, 1916; Commandant IRA Kerry 1920–1921

Mernin, Lily, Shorthand typist, Dublin Castle, 1914–1922; Co-operated with IRA Intelligence

Moane, Edward, Commandant IRA Mayo, 1921

Molony, Helena, Secretary Inghini 1907–1914; member Cumann na mBan, 1915–1921

Mooney, Martin, Commandant IRA Mayo, 1921

Moran, Christopher, Member IRA Fingal, 1921

Moran, John, Officer IRA Mayo, 1921

Morkan, Eamon, Brigade Officer, Waterford, 1919

Mulcahy, Mary J., Wife of General Richard Mulcahy, Secretary Cumann na mBan 1915–1916, Courier to Wexford, 1916

Mullen, Reverend E. J., Re. Shooting of a Black and Tan in Donegal

Mullins, William, Officer Commanding Communications, 1919; Officer IRB and IRA Kerry 1921

Murphy, Michael, Valet to Sir A. Vickers, shot Kerry 1921

Murphy, Sean, Captain IRA Cork, 1921

Neligan, David, IRA Intelligence Agent in British Police Service

Nevin, Eugene, Rev., Chaplain to Marrowbone Lane Post, Easter 1916

Nugent, Laurence, Officer IV and IRA Dublin, 1913–1921

Nunan, Sean, Secretary to President de Valera USA 1919; Registrar Dáil Bonds 1919–1921

O Boyle, Manus, Member IV London 1913–1916; IRB and IRA Belfast 1916–1921

O Buachalla, Donal, Member IV Maynooth, 1913–1916; Last Governor General of Ireland

O'Brien, Annie, Officer Cumann na mBan, 1916–1921

O'Brien, Henry, Captain IV and IRA, Westmeath, 1913–1921; Member ASU Westmeath

O'Carroll, Patrick, Officer IRA Kildare, 1921

O'Connor, Joseph, 2I/C IV Bolands Mills area, Dublin, 1916; OC 3 Battalion Dublin 1917–1921

O'Doherty, Felix, Captain IRA Cork, 1921

O'Donoghue, F. Major, Intelligence Officer Cork 1921; Member Advisory Committee attached to Bureau of Military History 1947–1948

O'Donoghue, Patrick, Member Sinn Féin Manchester 1908; Captain IRA Manchester 1921

O'Donovan, James, Director of Chemicals GHQ, 1921

O'Donovan, Kathleen, née Boland, sister of Harry Boland, killed 1922; Wife of Senator Sean O' Donovan

O'Gorman, John, Officer IRA Donegal, 1921

O'Hannigan, Donal, Senior Officer IV and IRA Dublin and Dundalk, 1916

O'Hannigan, Donchadh, OC Limerick Brigade IRA, 1921

O'Kelly, Michael, Organiser IV, President Sinn Féin, Kildare, 1921

O'Kelly, Sean T., President of Ireland 1945; Took part in Rising 1916; Speaker Dáil Éireann 1920; Irish Representative Paris, Rome 1920–21

O'Mara, Jack, Officer IV and IRA Waterford, 1913–1923

O'Mara, M. A., Widow of James O'Mara, member of first Dáil Éireann

O'Mullane, Brighid, Officer Cumann na mBan Dublin, 1917–1921

O'Nuallain, Nioclas, Assistant Secretary to the Government of Ireland; Re. Dáil Éireann appointments 1919–1921

O'Reilly, Eily O'H, Member Cumann na mBan, 1914–1921, sister of Michael O'Hanrahan, executed 1916

Perolz, Marie, née Flanagan; Member Inghini na hÉireann; Courier to Waterford and Cork 1916; Member Irish Citizen Army

Plunkett, Grace, née Gifford; Widow of Joseph Plunkett, executed 1916

Plunkett, Jack, Brother of Joseph Plunkett, executed in 1916; Lieutenant IV Dublin 1916; Member GHQ Engineering Staff IV and Staff IV and IRA

Power, Patrick J., Officer IRA Waterford, 1921

Quinn, John, Senior Officer, Clare County Council, 1919–1942

Rabbitte, Roger, Officer IRA Galway, 1921

Reilly, Michael, Captain IRA , Galway, 1921

Robbins, Frank, Member Irish Citizen Army 1916; Secretary IT&GWU

Robinson, Seamus, Officer IV Dublin 1916; Senior Officer IV and IRA, Tipperary, 1917–1921

Roche, Moses, Captain IRA Waterford, 1921

Ruane, Sean T., Senator, Officer IRA Mayo, 1921

Ryan, Mairin, née Cregan, wife of Dr James Ryan, Minister for Agriculture 1932–1948; Member Cuman na mBan, 1913–1921; Courier to Kerry, 1916

Ryan, Michael F., Brigade Engineer, Waterford, 1921

Ryan, Patrick, Lieutenant IRA Waterford, 1921

Scollan, John J., Commandant Hibernian Rifles Dublin, 1916

Shanley, Reverend T. J., New York friend of Eamon de Valera and IRA leaders, 1919

Sheerin, Michael, Officer IV and IRA Derry, Tyrone and Donegal

Sherry, Eugene, Captain IRA Monaghan, 1921

Shields, John, Member IRB, County Tyrone, 1913; Captain IV and IRA, 1913–1921

Short, James, Member IRB and IV Armagh, 1916; Lieutenant IRA Armagh, 1921

Shouldice, John, Lieutenant IV Dublin, 1916; Captain IRA Dublin, 1921

Slater, Thomas, Member IRB Dublin 1905; IV 1915–1916; IRA 1917–1921

Smith, Eugene, Official in Dublin Castle – the transfer of information to IV, 1913–1918

Smyth, James, Captain IRA Leitrim, 1921

Smyth, Nicholas, Vice Commandant IRA, South Tyrone, 1921

Spillane, Michael & others, Commandant IRA Kerry, 1921

Stack, Una, Widow of Austin Stack, member Cumann na mBan

Staines, Michael, IV 1913–1916, quartermaster; Member Dáil Éireann 1918–1923; first Commissioner Garda Siochana, 1923

Stephens, Edward H., Organiser National Land Bank, 1919

Sullivan, James, Member IRB and IV Monaghan, 1913–20; Commandant IRA Monaghan, 1921

Sweeney, Bernard, Member IV Leitrim 1917–19; Officer IRA Leitrim 1921

Thornton, Frank, Member IRB & IV Dublin 1913–16, Deputy Assistant Director of Intelligence IRA 1919–21

Togher, J., Intelligence Officer IRA Galway, 1917–21

Travers, John, Member IRA Donegal-Fermanagh, 1921

Traynor, Oscar, Captain IV Dublin, 1913–16; Officer Commanding, Dublin Brigade, IRA, 1921

Tully, James, Member Active Service Unit IRA Dublin, 1921

Tummon, Francis, Member IV & IRA Monaghan, 1916–22

Twamley, John, Member IV Dublin, 1913–1916

Tweedy, Robert N., Member, Dáil Commission on Industrial Resources, 1919

Tynan, W. A., Officer, IRA Laois, 1921

Ui Chonaill, Eilis Bean, Member Executive Cumann na mBan

Walsh, Liam, Member IRB Portlaoise 1909; Officer IV & IRA Waterford 1918–1921

Walsh, Mary, Officer Cumann na mBan Cork, 1917–21

Walsh, Patrick, Member IRB Kerry 1915; Lieutenant IRA Kerry 1921

Ward, Patrick, Formation of Fianna Éireann Dublin 1909; Member IV & IRA Dublin 1914–21

Waters, Thomas, Officer, IV & IRA Belfast, Cork and Tipperary, 1921

Wickham & others, Officer IRA Cork, 1921

Willis & Bolster, Member IV & IRA Cork, 1917–21

Wilson, Thomas, Captain IRA Galway 1921

Wordsworth, Mrs A. K., Niece of Mrs Alice Stopford Green; Housed IRA leaders 1921

Wylie, The Hon. E., British Prosecutor of leaders of 1916 Rising

Wyse Power, Charles, Member IV Dublin, 1913; Courier to Limerick, 1916; Counsel for Defence IRA prisoners

SUGGESTED FURTHER READING

R. F. Foster, *Modern Ireland 1600–1912*, Allen Lane

Sinead McCoole, *No Ordinary Women*, The O'Brien Press

Jim McDermott, *Northern Divisions*, Beyond the Pale Publications

Senia Paseta and Adrian Gregory (eds.), *Ireland and the Great War*, Manchester University Press

Terence Dooley, *The Decline of the Big House in Ireland*, Wolfhound Press

Dorothy Macardle, *The Irish Republic*, Wolfhound Press

Joseph Lee, *The Modernisation of Irish Society 1848–1918*, Gill & Macmillan

Eoin Neeson, *Birth of a Republic*, Prestige Books

James Durney, *On the One Road*, Leinster Leader

Patrick Murray, *Oracles of God*, UCD Press

Desmond FitzGerald, *Memoirs of Desmond FitzGerald, 1913–16*, Routledge & Kegan Paul

Leon O'Broin, *Revolutionary Underground: The Story of the IRB, 1858–1923*, Gill & Macmillan

Senia Paseta, *Before the Revolution*, Cork University Press

Martin Mansergh, *The Legacy of History*, Mercier Press

Angus Mitchell, *Casement*, Hans Publishing

Diarmaid Ferriter, *The Transformation of Ireland 1900–2000*, Profile Books

Padraig Yeates, *Lockout*, Gill & Macmillan

The Earl of Longford and T. P. O'Neill, *Eamon de Valera*, Gill & Macmillan

Michael Laffen, *The Resurrection of Ireland 1916–1923*, Cambridge University Press

David FitzPatrick, *The Two Irelands*, Oxford University Press

T. M. Healy, *The Great Fraud of Ulster*, Anvil Books

Owen McGee, *The IRB*, Four Courts Press

Hennessy Thomas, *Dividing Ireland*, Routledge

Tom Barry, *Guerrilla Days In Ireland*, Anvil Books

Lord Longford (Frank Pakenham), *Peace by Ordeal*, Sidgwick & Jackson

Michael Farrell, *Arming the Protestants*, Pluto Press

Con Costello, *A Most Delightful Station*, The Collins Press

Geraldine Plunkett Dillon, *All in the Blood*, A. & A. Farmar

Michael Hopkinson, *Green Against Green*, Gill and Macmillan

Sinead Joy, *The IRA in Kerry*, The Collins Press

WITNESSES

INSIDE THE EASTER RISING

ANNIE RYAN

'an entertaining book that gives us an insight into the way some of the ordinary people involved in the Easter Rising recalled that experience forty years later. Their voices come through with a lively immediacy that is very attractive.'

History Ireland

'A remarkable new book'

Irish Independent

€13.99 | ISBN 978–0–9545335–5–7

Available from all good bookshops and from www.LibertiesPress.com

DUBLIN NAZI NO. 1

THE LIFE OF ADOLF MAHR

GERRY MULLINS

'Gerry Mullins is admirably even handed through this fascinating biography of Mahr'

The Dubliner Magazine

'an edifying, wholly absorbing account which traces the tragic consequences when unquestioning patriotism surmounts reality'

Metro

'Intriguing'

Sunday Tribune

Hardback €25 | ISBN 978–1–905483–19–8
Paperback €16.99 | ISBN 978–1–905483–20–4

Available from all good bookshops and from www.LibertiesPress.com

EVERY DARK HOUR

A HISTORY OF KILMAINHAM JAIL

NIAMH O'SULLIVAN

€14.99 | ISBN 978–1–905483–21–1

Available from all good bookshops and from www.LibertiesPress.com

DUBLIN 1660–1860

THE SHAPING OF A CITY

MAURICE CRAIG

'rightly regarded as a classic . . . a most readable and entertaining political and social account of the city's growth . . . obligatory – and pleasurable – reading for anyone who wants to know Dublin'

Books Ireland

'As a readable and scholarly summary and a sensitive commentary upon "buildings and other artefacts" the book is without rival in its subject'

Times Literary Supplement

'A pleasure to read'

Sunday Tribune

€13.99 | ISBN 978–905483–11–2

Available from all good bookshops and from www.LibertiesPress.com

CAUSES FOR CONCERN

IRISH POLITICS, CULTURE AND SOCIETY

MICHAEL D. HIGGINS

'a brilliant compilation . . . a wonderful, absorbing book'

Western Writers' Centre website

Hardback €25 | ISBN 978–1–905483–09–9

Available from all good bookshops and from www.LibertiesPress.com

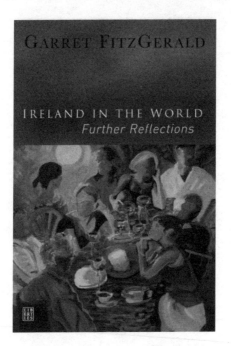

Desmond's Rising
Memoirs 1913 to Easter 1916
Desmond FitzGerald
Foreword by Garret FitzGerald

DESMOND'S RISING

MEMOIRS 1913 TO EASTER 1916

DESMOND FITZGERALD

'a beautifully written and thoughtful account of the period up to Easter 1916 . . . FitzGerald's account of Easter week in the GPO is wonderfully evocative'

Irish Times

'a unique take on that era and the events leading up to Easter Week. It describes in an intimate, very human and often gently humorous manner the build-up to the Rising and its immediate aftermath.'

Books Ireland

€13.99 | ISBN 978–1–905483–05–1

Available from all good bookshops and from www.LibertiesPress.com